The Politics of American Jews

Jewish voting is both distinctive and paradoxical. Stereotypes about the voting habits of American Jews include that they vote at unusually high levels, that they are all liberal, that they vote overwhelmingly for Democratic candidates in disregard to self-interest, and that policy on Israel is their most important issue. Not only are all of those claims wrong, but, more important, they obscure aspects of Jews' voting behavior that are much more interesting.

This book uncovers new perspectives on Jews' political choices by analyzing the unprecedented amount of survey data that is now available, including both surveys of Jews and surveys that permit contrasting the voting of Jews with that of comparable non-Jews. The data suggest several mysteries about Jewish voting. It is known that more Jews are Democrats than are liberals, but there has not been a previous exploration of why more politically conservative Jews are not Republicans. The Democratic presidential vote of Jews was about the same in 2012 as in 1932, paradoxical stability given that the same people would not have voted in these two elections. Jews have long yearned for social acceptance, but having finally achieved that acceptance, they remain politically wary of the social groups that accept them. While most American Jews care about Israel, most also are ambivalent about many of its policies; as a result, they are less likely to vote on the basis of what Israelis consider Israel's best interest.

A fresh picture of Jews' political behaviors shows that Jews are no longer politically monolithic. They vote on the basis of their self-interest and their values, but not all Jews share the same self-interest or the same values.

Herbert F. Weisberg is Emeritus Professor of Political Science at Ohio State University.

The Politics of American Jews

Herbert F. Weisberg

University of Michigan Press
Ann Arbor

First paperback edition 2021

Published in the United States of America by the
University of Michigan Press
Manufactured in the United States of America
Printed on acid-free paper
First published in paperback July 2021

A CIP catalog record for this book is available from the British Library.

Library of Congress Cataloging-in-Publication Data

Names: Weisberg, Herbert F., author.
Title: The politics of American Jews / Herbert F. Weisberg.
Description: Ann Arbor : University of Michigan Press, 2019. | Includes bibliographical references and index. |
Identifiers: LCCN 2019003161 (print) | LCCN 2019006626 (ebook) | ISBN 9780472125210 (E-book) | ISBN 9780472131358 (hardcover : alk. paper)
Subjects: LCSH: Jews—United States—Politics and government. | Jews—United States—History. | United States—Ethnic relations.
Classification: LCC E184.36.P64 (ebook) | LCC E184.36.P64 W46 2019 (print) | DDC 973/.04924—dc23
LC record available at https://lccn.loc.gov/2019003161

ISBN 978-0-472-03872-5 (pbk.)

Contents

Digital materials related to this title can be found on the Fulcrum platform via the following citable URL: https://doi.org/10.3998/mpub.10058621

Preface

When Lawrence Fuchs wrote the first book on the voting patterns of U.S. Jews in the mid-1950s, survey research was still in its infancy. National telephone surveys had not even been imagined. Now that several large-scale surveys of the Jewish population have been conducted, it is time for book-length analysis of the voting behavior of American Jews.

My background for this study comes from my research over the years in the fields of American political behavior and political methodology, including survey research. My intention is to apply a modern perspective on political behavior to the study of Jewish voting. After writing conference papers with my political science colleague Donald Sylvan based on the 2001 Columbus Jewish Population Study, I started analyzing national surveys of Jews for this book when I was a fellow at the University of Michigan's Frankel Institute for Advanced Judaic Studies in 2011. I took a fresh look at historical data on Jews' voting for a 2012 article in *Contemporary Jewry* entitled "Reconsidering Jewish Presidential Voting Statistics," and then I turned to the contemporary period with my 2014 article "Tradition! Tradition? Jewish Voting in the 2012 Election" in *PS: Political Science & Politics*. I put the project on temporary hold as the tumultuous 2016 election campaign developed, waiting to finish this book until there was data on whether the Trump victory would upset the "normal politics" of American Jews.

A few words on my personal background are appropriate. I come from a Minneapolis Jewish family. After my Weisberg grandparents were evicted from one Russian village, they moved to Kishinev in time to be there for its infamous 1903 pogrom; my mother's parents fled from anti-Semitic

Romania. Both sets of grandparents and their families immigrated to Minneapolis between 1886 and 1922. Unlike most American Jews, my ancestors and their descendants had little direct contact with New York City, with the Holocaust, or with Zionism. My mother's family was traditional Orthodox, my father's family became Conservative, and my family became Reform; being Jewish is a very significant part of our lives, though ours is not the Judaism of my grandparents.

The Minneapolis Jewish community in which I grew up was liberal in the traditions of progressive Farmer-Labor governor Floyd B. Olson, moderate Republican governor Harold Stassen, and liberal Democratic senator Hubert Humphrey. Minneapolis was described in 1946 as the "capital of anti-Semitism" in the United States, but it changed enough by the 1960s to elect a Jewish mayor. Minnesota has since become the first state to elect four Jews to the U.S. Senate: Republicans Rudy Boschwitz and Norm Coleman and Democrats Paul Wellstone and Al Franken.

This project has benefited from the release of Jewish survey data through the excellent Berman Jewish DataBank, jewishdatabank.org. I also appreciate the willingness of Jim Gerstein and of the National Jewish Democratic Council to share their data. Any opinions, findings, and conclusions or recommendations expressed in these materials are those of the author and do not necessarily reflect the views of the various survey organizations or their funding sources.

I owe a considerable debt to several people who have furthered my focus on this topic and encouraged me along the way. I have been fortunate to work with several graduate students who were interested in the fairly new field of religion and politics, including Kim Conger, Tobin Grant, Tim Hill, Ted Jelen, Erin McAdams, Steve Mockabee, Quin Monson, Anand Sokhey, and Clyde Wilcox. I especially value the discussions I had with Kenneth Wald at the University of Michigan's Frankel Institute for Advanced Judaic Studies, as well as the guidance I received there from Deborah Dash Moore and Zvi Gitelman. For thoughtful feedback on earlier drafts of this book, I thank Larry Baum, Paul Beck, David Campbell, Chris Devine, Steve Greene, Deborah Dash Moore, Goldie Shabad, Ira Sheskin, and Clyde Wilcox. Appreciation also for support of an Emeritus Academy Grant from the Ohio State University. Most of all, I am grateful to Judy Weisberg for pursuing our religious journeys with me.

Introduction

Having usually supported Republican candidates in presidential elections, the Jewish vote began moving to the Democratic side by the late 1920s. After the Great Depression began, the vote of Jews in 1932 was about 68% for Democrat Franklin Roosevelt, 24% for Republican Herbert Hoover, and 8% for minor-party candidates (Weisberg 2012). Although practically none of the 1932 voters would have been voting 84 years later, the Jewish vote had barely changed by 2016: about 70% voted for Democrat Hillary Clinton in 2016, 25% for Republican Donald Trump, and 5% for minor-party candidates. That amazing partisan stability over such a long time frame is the real puzzle of Jewish voting: how could it have remained so steadily Democratic over a period in which American Jewry and Judaism experienced remarkable change?

The argument offered in this book is that most Jews have incorporated being Democratic into their social identity as Jews, making their party identification unusually resistant to change. Contrary to usual claims, I contend that this incorporation is based on their self-interest, as they see it, as well as on their values, including their Judaic values. The other foundation of their Democratic partisanship is their minority consciousness—their recognition that they are a minority, their feeling that they are a vulnerable minority, and their view that the Democratic Party is best for protecting them. Together, Jews' social identity, their subjective self-interest, their Judaic values, and their minority consciousness lead to what can be termed a "politics of tradition."

The 1964 Broadway musical *Fiddler on the Roof* depicted Jewish life in a 1905 Russian shtetl (village). Tevye, the main character, explains at the beginning of the play that living in the village was like being a fiddler on a roof: it was dangerous and required balance, but the Jewish villagers kept their balance through "tradition." Being a Jew in modern America is much less dangerous than when Jews lived in Eastern European shtetls, though the news keeps reminding us that there are still dangers. Being Jewish is never easy; it still requires balance. Tevye was correct: tradition helps maintain that balance, and tradition makes the politics of American Jews very slow to change, even when fractures develop.

This book highlights several developing fractures that could lead to dramatic changes in Jews' political leanings, including an unnoticed large number of Jews with Libertarian views. Political developments in the early 2010s created a possibility for Jews to realign in the Republican direction. However, similar openings in the 1950s and 1980s proved to be illusions. The Jews' politics of tradition suggests that Donald Trump's electoral victory will effect another missed realignment opportunity.

The familiar descriptions of American Jews' politics are that Jews vote in unusually high numbers, that they are all liberals, that they vote overwhelmingly for Democratic candidates in disregard to self-interest, and that policy on Israel is the most important issue to them when deciding how to vote. Not only are all those claims incorrect, but they obscure much more interesting aspects of Jews' political behavior. Furthermore, Jews' voting has been characterized as paradoxical, such as when they seemingly vote against their self-interest. While this book argues that Jews do not vote against their self-interest, its chapters highlight other paradoxes, puzzles, and myths associated with Jewish voting.

This book uncovers new perspectives on Jews' political choices by analyzing the unprecedented amount of survey data now available, including both surveys of Jews and surveys that permit contrasting their political attitudes and behavior with that of comparable non-Jews. Jewish voting is still found to be distinctive, but the data suggest several important questions about Jews' politics: Are they as liberal on economics as they are on social issues? Why do many politically conservative Jews not consider themselves Republicans? Why do Jews remain politically wary of some social groups that are potential allies? Why do many Jews not base their votes on what Israelis consider to be in Israel's best interest?

Misconceptions about Jews' Politics

Jewish voting has long been viewed as cohesive, with an unusually high proportion of Jews being Democrats and liberals. The Democratic vote of most every other part of the New Deal coalition has fallen over the subsequent decades, but, as Shapiro (1991, 453) remarked, "the laws of American political gravity seemed to have been suspended when it came to Jews." American Jewry has, however, been changing, leading to several fissures in their vaunted political cohesion. They are still overwhelmingly Democratic and liberal, but changes in American Jewry could make their politics less distinctive—unless the Trump presidency causes Jews to reunite politically.

Jewish voting is not as monolithic as it is usually portrayed. There are divisions, and those fractures had been growing at least up to the 2016 election. There are three principal organized branches of Judaism: Orthodox, which is literal in its reading of the Torah; Conservative, which accepts Jewish law as binding but as evolving to fit the modern age; and Reform, which emphasizes social justice and morality more than Jewish law. Contrary to the Democratic voting pattern usually attributed to Jews, Orthodox Jews have been voting predominantly Republican. Jews from the former Soviet Union are also more politically conservative and Republican than other Jews. Regardless of usual claims, there are some economic differences among Jews in their voting, with higher-income Jews being somewhat more likely to vote Republican when other factors are controlled. Furthermore, attitudes on Israel split the Jewish community, with those who are supportive of the specific policies of Israel's government (e.g., on the West Bank settlements) being more Republican in their voting. However, even taking these several divisions into account, the Jewish vote in presidential elections remains overwhelmingly Democratic.

Most Jews are Democrats, and more are liberal than are conservative, but those familiar facts obscure two noteworthy patterns. First, many Jewish political conservatives are not Republicans and are primarily conservative on economic issues rather than social ones. Second, a substantial number of Jews are liberals on social issues and favor a smaller government. These "Libertarians" do not fit comfortably into either party, so they could realign politically if the Republicans nominate presidential candidates who enthuse them.

In contrast to the claim that "similarity among Jews rather than division is the most prominent feature" of their politics (Smith 2005, 50), these divisions show that Jews are not as united as they are usually portrayed. Fractures are evident, even if Jews still give a large majority of their votes to Democratic candidates. Lefkowitz (1993, 38) described Jews as having "a virtually congenital proclivity to pull the Democratic lever," but these divisions suggest that mutation in the Jewish political DNA may be occurring.

The writing of this book has been finalized in the aftermath of the 2016 presidential election. After failing to move the Jewish vote away from the Democrats in the 2008 and 2012 elections, the Republican Party was ready to base a major 2016 campaign argument on the Iran nuclear accord negotiated by the Obama administration. Israeli opposition to the accord threatened to tear apart the American Jewish community. However, after Donald Trump's candidacy upended traditional party competition, the accord played only a minor role in the 2016 election. Surveys found that the level of Democratic voting by Jews in that year was virtually identical to four years earlier. Still, Trump's election may lead to changes in the Republican Party that could modify the basis of future party competition.

The argument in this book is that Jews' political positions have changed. The political unity of Jews has eroded. To just describe Jews as liberal and Democratic would miss the considerable complexity of their politics. While Jews have not realigned politically, they have become disunited, which has created a potential for larger transformation. The question becomes whether the effects of the Trump administration will cause the Jewish community to come back together or will further exacerbate their divisions. That question makes this an appropriate time to assess the state of Jewish voting as a prelude to understanding how it could shift in the future.

Paradoxically Distinctive Politics

Political analysts agree that Jewish voting in the United States is distinctive. As survey research expert Tom Smith (2005, 59) aptly concluded in his extensive analysis of Jews' political attitudes, "while all ethnic/racial and religious groups are unique, Jews are more unique than others." Most obviously, Jews are more liberal than the overall population and more Democratic in their leanings and voting. Of course, Jews are not the only social group in the United States that is distinctive politically, but the political distinctiveness of American Jews is unusual and paradoxical.

A well-known example of how Jews' politics seem paradoxical is that though most Jews are relatively well-off, they vote like groups that are much poorer. They seem to ignore self-interest when they cast ballots for Democratic candidates when Republican voting might better fit their economic interests. Equally paradoxical, Jews are more united in their politics than in their religion. There are different religious branches among Judaism, but none has as many adherents as there are Democrats in the Jewish community. Similarly, polls show that more Jews vote Democratic than keep kosher, fast on Yom Kippur, or light Sabbath candles.

One of the most surprising findings in this book is that Jewish political conservatives are not particularly Republican in their politics. Not only are political conservatives a minority among Jews, but many are conflicted on issues and therefore less Republican than one would expect. Few Jews are consistent political conservatives; more are Libertarians (even if they would not describe themselves as such), and these Libertarians are not politically cohesive. Jews' political views are sometimes described as a reaction against the large role that evangelical Christians play in the Republican Party, even though evangelicals are very supportive of Israeli government policies—indeed, more supportive than many American Jews.

Jews' political views are often ascribed to fear of anti-Semitism, but surveys find that anti-Semitic attitudes are near historical lows. There have been increased tensions between Jews and African Americans, but Jews have remained loyal Democratic voters, even when the nomination of Barack Obama tested whether they would support a black for the presidency. Jews care about Israel, but they have remained fairly immune to GOP ads attacking the Democrats as weak on Israel.

Jews are one of the most educated social groups, and they score high on survey questions regarding political knowledge and interest in politics. How, then, can they ignore what others consider their economic self-interest, not follow the lead of prominent Republican Jews, support Democratic candidates regardless of the Israel issue, and confound expectations in so many other ways? This situation is not just paradoxical; it is a multiplicity of paradoxes. The intention behind pointing out these paradoxical aspects of Jews' political distinctiveness is not to say that there is anything wrong or irrational about the politics of Jews. Rather, it is intended to focus attention on the need for explanations, which requires good data about their politics.

Studying Jews' Politics

The first studies of Jews' political views were necessarily based on limited evidence. Claims about their views in the 19th century are mainly based on the positions of a few prominent Jews; we have little solid information about the politics of most Jews of that period. There were enough Jews living in some predominantly Jewish voting precincts by the early 20th century that their politics then can be inferred from voting statistics, though the inferences could be wrong, since Jews who lived in religiously diverse areas might have voted differently. Lawrence Fuchs's (1956) pioneering analysis in *The Political Behavior of American Jews* was mostly limited to precinct data and surveys of a few cities.

Jewish Surveys. National surveys of the general public became prevalent by the mid-20th century, but few included interviews of enough Jews to permit reliable generalizations. Since Jews are only about 2% of the U.S. population, most national surveys have fewer than a hundred Jewish respondents; very few include interviews of as many as a thousand Jews.[1] Fortunately, useful results can now be obtained by combining data for several years in some of the long-running probability-based academic surveys, particularly the American National Election Studies and the General Social Survey. The national exit polls, which were started in 1972, are less useful because they do not ask enough questions about political issues.

The most important development is that there are now several national surveys of Jews that include political questions. One of the first large-scale surveys of Jews, the National Jewish Population Survey (NJPS), was mainly intended to estimate the Jewish population size and to measure the changing character of American Judaism. The 2000–01 NJPS used random sampling, but its methodology became so controversial that there was no 2010 Jewish population study (Rosenblatt 2011). The Pew Research Center stepped into this breach in 2013 by using random-digit dialing (RDD) to conduct a telephone survey of 3,475 Jews, which is more than three times the size of most other Jewish surveys. Pew used a complex stratified sampling approach (Pew Research Center 2013, 124–29), phoning cell phones as well as landlines and even conducting interviews in Russian when necessary. The 2012 Jewish Values Survey sponsored by the Public Religion Research Institute also included several political questions. The American Jewish Committee's Annual Survey of American Jewish Opinion is also useful, particularly since its adoption of RDD sampling in 2016.

This book utilizes a combination of these surveys (see the data appendix) to assemble an unusually broad portrait of Jews' political behavior. None of these surveys is perfect, partly because no system for sampling Jews is flawless. All these surveys have been criticized on sampling grounds. Even the 2013 Pew Survey of U.S. Jews, which is considered the gold standard in the field, has been criticized because of its low response rate (Klausner 2013), although a low rate is common in this era when people feel oversurveyed.[2] The accuracy of surveys depends on many factors, including the wording and ordering of questions. As one means of trying to handle those limitations, results presented in this book have been checked by performing parallel analysis of two different surveys whenever possible.

Limitations. Before proceeding further with this study, it is appropriate to mention its limitations. While there were enough surveys of Jews for an extensive analysis by the mid-2010s, no single survey yet covers all the topics pertinent here. The following chapters piece together an understanding of Jews' politics by looking at several surveys that each asked some relevant questions, but a complete examination of Jews' voting would require a comprehensive survey that covers a broader range of topics at once.

This book gives little attention to topics for which there is not much systematic information, particularly voting for offices other than the presidency. The real debate about Jews' politics is about their presidential voting. American Jews' presidential choices will ultimately determine whether their politics will change further or will remain paradoxically distinctive.

An optimal study would have three additional components: (1) in-depth individual interviews on religion and politics, rather than relying totally on closed-ended questions; (2) focus groups, to see how opinions develop in the setting of group discussion; and (3) interviews with respondents' family and friends, to assess primary-group influences. Considering the contours of an ideal study clarifies the limitations of the current study, though an ideal study would be too costly to be practical. This study still provides a baseline so we can better understand the forces that lead to any subsequent changes in Jewish voting.

Explanations of Jews' Politics

Several different explanations of Jews' politics have been offered over the years and are reviewed in the chapters of this book. Most analysts have discarded explanations of Jews' politics based on their self-interest and their values. After all, Jews seem to be voting against their self-interest when they vote liberal and Democratic while being relatively affluent. Judaic values seem to be irrelevant to their politics, since the most observant Jews—the Orthodox—are the most politically conservative and Republican. However, the following chapters argue that these explanations are essential for understanding how most Jews became liberal and Democratic. They see being liberal and Democratic as in their general self-interest, even if it is counter to their economic self-interest, and Conservative and Reform Jews apply Judaic values to their politics, even if their Judaic values differ from those of Orthodox Jews.

Two other elements are more important yet in explaining Jews' politics. Social identity and minority consciousness are strong influences on Jews' politics. As to social identity, most Jews have come to think of being liberal and/or Democratic as part of their being Jewish. It has become ingrained in their thinking, and that political identity is reinforced as they talk to Jewish friends and relatives who are mostly liberal and Democratic. As for minority consciousness, Jews have learned that being a minority leaves them in a vulnerable position, so it is important to them to favor political views that help support minorities. Their minority consciousness has caused most Jews to have universalistic values and to have a self-interest in protecting their religious liberty. Their minority consciousness, values, and self-interest have led to most Jews becoming liberal and Democratic.

These elements are brought together in Jews' politics of tradition. Being liberal and Democratic has become part of the political tradition of a people who value tradition. They have been secure and have prospered in the United States since the mid-20th century under a relatively liberal political regime and by voting Democratic. It is possible that they would benefit more by moving over to the politically conservative side and voting Republican, but that could be a risky strategy. Jews are used to being hurt by drastic shifts in the political regimes of other nations. It seems much safer to stick with tradition than to take the chance of going for change. Unless the Democratic Party turns against them, they see insufficient reason to switch politically.

Before leaving this point, it is essential to avoid a potential misunderstanding. To say that Jews are predominantly liberal and Democratic is not meant to understate the fact that many Jews are conservative and Republican. Indeed, the Pew survey estimates that there are nearly a million Jewish political conservatives and Jewish Republicans. Recognizing why some Jews are conservatives and Republicans helps us to understand why more are liberals and Democrats.

Analyzing Jews' voting does not imply that their individual decisions involve consciously thinking about which party or candidate would be better for Jews and/or for Israel. Instead, patterns found in their voting may be due to their social demographics and to values that most Jews share. Jews, like other Americans, take numerous matters into account in deciding how to vote, but there are some distinctive patterns for Jews because of what they have in common with one another.

Conclusions

In many ways, Jews are a people who enjoy paradoxes. Early rabbis endlessly debated the meaning of phrases in the Torah (the five books of Moses in the Old Testament), with their debates written down in the Talmud. It is only fitting for a people who are used to Talmudic debates about fine points of interpretation to have politics that are paradoxically distinctive, and perhaps that is not entirely coincidental.

The paradoxical nature of Jewish voting means that there is an opening for larger partisan change. The possibility of realignment has been discussed for decades. However, every time the beginnings of realignment have been spotted, Jews quickly reverted to strong Democratic voting. In the end, what matters is whether long-term change occurs, and that can only be judged through the lens of history.

A fresh picture of Jews' political behaviors emerges from this effort. Jews are no longer politically monolithic. Fractures are developing in their politics. They vote on the basis of their self-interest and their values, though not all Jews share the same self-interest or the same values. Most have incorporated being Democratic into their social identity, though many are instead Republican. Jews may have been moving away from the Democratic Party as New Deal issues receded in salience, but they returned to that party because of a new set of social issues. At the same time, politically conservative Jews have not necessarily flocked to the Republican Party, often because of the association of the Republicans with the Christian right's desire for government regulation of individual choice in the morality sphere. In the first two decades of the 21st century, the Republican Party has tried to turn Jews into Republicans by being unconditionally supportive of Israel, without recognizing that most American Jews have ambivalent feelings about Israel because of its policies. While there are fissures in Jewish support of the Democratic Party, the GOP's hope for a realignment of Jews is unlikely to be successful in the near future unless there are permanent changes in the Republican Party.

Jews constitute only 2% of the U.S. population, though a larger portion of the active electorate. They are more involved in politics than most groups and are disproportionately important political donors. As is described later in this study, they are concentrated in a few states, including some battleground states where a few votes may make a large difference, especially in low-turnout primary and midterm elections. They constitute an important case study of a group that maintains its political tradition long after seemingly comparable groups have realigned.

The chapters of this book resolve some of the paradoxes of Jews' voting but do not solve all the mysteries. As American politics and political parties evolve, Jewish voting will continue to mutate. As some puzzles are answered, new ones will develop. Jewish voting will never be straightforward, because Jews will always regard their status in this country as fragile.

The Plan of This Book

There have been numerous studies of Jewish politics since Lawrence Fuchs's (1956) pioneering book. Most notable is Maisel and Forman's ([2001] 2004) excellent compendium *Jews in American Politics*. Sheskin (2016) and Abrams and Cohen (2016) have provided recent broad data-based overviews. There are several sources on Jewish voting in specific elections (e.g., Forman 2004; Wentling and Medoff 2012; Uslaner 2015; Weisberg 2014), as well as high-quality reconstructions of Jewish voting over the years by the Solomon Project (Mellman, Strauss, and Wald 2012) and Weisberg (2012).

The goal of this book is to provide a summary of Jewish political behavior, while paying attention to the changes that have occurred in their voting. The usual explanations of Jewish voting are here reconsidered, and stronger theory-based explanations are suggested, allowing for consideration of the circumstances under which Jewish voting may change. The analysis of surveys is inherently statistical, but most of their results are presented in this book in a nontechnical manner, so that the book can be more easily read by a general audience that is interested in religion and politics.

Part I of this book introduces American Jewry, including their religion, their religious practice, and their views on their religion, with an emphasis on how those topics might affect their politics. Part II considers explanations of Jewish voting, arguing for the importance of social identity theory, self-interest, values, and minority consciousness. Part III analyzes the political behavior of Jews, including their political participation, partisanship, and ideology. Jews are shown to be more Democratic than liberal, to be less distinctive on economic issues than on new "values issues," and to have politicized attitudes regarding Israel. This analysis importantly leads to discovery of "missing Jewish Republicans" and Jewish ideological Libertarians. Part IV assembles the different aspects considered in the previous chapters, starting with an integrative analysis of Jews' voting, followed by examination of the possibility of Jews realigning politically and analysis of the 2016 presidential election. The final chapter provides a brief summary of the Jews' politics of tradition.

PART I

An Introduction to American Judaism and American Jewry

The starting point for understanding the politics of Jews in the United States is to understand the nature of contemporary Judaism and Jewry. Judaism is the oldest of the three Abrahamic religions, with Jews being the descendants of the biblical Hebrews. Nowadays, however, Judaism is both more and less than a religion. It is more than a religion in that being Jewish has become an ethnocultural identity for most Jews. Yet it is less than a religion because that ethnocultural identity has become the sole basis of being Jewish for many Jews who are not at all religious, which implies that their religion per se is not likely to be the basis of their political attitudes and behaviors. Still, the ethnocultural ties are strong enough to provide a basis for cohesion among Jews.

While cohesion among Jews is at a high level, there is also fracture. Just as there are several separate Protestant denominations, so there are different organized movements in Judaism, with an order from the most observant to the least. This "denominational ladder" is relevant to Jews' politics, with the two poles differing considerably on public policy issues and in political leanings. Jews in the middle of this continuum turn out to be the most concerned about Israel and the most focused on social justice concerns, again affecting their politics. This first part of this book expands on these themes of cohesion and fracture in American Judaism and American Jewry. Data from the 2013 Pew Survey of U.S. Jews and other surveys are used to document these themes.

CHAPTER 1

Religion and/or Culture

Jews have been in the United States since 1654, when a group of Portuguese Jews sailed from Recife in Dutch Brazil to present-day New York. But Jews were such a miniscule minority until the 1890s that most Americans would have had little direct knowledge of them. Since then, Jews have become part of the nation's fabric, with most Americans having heard of successful U.S. Jews, including prominent businesspeople, entertainers, and scientists. Even more important, Americans have increasingly come to know Jews personally through their workplaces, their neighborhoods, and even their families.

In focusing on the voting of American Jews, are we studying the members of a religious group or of an ethnic group? In the first book-length study of Jewish voting, Fuchs (1956, 15–20) treated Jews as an "ethnoreligious" group, assuming that they were Jewish in both religion and ethnicity. That assumption no longer fully holds. The contrast between these two perspectives is exemplified by the differences between two of the leading American Jewish politicians of the early 21st century, Joe Lieberman and Bernie Sanders. Lieberman became the first Jewish major-party nominee for national office when Al Gore chose him as his vice presidential running mate in 2000. A former senator, Lieberman is an observant Orthodox Jew. Since Orthodox Jews do not drive on the Sabbath, Lieberman would walk four miles to get to the U.S. Capitol when his vote was needed on Saturdays. Sanders was the first Jewish presidential candidate to mount a serious run for a party's presidential nomination, winning several presidential primaries and contesting the Democratic nomination up through its 2016 national convention. Senator Sanders is a secular Jew, so nonobservant that he spoke to Jerry Falwell's fundamentalist Liberty University in 2015 on one of the most sacred Jewish religious holidays. Yet Sanders has stated, "I am very proud of being Jewish, and that is an essential part of whom I am as a human being." Being Jewish is an important part of the lives and histories of both Lieberman and Sanders, but these two politicians are near the opposite ends of a spectrum from religious to ethnocultural Jewish.

Understanding the politics of American Jews requires recognition that being Jewish is not just a religious identity. It is also an ethnocultural identity, rooted as much in heritage and traditions as in belief. Furthermore, being Jewish is an identity that is usually interpreted by individual adherents rather than dictated by religious leaders. The first sections of this chapter treat these two aspects: Judaism as a religion and Jewishness as an ethnocultural identity. Then, the individuality of religious decisions is described. Finally, the question of who is Jewish is discussed, along with how surveys define who is Jewish. Throughout the chapter, implications for politics are stressed, particularly whether the politics of most Jews flow from their religious doctrines or are based primarily on their shared ethnocultural identity.

Judaism as a Religion

Jews have become a familiar minority, and many people are acquainted with the Judaism of the ancient Hebrews, but contemporary Judaism has become a considerably more complicated topic. Not only are there three major organized branches of Judaism, with somewhat different philosophies and practices, but the Conservative movement is not the most conservative of the major branches, and the more conservative Orthodox branch of Judaism is splintered into at least a dozen different elements. It is not necessary to understand all the details of Judaism to analyze Jews' politics, but it is important to have some general level of knowledge about contemporary Jewry. This section begins by reviewing some of the doctrines of traditional Judaism. It should be emphasized that Jewish philosophers and rabbis have reinterpreted some of these doctrines and that there is considerable difference between Jewish law and how most American Jews practice their Judaism.

Traditional Judaism. Judaism is the monotheistic religion of the Old Testament Hebrews. Its Bible includes the Torah (the "five books of Moses") plus the Prophets and Psalms, amplified by early rabbinic interpretation in the Talmud. The Old Testament is considered holy by adherents to Christianity and Islam, though they believe that it is superseded by the New Testament and the Qur'an, respectively. While Jewish prayers are in ancient Hebrew, the mother language of most Jewish immigrants from Central and Eastern Europe was Yiddish, an amalgam of Hebrew, German, and other European languages. The traditional conception of God in Judaism is that God is the creator and ruler of the world. Crucially, Judaism views God as the only God. The Talmud lists three basic tenets of Judaism: the Torah (which can be interpreted more broadly as an emphasis on learning), service to God (prayer, which is often read as leading an ethical life), and righteous giving (charity and, more generally, human kindness).

The two most holy Jewish religious days are in early autumn (the dates move around because the Jewish calendar is lunar rather than solar). Rosh Hashanah marks the start of the religious new year. Yom Kippur, the Day of Atonement, is when Jews pray individually and collectively for forgiveness for their sins. Many Jews who do not customarily go to synagogue throughout the year attend services for those two High Holidays, as many Christians do on Easter. There are several other Jewish holidays, the best known of which are two family festivals that are celebrated mainly at home: Passover in the spring, commemorating the exodus from Egypt, and Hanukkah in the winter, marked by lighting an additional candle each night for eight nights. Jewish life-cycle rituals include circumcision of male infants in recognition of Israel's covenant with God, bar and bat mitzvah celebrations when children reach adulthood (age 13 for boys and, depending on the denomination, 12 or 13 for girls), the ritual bath (*mikveh*) especially for women, and mourning practices ("sitting *shiva*").

Jewish days start at sundown. The Jewish Sabbath is on Saturday, starting at sundown on Friday. There are restrictions against work on the Sabbath, which extend to prohibitions on using money, driving, and turning electricity on or off. A large number of laws involving Jewish practice emanate from the Torah and/or later commentary. Most widely known are the dietary laws for keeping kosher, including restrictions on what to eat (e.g., no pork or shellfish), rules for how animals should be slaughtered if they are used for food, and prohibitions on combinations of food (meat and milk in the same meal). The traditional practices described in this section serve to keep Jews "a people apart" from the general society.[1] As is described in this chapter and in chapter 2, fewer Jews observe some of these practices as they have acculturated to American society, and some branches of Judaism have relaxed various restrictions.

Beliefs. Given that monotheism is a basic precept of Judaism, one would expect that Jews would believe in God. However, about half of self-identified Jews in the U.S., more than adherents of other religions, tell pollsters that they are not sure they believe in God (Putnam and Campbell 2010, 23). The 2013 Pew survey found that only 35% of Jews answered that they are "absolutely certain" in their belief in God or a universal spirit, versus 69% for the population as a whole; 20% of Jews definitely do not believe in God, compared to just 7% among the general American public. Thus, in practice, belief in God is not necessarily a criterion for saying that one is Jewish.

The 2014 Religious Landscape Study (RLS) found that compared to other religions, lower proportions of Jews believe that the Bible is the word of God and that it should be interpreted literally (Pew Research Center 2015; see also Lugo 2008).[2] (The RLS and other surveys used in this book are described in the data appendix.) Jews were about half as likely as non-Jews (26% v. 48%) to feel that their religion should preserve its traditional beliefs and practices.

A report about Jews based on the 2007 RLS (Cohen and Blitzer 2008) was entitled "Belonging without Believing" and argued that Americans who consider themselves Jews (those who "belong") do not accept the religious tenets of Judaism (they do not "believe"). That title was an exaggeration, since many American Jews do believe, but it points to the fact that American Jewishness is more than a matter of religious beliefs. This limits the extent to which the political views of Jews are likely to be based on their religious beliefs.

Jewishness as Identity

A person walks into a neighborhood restaurant, and the Jewish owner says, "You don't look familiar; you must be new here. Tell me your religion: are you Protestant, Catholic, or Jewish?" The person uncomfortably answers, "None of those—I'm an atheist." The restaurant owner keeps pushing, asking him, "Ok, but are you a Christian atheist or a Jewish atheist?" The fellow answers, "I guess I'm a Jewish atheist," and the owner enthusiastically welcomes him as a fellow Jew and offers him a free dessert with his meal. Theology was not the issue; ethnicity was what mattered.[3]

While the preceding scenario is an adaptation of a popular joke, it is true that many people who are not religious in belief and/or practice still consider themselves Jewish. Thus, "being Jewish" does not necessarily refer to religion. For many people, being Jewish today is more a matter of ancestry, ethnicity, and/or culture, rather than an emphasis on religion, which explains why "Jewish atheists" can be considered Jews.

While Judaism is a religion, being Jewish is an identity. The concept of identity refers to how people define themselves. Jewish identity is a complicated topic, because people view their Jewishness in different ways. Studying American Jewry requires understanding what Jewish identity means to American Jews.[4] Five hundred years ago, being Jewish represented a religious, cultural, and ethnic identity all at once, with no need for Jews to separate these different aspects. Today, however, many Jews see being Jewish as identifying with a people, culture, or ethnicity rather than as a religion, which means that their politics may be based on their feeling Jewish rather than on their Judaism.

Ethnocultural Identity. Social scientists recognize that some ethnic groups share a religion, so their ethnicity and religion reinforce each other. Irish Catholics and Dutch Calvinists are examples of "ethnoreligious" groups. Such groups typically have common ancestry, language, culture, and religious practices. American Jews differ from most ethnoreligious groups in that they came to the United States from a variety of different nations. Additionally, there are religious differences between the branches of Judaism to which they belong. Thus, there are more differences among American Jews than is typical for an ethnoreligious group.

However, a common focus on Jewish culture helps maintain Jews as an "ethnocultural" group. For example, many Jews who do not regularly participate in religious activity maintain their Jewish identity through what Gans (1994) describes as "symbolic religiosity," such as attending relatively nonreligious Hanukkah celebrations, family Passover seders, or Jewish film festivals. Even some people of Jewish ancestry who do not practice Judaism could be considered "culturally Jewish" through their commemorating the Holocaust, participating in solidarity events with Israel, and/or enjoying lox and bagels on Sunday mornings.[5] Furthermore, as argued in chapter 3 of this study, politics has become ingrained in the ethnocultural Jewishness of many Jews.

Transnational Identity. Jews are a diasporic people, having been exiled from Israel after the Romans quelled a Jewish revolt in 135 AD. Additionally, American Jews have been transnational in their focus, feeling connected to Jews in other countries. The diaspora aspect of Jews is evident in standard Jewish prayers that mention Israel. Even the Passover seder ceremony ends with the proverbial statement "Next year in Jerusalem!" While some American Jews have emigrated to the State of Israel since it was established in 1948, the vast majority consider themselves proud Americans, albeit concerned about Israel's security.

Unlike most immigrants, American Jews have never retained much identification with the dozen or so countries that they left to come to the United States. Many Irish Americans feel a tie to Ireland, and many Italian Americans have nostalgia about Italy. By contrast, most Jewish immigrants did not feel any allegiance to the country where they were born. For example, Jews who came from Russia at the beginning of the 20th century remembered it as a place they fled because of pogroms (anti-Jewish riots), not as their homeland. This made it easy for Jewish immigrants to transfer their loyalty to America.

Still, Jews have always been interested in the fate of their coreligionists abroad, partly due to natural concern about relatives who remained in Europe, but also due to a generalized concern for fellow Jews wherever they lived (Lederhendler 2017, 191). Jewish newspapers in America have long included articles about problems that Jews encounter across the world, which made American Jews more transnational in their focus and interested in news from a variety of other countries. As a result, foreign affairs can affect the politics of Jews more than is the case for most other Americans.

How Jews View Their Identity. Surveys of Jews help show how they view their identity. The 2004 Survey of American Jewish Opinion conducted by the American Jewish Committee (AJC) asked a consumer panel which of four qualities people considered most important to their Jewish identity: (1) religious observance, (2) support for Israel, (3) being part of the Jewish people, or (4) commitment to social justice. As shown in figure 1.1,

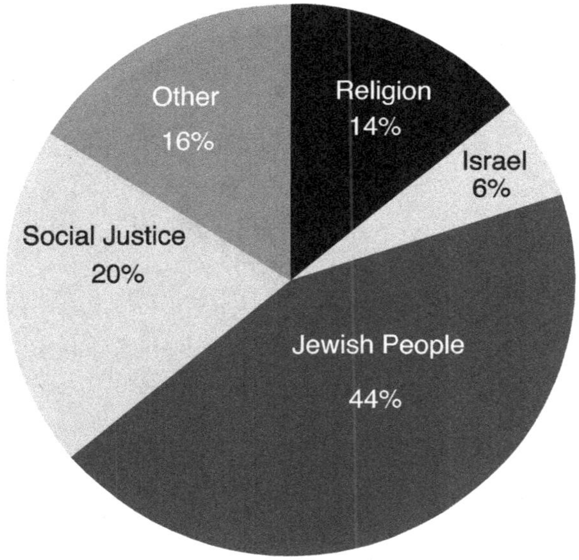

Fig. 1.1. What Jews consider most important to their Jewish identity (*Note:* Data shown is an analysis of 2004 American Jewish Committee survey.)

the most popular answer (44%) was peoplehood. By contrast, 20% of respondents emphasized social justice, and only 14% focused on religious observance. Even fewer respondents (6%) chose support for Israel, showing that it is not of paramount importance. While none of the choices received majority support, the results make clear that religious observance was not seen as the most crucial part of Jewish identity.

That finding was bolstered when the 2013 Pew survey asked if being Jewish is mainly a matter of religion, ancestry, or culture. As in the AJC survey, "religion" was not the most common answer: few respondents (15%) chose "religion" only, while a majority (62%) chose "ancestry" and/or "culture," with the rest (23%) choosing both "religion" and "ancestry/culture" (fig. 1.2).[6] These results suggest that the Jewish religion is secondary in terms of most Jews' politics. Religion may be the basis of the politics of some Jews, but their Democratic partisanship and liberal views are more likely to be based on their ethnicity and culture.

The 2013 Pew survey also asked respondents which of several topics were essential to what being Jewish means to them. Figure 1.3 shows the relative emphasis on these different topics. Remembering the Holocaust retains paramount resonance (73%), with leading an ethical life also being widely cited (69%). Next were social justice (57%) and being intellectually curious (50%). Many Jews see caring about Israel as essential, but the 43%

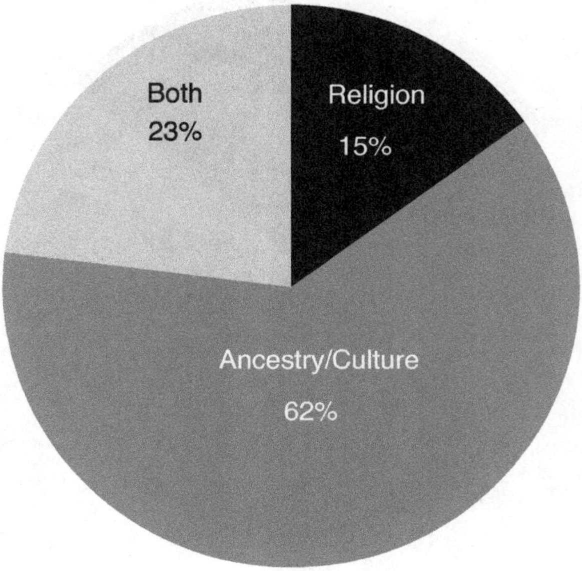

Fig. 1.2. Proportion of Jews viewing being Jewish as a matter of ancestry/culture, religion, or both (*Note:* Data from 2013 Pew Jewish survey, recomputed with noncitizens excluded.)

of respondents selecting that topic is merely equivalent to the percentage who view a sense of humor as essential. The least-popular topics were being part of a Jewish community,[7] observing Jewish law (*halakha*), and eating traditional Jewish foods.

Additional Pew results show that being Jewish is important to most American Jews: 94% of respondents said they were "proud to be Jewish," and 80% described being Jewish as very or somewhat important in their lives. However, only a little more than half (56%) considered religion to be very or somewhat important in their lives. Thus, being Jewish trumps being religious for many American Jews.

Contemporary Jewishness

Not only have American Jews become less religious, but their Jewishness is different than it was decades earlier. Most Jews identify with one of the major denominational movements, but their denominational choice does not suffice in describing their approach to Judaism. Scholars seeking to describe Jews' approach to their Judaism in contemporary America instead emphasize the individualism of Jews, as well as social influences.

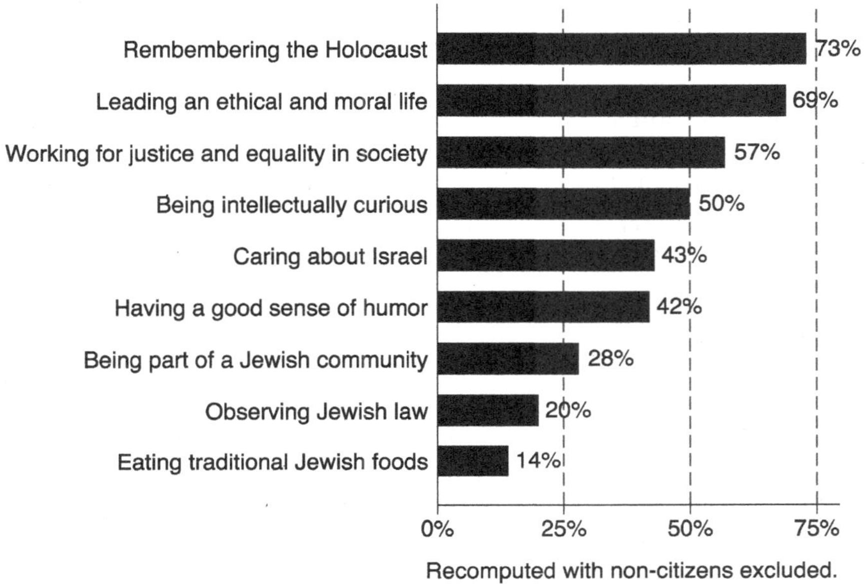

Fig. 1.3. Which topics Jews consider an essential part of their being Jewish
(*Note:* Data from 2013 Pew Jewish survey, recomputed with noncitizens excluded.)

Religious Individualists. Jews choose to experience their Jewishness in a variety of different ways, some of which do not correspond to what previous generations would have viewed as "authentic." Cohen and Eisen (2000, 183–85) insightfully describe individual Jews as dedicated to a "sovereign self" and deciding for themselves what combination of Jewish practices to follow. Some light Sabbath candles whereas some do not, some keep kosher whereas some do not, and so on. Besides the expected differences between Jewish denominations in their level of observance, there is also considerable variation within denominations. Most Jews decide for themselves which practices to follow, rather than accepting rabbinical decisions.

Participating in Jewish culture has become an important part of being Jewish, with many finding cultural ways of expressing their Judaism to be more meaningful than traditional observances. Of course, many Jews still belong to synagogues, regularly attend religious services, participate in Jewish adult education, and try to follow Jewish values in their daily lives. Yet family activities like Passover seders have become the means by which "Jewish meaning is routinely and legitimately accessible to [American Jews], in concert with those most dear to the self, in the privacy of their own homes" (Cohen and Eisen 2000, 198). Cohen and Eisen saw this shift as an instance of Jews' emphasis on their individuality, noting that American Jews are not looking for formal theologies to systematize their beliefs but, instead, expect their Judaism to provide them with "experiences of meaning in family and community contexts that leave them free in other respects to be the selves they want to be" (2000, 197). Moreover, American Jews do not simply decide on how they will be Jewish; it is a process with changes in their religious journeys over the years (Horowitz 1998).

Social Construction. Kelman et al. (2017) suggest that social ties construct the Jewishness of generations of American Jews born after the baby boom. In contrast to earlier generations, post-boomers have non-Jews as well as Jews in their families and in their peer networks, and their Jewishness has been forged by those social interactions. The qualitative interviews by Kelman et al. discovered three basic narratives for different people: some described how relationships with other Jews were important to their sense of being Jewish ("connections"), other constructed their Jewish identity by contrasting themselves with non-Jews ("comparison"), and still others explained how discomfort in social settings with non-Jews contributed to their feeling more Jewish ("conflict").

Kelman et al. assert that a "social self" characterizes the Jewishness of this new generation, rather than the "sovereign self" Cohen and Eisen claimed. Similarly recognizing the importance of this social self, Wolfson's influential book *Relational Judaism* (2013) argues that Jewish institutions must adapt to the 21st century through fostering social interactions and connections among their potential members. There is also a social self as regards the family unit. One's family of origin is of critical importance in shaping one's reality (Berger and Luckmann 1966). That role holds for religion, especially for a religion, like Judaism, in which the celebration of several holidays is primarily at home. Young Jews naturally assume that how their family observes Judaism is how Judaism is practiced universally, and the same assumption holds for how their family views politics. Marriage always involves negotiation between the realities of the spouses, and negotiation is needed not only among intermarried couples but also among inmarried Jews whose parental families differed in how they practiced their Judaism. When there are differences, that negotiation is likely to spread out to negotiation about politics as well.

American Jewishness. What, then, is the essence of American Judaism? Two social scientists have attempted to distill that essence in short lists. Charles Liebman (1971, 68–69) delineated six basic principles of the "folk religion" of American Jews, while Jonathan Woocher (1986, 67–68) described seven tenets of their "civil religion" (adapted from Bellah 1967). Table 1.1 shows the two lists and attempts to coordinate them.

Both lists emphasize Jewish peoplehood and the importance of its survival. Liebman's principles emphasize Jewishness rather than Judaism, while Woocher's tenets emphasize ethnicity rather than religiosity. Woocher (1986) admitted that the Jewishness he described was "religion without theology" (91), indicating that it "prescribes a model of Jewishness which synthesizes ethnicity and religiosity and places both firmly within the embrace of American pluralism" (20).

Not every Jew would accept all these principles or tenets, but Liebman's and Woocher's statements nicely summarize some core views of many Jews in the 1970s and 1980s. How these will hold for the millennial and post-millennial generations remains to be seen. In any case, these statements imply that Jews' political positions are likely to be grounded more in their Jewishness than in their Judaism.

TABLE 1.1. Core Principles of American Jewry

Liebman	Woocher
Jews are an indivisible people regardless of denominational differences	The unity of the Jewish people
The survival of the Jewish people is more important than theological matters	Jewish survival
Rituals are important, but people should decide themselves which to observe	Jewish tradition
Every Jew should support Israel's survival	The centrality of Israel
Being a good Jew and a good American are not incompatible	"Americanness"
Separation of church and state is essential to protect Judaism and Jews	
	Jews' mutual responsibility
	Charity (*tzedakah*) in the forms of philanthropy and social justice

Source: Based on Liebman 1971 and Woocher 1986.

Who Is Jewish?

The question of what makes a person Jewish is fundamental to examining their politics. The interplay between Jewish religion, ethnicity, and culture is complex. Discussing the Jewishness of a variety of some public figures provides a means of illustrating the different possible combinations. For example, what do Bill Clinton's grandson Aidan Mezvinsky and Donald Trump's grandson Theodore Kushner have in common with Barry Goldwater? Each has some Jewish grandparents.[8] But are they Jewish?

Intermarriage. Chelsea Clinton and Ivanka Trump both married Jews, so their children have a pair of Jewish grandparents. Intermarriage is not new and has become fairly common among Jews. The 2013 Pew Research Center Survey of U.S. Jews (Pew Research Center 2013, 35–36) found that 44% of its married Jewish respondents were currently intermarried, including a majority of those who got married in the 1995–2013 period. Those rates seem high, but Putnam and Campbell (2010, 156) found that the percentage of Jews who intermarried (53%) is comparable to the percentage for evangelical Protestants (51%) and less than the percentages for mainline Protestants (60%) and non-Hispanic Catholics (58%).

The Trump and Clinton intermarriages differ in that Ivanka Trump converted to Judaism whereas Chelsea Clinton did not. Their husbands, Jared Kushner and Marc Mezvinsky, were both "Jews by birth," whereas, as a convert, Ivanka became a "Jew by choice." Ivanka and Jared's children are considered Jewish because their mother converted to Judaism. The traditional doctrine is that being Jewish follows matrilineal descent, so Ivanka's conversion qualifies her children to be considered Jewish. In contrast, even though Marc is Jewish, Chelsea and Marc's children would not be considered Jewish by an Orthodox rabbi, because their mother is not Jewish.

The three Kushner children are being raised Jewish, while there has not been a statement yet as to how the two young Mezvinsky children will be raised. Some intermarried couples raise their children as Jewish, others raise them as Christian, and still others acquaint their children with both religions. For example, an intermarried couple who put their children in a local Jewish pre-school explained that they want their children to participate in both Jewish and Christian religious activities and to learn about the traditions of each. Intermarriage is often regarded as threatening the long-term survival of the relatively small American Jewish community because only 43% of children of intermarried couples grow up to identify as Jews (S. Cohen 2018). However, Alan Cooperman (in Johnson 2017, 52), who had a lead role in organizing the 2013 Pew survey, counters that 63% of the intermarried are raising their children Jewish "in some way," and social psychologist Leonard Saxe (in Johnson 2017, 52) contends that intermarriage is "contributing to an increase in the [Jewish] population."

The prevalence of intermarriage has decreased Jews' separation from the larger society. The Clintons and Trumps are like an increasing number of Christians who now have Jews in their family. In the long term, this increased personal acquaintance is likely to reduce feelings of anti-Semitism. At the same time, Jews have become more accustomed to having non-Jewish relatives. Many join extended family in celebrations of Christian holidays or in hybrid celebrations such as "Chrismukkah," which is likely to minimize the extent to which their children will see their Jewishness as setting them apart from the general culture. Jews have been called "a people apart," but the increased connections through intermarriage are one of many ways in which American Jews are less "apart" than they used to be. They have become part of the general society and culture in ways that were unimaginable a century ago, though they remain much more liberal and Democratic than any other religious group. That is a paradox: if being Jewish is finally being accepted, why are their politics still so distinctive?

Partly Jewish. Surveys find that some people consider themselves "partly Jewish." Someone who grew up in an intermarried family might explain, "I am Jewish when I'm with my father's family, but I'm Protestant when I'm with my mother's family." Even some Jews who grew up in inmarried families have come to value experiencing multiple religions. They might explain, "Celebrating two religious traditions allows me to explore my spiritual side more than just one would."

The 2013 Pew survey did not classify as Jews the partly Jewish who also practice another monotheistic religion. However, the 2015 Greater Boston Jewish Community Study (Aronson et al. 2016) included "Jews of multiple religions," who constituted 3% of Boston Jewry. Indeed, having multiple religions is not unique to Jews: the 2014 Pew Religious Landscape Study (RLS) found that 6% of Americans belong to more than one religion (Lipka 2016).

Religious Fluidity. As is the case with other religions, there is considerable religious fluidity in the American Jewish community. The 2014 RLS survey (Pew Research Center 2015, 39) reported that a quarter of adults who were raised as Jewish do not identify as Jewish. While that fluidity may seem high, it is substantially lower than the parallel statistics for mainline Protestants (55%), Catholics (41%), and evangelical Protestants (35%).

This religious fluidity was exemplified by three cabinet secretaries in the late 20th century who were Jewish by descent but did not practice Judaism. James Schlesinger, Casper Weinberger, and William Cohen were Republicans who served in the position of secretary of defense for Presidents Nixon, Reagan, and Clinton, respectively. Weinberger's paternal grandparents had left Judaism; he was raised with a nondenominational Christianity and became Episcopalian. Schlesinger's parents were Jewish, but he converted to Lutheranism as a young adult. Cohen's father was Jewish, but Jewish lineage is traditionally through the maternal line; leaving Judaism when he was told he would have to go through conversion to have a bar mitzvah, he eventually became a Unitarian Universalist. When Reform Judaism began to consider accepting as Jewish those children who have Jewish fathers and are raised as Jews, Cohen, then a senator, reportedly wrote the president of the Union of American Hebrew Congregations, "If you had been around 30 years ago, I might still be a Jew." None of these three defense secretaries identified as Jewish. The 2013 Pew report would not have classified any of them as Jews, since they were practicing another monotheistic religion.

According to the 2014 RLS, only 7% of Jews left their childhood religion to join another faith as did Schlesinger, Weinberger, and Cohen. The more common pattern is becoming unaffiliated, which is the pattern for 18% of those who were raised Jewish. That value is within 2 percent of the values that the RLS found for people who were raised as Catholics or evangelical Protestants, and it is less than the 26% of those who were raised in mainline Protestant churches but are currently unaffiliated.

Jews of No Religion. Many prominent people can be cited as examples of those who were raised Jewish but became unaffiliated. David Silverman, the current president of the American Atheists organization, was raised Jewish and had a bar mitzvah. Economist Milton Friedman was raised Jewish but considered himself agnostic, as was and did Felix Frankfurter, who served on the Supreme Court from 1939 to 1962 (Dalin 2017, 129). Many American Jewish scientists are in this category, including evolutionary biologist Stephen Jay Gould (who called himself a Jewish agnostic) and theoretical physicist Richard Feynman. Playwright Arthur Miller, composer Aaron Copland, comedian Sarah Silverman, and screenwriter Woody Allen are just a few of the many Jews in the arts who fit this pattern.

The 2013 Pew report labeled them as "Jews of no religion" (JNR). Most Jews are "Jews by religion" (JBR), who say they are Jewish when asked if their religion is Protestant, Catholic, Jewish, or something else. "Jews of no religion" do not practice any religion but consider themselves Jewish, often because of Jewish heritage. When asked their religion, typical JNRs might answer, "I don't believe in any religion." When probed further, they might say that they are Jewish because they were raised Jewish and/or because their parents were Jewish.

The JNR are meaningfully different from those who have left Judaism for another religion. Secretaries Weinberger, Schlesinger, and Cohen had Jewish ancestry but actively practiced a different religion, whereas the JNR do not believe in any religion. Indeed, most Jews in this category do not consider themselves atheists or agnostics; they simply do not think of themselves in any religious terms. Still, most retain some bond with being Jewish. A good friend of mine exemplifies this category. He would not say he has a religion, but like many other JNRs, he celebrates Hanukkah with his extended family and attends friends' Passover seders, as evocative reminders of his Jewish heritage. The notion of "Jews of no religion" is intrinsically paradoxical, but it exemplifies the complexity of contemporary Judaism.[9]

Defining Jews. These definitional matters directly affect estimates of the size of the Jewish population. A careful estimate put the U.S. Jewish population at 6.85 million in 2017 (Sheskin and Dashefsky 2018, 179). However, defining Jews solely based on their religion would miss as many as 15–20% of people who consider themselves Jewish (Cohen, Ukeles, and Miller 2012).[10]

These issues are also relevant for surveys that seek to measure Jews' opinions and voting. Surveys of the general population, including exit polls following recent elections, generally ask people to identify their religion.[11] People who answer "Jewish" qualify as "Jews by religion," which excludes many people who consider themselves "culturally Jewish" while not practicing Judaism. Surveys that seek to estimate the size of the Jewish community therefore generally ask further screening questions of people who do not give their religion as "Jewish." These questions include whether the person had Jewish parents, was raised Jewish, or considers himself or herself Jewish for any reason, so the "Jews of no religion" can also be identified.

Analysts of Jewish surveys must decide whom to include in their reports (Perlmann 2010). The 2000–01 National Jewish Population Survey (NJPS) included as Jewish those who considered themselves Jewish and either had a Jewish parent or were raised Jewish, even if they also had another nonmonotheistic religious affiliation (e.g., Buddhism). The 2013 Pew report included JNRs who consider themselves Jewish in some way but do not have any religious beliefs;[12] they constitute 23% of the Jews in the Pew report. Slightly less than half of them described themselves as atheists or agnostics, the rest as nothing in particular.

As is shown in later chapters of this study, JNRs are somewhat more liberal and Democratic than JBRs. As a result, media surveys and election exit polls that ask people their religion but do not include further screening questions are likely to interview a more politically conservative set of Jews than those responding to the Pew survey questions. This book follows the Pew report's practice of including JNRs as Jews. However, some surveys cited in this book omit JNRs by asking people their religion without including further screening questions, and that omission is indicated when references are made to those surveys.

Conclusions

There is more to religion than being a member of that religion. What is important to Jewish identity is feeling Jewish. Family connections, embellished by family traditions and rituals, are crucial to that feeling. The synagogue acts like an extended family for many Jews, enmeshing members in interlacing friendship groups. Many other Jews do not belong to synagogues but still enjoy participating in cultural Judaism with their friends. The tenets of the religion are important to some people, but for many Jews, those tenets are secondary to feeling Jewish because of ancestry, heritage, and culture.

Jews have many characteristics of an ethnoreligious group, but some Jews identify primarily with the religious part, while more identify with ethnicity and culture. A plurality interprets their Judaism as "being part of the Jewish people," and most feel that being Jewish is more a matter of ancestry/culture than of religion. Being Jewish is still important to the overwhelming majority of Jews, but for many American Jews, practicing their religion has mainly become their way of exhibiting and celebrating their ethnicity and culture with family and friends.

Since a significant number of Jews do not emphasize the religious aspect of being Jewish, the politics of many Jews are not affected by their religion directly as much as by other aspects they share with other Jews. The findings in this chapter imply that religion per se is not likely to be important as a source of Jews' predominantly liberal views and Democratic leanings; their ethnocultural identity as Jews is likely to be more important to their politics. However, the denominational fracture among Jews has some implications for Jews' politics. The next chapter explores these implications, with emphasis on the distinction between Orthodox and non-Orthodox Jews.

CHAPTER 2

Differences among Jews

Shortly after the Pew Survey of U.S. Jews was released in 2013, I attended a symposium about changes in American Jewry. A presenter seemed to say that one of the most important changes was an increase in the number of Jewish nuns. There was considerable consternation in the hearing audience as people mulled over the possibility that large numbers of Jews were joining Catholic convents, until the speaker explained that these people were not "n-u-n-s" but "n-o-n-e-s." The Pew survey had asked Jews if they were Orthodox, Conservative, or Reform, and the "nones" were people who answered that they were none of those—that they were "just Jewish."

These "just Jewish," along with the "Jews of no religion" (JNR) introduced in the previous chapter, emphasize the vast differences among contemporary American Jewry. Back in the 1500s, Jews were simply Jews: they accepted monotheism, respected the Torah, believed in the continuity of the Jewish people, and understood that they were supposed to observe the many commandments in the Torah—though certainly not all did. Nowadays, there are three principal branches of Judaism—Orthodox, Conservative, and Reform—a distinction that is somewhat similar to the different denominations in Protestantism. These branches differ in their underlying philosophies and their levels of observance. Because the divisions carry through to Jews' political views, it is important to the present discussion to understand the differences between these major movements in organized Judaism, as well as between them and Jewish "nones."

It is reasonable to expect that those who identify with the stricter, Orthodox branch of Judaism would be more likely to emphasize the religious aspects of Judaism, with a decrease going down the denominational ladder and with least emphasis on religion among the "just Jewish" JNR. However, some other aspects of Judaism may not follow the denominational ordering, and examining them would illuminate other aspects of feeling Jewish.

A quick introduction to the history of Jewish immigration to the United States is useful for the discussion of Jewish denominations. There were a few Jews on the ships that Christopher Columbus sailed to America, but Jews' first actual settlement in what is now the United States occurred in 1654, when a ship of Jews landed in New Amsterdam, modern-day New York City. A simplified account is that there have been five main waves of migration of Jews into the country. The earliest consisted of Sephardic Jews, the descendants of exiled Spanish and Portuguese Jews. Roughly from 1820 to 1880, there was a second, larger migration from German-speaking countries (Prussia, Austria, etc.). The largest Jewish immigration was the third wave from Russia and Eastern Europe around 1881–1924. Immigration was tightened considerably in 1924, by imposing immigration limits based on the national origin of the U.S. population in 1890, before the large-scale migration of Eastern European Jews. The quotas severely limited the ability of Jews fleeing from Nazi Europe to escape to the United States, but a small, fourth wave of immigrants managed to enter, as did some displaced persons right after the war.[1] With a relaxation of immigration laws, a fifth migration wave entered in the 1950s–90s, from nations under Soviet domination during the Cold War and from the former Soviet Union.

This chapter begins by introducing the Jewish denominations, along with the political differences between Orthodox and other Jews. Next, the religiosity of American Jews is discussed, since it is common for more religious Americans to be more politically conservative. Finally, the aspects of Judaism emphasized by adherents to the different branches of Judaism are compared, to determine if there are other differences that could affect their politics.

The Orthodox

Orthodox Jewry accepts the Torah as representing the exact word of God and emphasizes Jewish law (*halakha*). There can be questioning of what God requires, but questions must be answered within the Torah and Talmud. Orthodox religious services are conducted almost exclusively in Hebrew. Most Orthodox Jews keep kosher in their dietary practices (both at home and outside the home), do not work on the Sabbath, observe all the religious holy days, and follow the other traditional practices.

A Revitalized Movement. Most Jewish immigrants had been traditional in their Judaism in the old country. Many moved away from that position when they were in the United States. By the middle of the 20th century, it seemed that Orthodox Jewry would soon disappear in America. Yet the most recent two immigration waves have reenergized Orthodoxy.

The immigration wave just before and after World War II included many professionals, most of whom were assimilated Jews who fit very well into Conservative or Reform Judaism. However, an exception in the national origin law for ministers of any religious denomination (Sarna and Eleff 2017) permitted non-quota immigration of leaders of several important ultra-Orthodox sects. In particular, Yosef Yitzchak Schneersohn, who later became the rebbe of the Chabad movement, came to the United States in 1940, and Joel Teitelbaum, the rebbe of the Satmar Hasidic dynasty in Hungary, escaped the Holocaust and moved to the United States in 1946. Schneersohn made the Chabad movement influential by establishing a set of Chabad houses around the world in an attempt to reach out to lapsed Jews. Keren-Kratz (2017) describes how Teitelbaum established himself as a major figure and thereby increased the importance of the Satmar Hasidim by adopting an anti-Zionist perspective after Israel was formed. As a result, the Chabad and Satmar movements have since grown exponentially in America, providing considerable energy to Orthodox Judaism.

The immigrant wave in the second half of the 20th century by Jews from nations (including Cuba) that had been under Soviet domination during the Cold War and from the former Soviet Union consisted mainly of older Jews who still spoke their mother tongues. Under Communism, they had not been allowed to learn about their Jewish heritage. Orthodox Judaism in the United States was more successful in reaching out to them than were the other movements (Kliger 2011).

Deborah Dash Moore (personal communication) has suggested an additional dynamic for accounting for the growth in the Orthodox community. Before World War II, the Orthodox considered themselves to be the norm and the majority in the American Jewish community; afterward, they realized they were the minority and gradually adopted the perspective of being a minority. Recognizing their minority status allowed them to revitalize their movement in ways that were unnecessary when they assumed that they were the majority. For example, the yeshiva (seminary) movement grew considerably among the ultra-Orthodox, followed by growth in Jewish day schools.

The Varieties of Orthodoxy. There are two main parts to contemporary Orthodox Jewry. The ultra-Orthodox (*Haredi*), particularly the Hasidim, are insular, practicing separation from secular culture. The Modern Orthodox work outside the home but accept Jewish law as binding and remain observant. Modern Orthodoxy emphasizes secular knowledge as well as the Torah.

Heilman and Cohen's (1989) analysis of 1979–80 data found that there were more Modern Orthodox than ultra-Orthodox Jews, though those authors recognized that Orthodoxy was growing and would become more traditionalistic. Not only did the immigration of Hasidic dynasties and Jews from Communist and ex-Communist nations bolster Orthodox numbers, but the high fertility rate of the ultra-Orthodox has considerably increased their population's size. The 2013 Pew survey found that the ultra-Orthodox now outnumber the Modern Orthodox by roughly two to one. Recent trends (Ferziger 2015) are toward diminished differences between the two, as the Modern Orthodox have become more observant in their ritual and social practices.

There has been some tension between the Orthodox and the non-Orthodox. By the 1970s, many Orthodox Jews viewed the non-Orthodox as inauthentic Jews, while many non-Orthodox regarded the ultra-Orthodox as an outdated sect. That tension has subsequently decreased as the ultra-Orthodox have practiced outreach to try to bring less-religious Jews back into the fold (Ferziger 2015). Still, the Orthodox movement has operated so separately from the rest of organized Judaism that discussions of contemporary American Jews often ignore the Orthodox.

The distinction between Orthodox and non-Orthodox Jews is important for studies of Jewish politics because, as is shown in later chapters in this book, the Orthodox are distinctly more politically conservative and Republican than other Jews. Like fundamentalist Christians, they are more conservative on most political issues than are other denominations, though their impact is limited because they are the smallest of the major branches of Judaism. The Pew estimate that only 10% of Jews are Orthodox is fully consistent with other surveys but could be marginally understated; as part of their insularity from general society, the ultra-Orthodox may be less willing to participate in surveys (Fischer 2013).[2]

The Non-Orthodox

The Early Jewish Immigrations. The early Jewish settlers in the American colonies were descendants of Sephardic Jews who left Spain and Portugal after the Christian reconquest of Spain led to expulsion of its Jews in 1492. By the time of the American Revolution, Jews had come to the colonies from the rest of western Europe, but Jews were a miniscule 0.05% of the U.S. population.

The large wave of Jewish immigration from Germany and Central Europe between 1820 and 1880 brought Jews up to 0.50% of the total population. This immigration began after anti-Semitic riots in 1819 and 1832 and accelerated after the failed 1848 revolutions in the German states. These immigrants were primarily enlightened urban Jews, often younger sons in families whose property would be inherited by the oldest son. Many became prosperous middle-class merchants in the United States by the middle to late 1800s.

Many of those "German Jews" adopted Reform Judaism. The Reform movement had started in the early 19th century in Germany as part of the Jewish Enlightenment (Haskalah). In 1824, Congregation Beth Elohim (House of God) in Charleston became the first synagogue in America to experiment with reforming its practices. In adapting to American society, the early Reform movement swept away many traditional Jewish practices. By the late 1800s, Reform congregations were holding religious services primarily in English, observing the Sabbath on Sunday, and not following kosher dietary restrictions.

Emigration from Eastern Europe. The "Great Migration" of two million Eastern European Jews from 1881 through 1924 brought Jews up to just over 3% of the U.S. population. They were fleeing Russia, Romania, and other Eastern European countries where direct anti-Semitism periodically culminated in murderous anti-Jewish riots (pogroms). Many of these "Russian Jews," eager to adapt their traditional religious practices to their new country but finding the Reform movement too radical and dominated by middle-class German Jews, joined the new Conservative movement, which had its origins in Germany in the mid-19th century and came to the United States in the early 20th century. The Conservatives became the largest branch of Judaism in America by the 1950s.

Conservative Judaism accepts Jewish law as binding but regards it as evolving to fit the modern age. It relaxes many of the stringent rules, rather than totally eliminating them. It maintains more rituals and uses more Hebrew in its religious services than Reform Judaism does, while still adapting to the general culture more than traditional Judaism did. A typical compromise is that most Conservative Jews will eat at restaurants and people's houses that are not strictly kosher, though many keep kosher at home. Conservative Jews vary in how they handle this, some avoiding meat at restaurants. For example, Eric Cantor, majority leader in the U.S. House of Representatives from 2011 to 2014, is Conservative and has stated that he is "basically a vegetarian" when eating out, because he does not eat nonkosher meat or chicken (Greenberger 2009).

The Modern Reform Movement. The Reform movement has continued to evolve. It emphasizes social justice more than Jewish law but has brought back many traditional religious practices. Its Sabbath has been returned to the traditional Saturday observance. There is considerable Hebrew in its religious services, though those services are still shorter than Orthodox or Conservative services. Relatively few Reform Jews keep kosher, even at home.

The Reform movement has been particularly progressive in attracting adherents. It was the first of the major movements to accept gender equality in services and to be open to gays and lesbians, and it remains more acceptant of intermarried couples. Since 1983, it has accepted children born of a Jewish father as Jewish if they are raised Jewish, as well as the traditional practice of matrilineal descent. Partly because of its greater openness in these regards, the Reform movement has become the largest branch of American Judaism.

The Jewish "Nones." Many Jews today do not identify with any of the major branches of Judaism. Some grew up in one tradition but currently attend a synagogue from a different tradition, for reasons of family or convenience, and are uncomfortable being labeled. Others do not belong to a synagogue and therefore do not consider denominational distinction relevant. When surveys ask their denomination, they often answer that they are "just Jewish," so that term is used in this book to refer to these nondenominational Jews.

As is true for the general public, young Jewish people are particularly likely to be nondenominational. According to Pew data, 42% of Jews who are 18 to 29 years of age do not identify with a denomination, versus 37% of Jews between 30 and 49 years old and only 27% of Jews 50 years old and older. Eventually, nondenominational young people might choose a denomination when they get married and might affiliate with a synagogue in order for their children to meet other Jews and have bar/bat mitzvahs. However, general population trends suggest that even as they age, the millennial generation may not become as denominational as previous generations.

Other Distinctions. Judaism includes three smaller movements that are less traditional. Reconstructionism views Judaism as a civilization more than a theology, the Humanistic movement emphasizes Jewish culture rather than theology, and the Renewal movement stresses spiritual aspects of Judaism over philosophical ones. In this book, Jews who affiliate with these three movements are included among the "just Jewish."

Early Jews in the Americas were Sephardic, while most Jews in America today come from Ashkenazi (Central and Eastern European) roots. There are still sizable concentrations of Sephardic Jews from Turkey and Rhodes in Seattle and of Mizrahi (Eastern) Jews from Iran in Los Angeles. The differences between Sephardic and Ashkenazi Jews are a matter of customs more than theology, though Sephardim are more likely to be traditional Orthodox rather than Conservative or Reform.

Two related movements are generally not considered Jewish. Karaites follow the Torah but do not accept the postbiblical interpretations given by the Talmud and later rabbinic Judaism. Many Karaites do not consider themselves to be Jewish, and they avoided the Holocaust by convincing Nazi Germany that they were not Jewish. The Messianic Jews for Jesus movement is also not considered to be Jewish.

Other Jewish movements include Kabbalah, which employs mystical interpretation. The Hasidic movement emphasizes spirituality, but with more emphasis on joy than on the intellectualism of Kabbalah. The Chabad movement stresses outreach to encourage nonobservant Jews to return to traditional Jewish practices. Incidentally, Zionism is not a separate religious movement; it is a nationalist movement for a Jewish state in Israel (Zion).

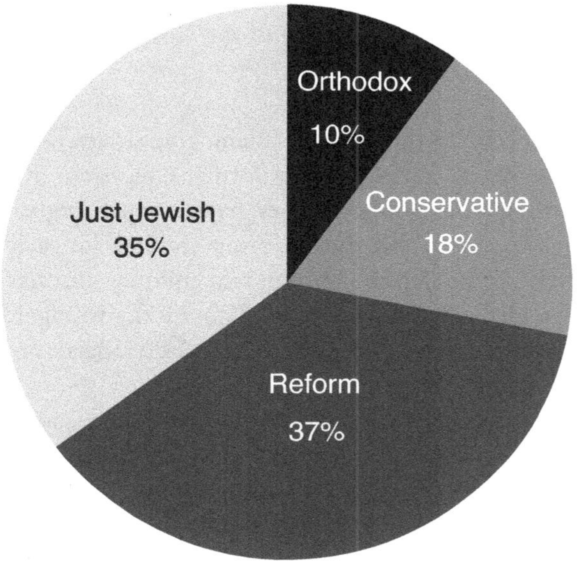

Fig. 2.1. Size of Jewish denominations
(*Note:* Data from 2013 Pew Jewish survey, recomputed with noncitizens excluded. The Just Jewish category includes 6% of the sample that identifies with other denominations.)

Denomination Size. Figure 2.1 shows the size of the three major streams of American Judaism today. The Reform movement is largest (37%), the Conservative movement is second in size (18%), and the Orthodox group is smallest (10%). The figure also shows that many Jews today consider themselves "just Jewish" rather than identifying with any of these movements (35%).

Not surprisingly, the "just Jewish" are particularly prevalent among Jews of no religion, with nearly three-quarters of JNR being "just Jewish," compared to slightly over three-quarters of Jews by religion (JBR) who identify with one of the major branches of Judaism. As table 2.1 shows, Orthodox and Conservative Jews are overwhelmingly JBR, as are a large

TABLE 2.1. Denominations of Jews

Denomination	Jews by Religion	Jews of No Religion	Total
Orthodox	10%	0%	10%
Conservative	17%	1%	18%
Reform	32%	5%	37%
Just Jewish	18%	17%	35%
Total	77%	23%	100%

Source: Analysis of the 2013 Pew Jewish survey, recomputed with noncitizens excluded.

majority of Reform Jews. By contrast, nearly half of the "just Jewish" are JNR.

Demographic Differences. The Orthodox differ demographically from other Jews in important respects. They have less formal education and lower median income than Jews as a whole. They have a much higher fertility rate; the Pew survey reported that there are four children for each Orthodox adult aged 40–59, compared to less than two children for each Jewish adult generally. The ultra-Orthodox are also dramatically younger, with a median age of 35, versus a median age over 50 for the Modern Orthodox, Conservative, and Reform groups.

Additionally, compared to other Jews, the Orthodox intermarry with non-Jews at a lower rate (only 2% in the Pew survey). Pew found that among the Orthodox under age 50, the cross-generation retention rate (the proportion remaining in the same denomination as their parents) is much higher than for other branches of Judaism. However, William Helmreich, who has extensively studied the Orthodox, claimed (in Johnson 2017, 50) that the real defection rate among the Orthodox is unknown; he implied that it is likely higher than generally recognized.

Because of these demographic differences, the Orthodox community is likely to grow over the coming decades. At the same time, trends suggest that the numbers of non-Orthodox Jews will decline. Sociologist Steven M. Cohen[3] (2018) points to the low fertility rate and high intermarriage rate of non-Orthodox Jews and emphasizes that only 43% of children of intermarried Jewish parents grow up to identify as Jews. Orthodox Jews are very engaged religiously, while, at the other end of the spectrum, the "just Jewish" are not very engaged. Cohen identified the engaged "Jewish middle" as those non-Orthodox who say that being Jewish is at least somewhat important to them, attend a Passover seder, and have some close friends who are Jewish, and he found that the number of Jews in this engaged middle falls from 53% in the 55–69 age-group to just 35% among those 25–39 years old. This led him to conclude that the Jewish middle is shrinking, which raises concern about the future of American Judaism. The counterargument is that intermarriage has led to many more households with a Jewish adult and many more children who may identify as Jewish in adulthood (McGinity 2009; Thompson 2014). Sasson et al. (2017) find that with the greater openness to intermarriage, children of intermarried parents in the millennial generation are more likely to be raised Jewish, to have a Jewish education, to identify as Jewish as adults, and to engage in Jewish practices.

Political Implications. As mentioned briefly above, these denominational distinctions are important to studies of Jewish politics because the Orthodox are more politically conservative and more Republican in their party ties than the non-Orthodox. For example, according to the 2013 Pew data, Republicans outnumber Democrats by 58% to 37% among Orthodox Jews, and political conservatives outnumber liberals even more strongly, 59% to 13%. Both of those findings are in sharp contrast to the Democratic and liberal leanings of Reform and Conservative Jews. Indeed, the attitudes of Orthodox Jews on many political questions are closer to those of fundamentalist Christians than to those of other Jews. If current political alignments continue, growth of the Orthodox would lead to greater support for political conservatism and the Republican Party among the Jewish community. These trends mean that the Orthodox might lead a reversal of the political leanings of American Jews, though, of course, unforeseen political events could easily overtake and overturn these political implications.

The consequences of denominational differences for Jews' political attitudes and for the possibility of political realignment are discussed further in later chapters of this book. The political differences between Orthodox and non-Orthodox Jews are large enough to confound other political differences among Jews. As a result, some of the analyses in later chapters check whether effects that are found are just due to differences between the Orthodox and non-Orthodox.

Importance of Religion

The literature on religion and politics routinely finds political differences according to how religious people are—their "religiosity." In particular, those who most frequently attend religious services generally vote more Republican than those who rarely attend. Such differences are largely denominational, with fundamentalist denominations attending services more often and voting more Republican. This finding is strong enough that it is important to examine the correlates of religious observance among Jews.

Surveys routinely find that Jews are relatively low on the common measures of religiosity. Many Jews do not belong to synagogues, do not attend services frequently, and do not observe several traditional Jewish religious practices. The lower apparent level of religiosity among Jews is partly due to the difference in expectations across the different branches of Judaism, but it also reflects Jews' attitudes about religion.

Religiosity. Surveys usually use reports of church attendance as a behavioral indicator of "religiosity." Jews' synagogue attendance is low compared to the level of church attendance in other religions. For example, only 29% of Jews by religion in the 2013 Pew report attended Jewish religious services at least monthly, compared to 50% for the general public (Pew Research Center 2013, 75–76). Synagogue membership is indeed low: only 39% of JBR in the Pew survey were members.[4]

These statistics are misleading for several reasons. First, unlike Christian churches, many synagogues require membership dues, especially for attending High Holiday services. These dues are often upwards of $2,000 annually, which deters many Jews from joining synagogues and leads some parents to drop their membership after their children have had their bar and/or bat mitzvahs. Second, synagogue attendance is not necessarily an appropriate measure of religiosity for Jews, because it is not a prerequisite for practicing Judaism. Even a rabbi is not necessary for conducting prayers, since a rabbi is technically a teacher rather than a prayer leader. By traditional standard, all that is required for collective prayer is a minyan, a quorum of ten males aged thirteen or over, with Reform and Conservative synagogues now counting women as part of a minyan. Third, most Jews do attend synagogue services on the most religiously important Jewish holidays, the autumn High Holidays of Rosh Hashanah and Yom Kippur. In the Pew survey, 69% of JBR said that they attend services at least a few times a year, such as for the High Holidays. Fourth, the celebration of some Jewish holidays is in homes with family and friends rather than at the synagogue. Surveys find that these are some of the most prevalent Jewish behaviors nowadays. For example, 70% of the Pew sample indicated that they attended a Passover seder the previous year, and 72% of the sample for the 2000–01 National Jewish Population Survey (NJPS) said they light Hanukkah candles. Thus, the level of Jews' religious practice is higher than would be obtained by measuring Jews' religiosity by weekly or monthly synagogue attendance.

An alternative measure of religiosity that is frequently used is how often people pray. However, reports of the frequency of Jews' praying vary widely, depending on how the question is worded. Only a quarter of Jews in the 2014 Pew Religious Landscape Study prayed outside of religious services daily, versus half of Americans as a whole. Half of Jews in the 1972–2012 data from the General Social Survey reported praying at least once a week, versus three-quarters of non-Jews. Yet three-quarters of the 2000–01 NJPS respondents answered that they pray using their own words outside of religious services. These results are too inconsistent for a firm conclusion about the frequency of praying by Jews, other than that it seems lower than among American Christians.

The Importance of Religion. The 2013 Pew survey asked respondents how important religion is in their lives. The responses indicate that Jews focus less on religion than non-Jews do. Only 26% of Jews said religion is very important in their lives, compared to 56% of the general public (Pew Research Center 2013, 72).

The first two pairs of columns in table 2.2 show large differences across denominations with respect to belief in God and viewing religion as important. The first row shows ultra-Orthodox Jews to be virtually unanimous in their absolute certainty in believing that there is a God. The vast majority of them also consider religion an important part of their lives: 89% describe it as very important, and the rest call it somewhat important. The Modern Orthodox are also at very high levels in these regards. Given this emphasis on religion among the Orthodox, they are most likely to

TABLE 2.2. Religiosity of Jews by Denomination

	Belief in God		Importance of religion in your life		Importance of being Jewish in your life	
Denomination	Absolutely certain	Absolutely or fairly certain	Very important	Very or somewhat important	Very important	Very or somewhat important
Ultra-Orthodox	97%	98%	89%	100%	89%	100%
Modern Orthodox	77%	93%	73%	94%	84%	99%
Conservative	43%	76%	43%	83%	69%	93%
Reform	30%	59%	16%	55%	44%	87%
Just Jewish JBR	25%	51%	16%	45%	39%	80%
Just Jewish JNR	16%	29%	5%	13%	8%	39%
All Jews	35%	59%	26%	56%	46%	80%

Source: Analysis of the 2013 Pew Jewish survey, recomputed with noncitizens excluded.

base their politics on their religion. As expected, both belief in God and importance of religion diminish as one goes down the denominational ordering in the table.

The Importance of Being Jewish. As shown in chapter 1, the Pew survey found that Jews emphasized being Jewish more than religion. However, the last pair of columns in table 2.2 show differences between denominations, again following the denominational ordering. More people in the Conservative and Reform movements consider being Jewish important than consider religion important. A 69% majority of those identifying with the Jewish Conservative movement consider being Jewish very important, just 43% of them view religion as that important, and only 43% are absolutely certain in their belief in God. Fewer than a majority of Reform Jews give the most positive answers on these questions, yet 87% of them view being Jewish as at least somewhat important in their lives, 55% view religion as at least somewhat important, and 59% are at least fairly certain in their belief in God, though many might have a nontraditional conception of God. These results imply that Conservative and Reform Jews are more likely to base their politics on their understanding of being Jewish than on Judaism's religious tenets.

While a majority of all three main branches of Judaism view religion and being Jewish as important in their life and believe in God, the "just Jewish" are lowest in these regards. Only half of the "just Jewish" who are Jews of no religion are at least fairly certain that there is a God, though 80% of them regard being Jewish as at least somewhat important in their lives. As to be expected, the "just Jewish" JNRs are least religious on these measures, yet still more than one-third of them (39%) consider being Jewish somewhat important in their lives.

The denominational order also fits for adherence to matters of ritual observance, as shown in table 2.3. On these behaviors, the Orthodox score highest, while the Reform and especially the "just Jewish" score lowest. The only deviation in the results is that Modern Orthodox Jews attended religious services somewhat more than the ultra-Orthodox.

Political Implications. As stated above, studies of the general public routinely show that those who are more religious vote more Republican. That tendency is also true for Jews: for example, 60% of those who attend services more than once a week are Republican, versus only 12% of those who never attend services. However, that dramatic difference is because the frequent synagogue attenders are primarily Orthodox while the nonattenders are primarily Jews of no religion.

The differences are milder among the non-Orthodox Jews by religion: those who consider religion to be at least somewhat important are only slightly more Republican than those who consider it less important (24% to 12%). Similarly, those who regard being Jewish as at least somewhat important are just slightly more Republican than those who view it as less important (21% to 14%). Thus, most of the effect of religiosity on Jews' politics involves their sorting themselves into the different branches of Judaism.

Jewish Identity

The 2013 Pew survey results show that the denominational ordering accounts for some, but not all, of the differences in people's Jewish identity. As shown in figure 2.2, the expected denominational order is followed by respondents' answers to whether they view their being Jewish as mainly a matter of religion, ancestry, or culture. Predictably, the Orthodox were most likely to choose "religion" as the answer, with a majority of the ultra-Orthodox choosing "religion" only. By contrast, fewer than one-sixth of the non-Orthodox chose "religion" by itself. Instead, sizable majorities of the Reform and "just Jewish" chose "ancestry/culture" without "religion," as did nearly half of Conservative Jews.[5] The relative emphasis on culture and ancestry reveals different views of being Jewish. Reflecting their enjoy-

TABLE 2.3. Religious Observance of Jews by Denomination

Denomination	Attend religious services at least monthly	Attend Passover Seder	Fast on Yom Kippur	Keep kosher at home
Ultra-Orthodox	71%	100%	100%	98%
Modern Orthodox	77%	98%	94%	84%
Conservative	40%	80%	81%	32%
Reform	17%	77%	59%	7%
Just Jewish JBR	13%	57%	41%	14%
Just Jewish JNR	2%	37%	20%	10%
All Jews	24%	70%	57%	22%

Source: Analysis of the 2013 Pew Jewish survey, recomputed with noncitizens excluded.

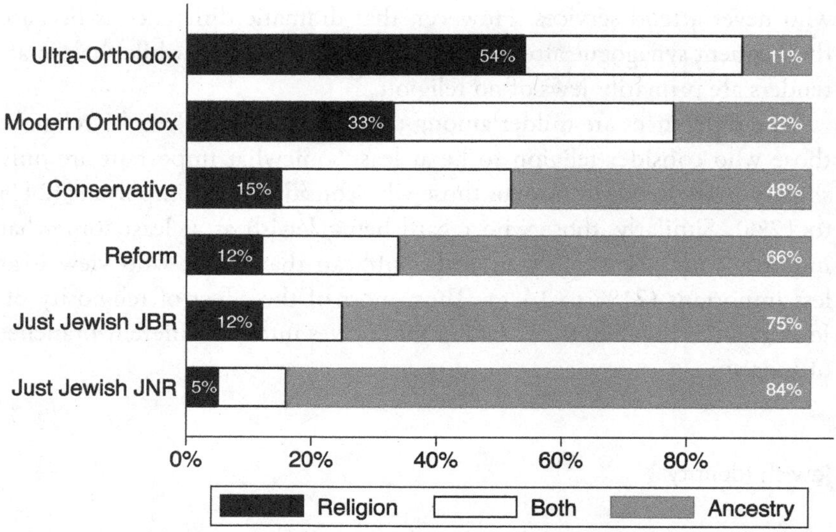

Fig. 2.2. Denominational differences in viewing being Jewish as a matter of ancestry/culture, religion, or both

(*Note:* Data from my analysis of the 2013 Pew Jewish survey; percentages in the middle bars omitted to improve readability.)

ment of Jewish culture, more Conservative and Reform respondents chose "culture" by itself than chose "ancestry" by itself. By contrast, more of the "just Jewish" chose "ancestry" rather than "culture," because their main tie to Judaism was having a Jewish parent.

As shown in table 2.4, the denominational ordering was not necessarily followed when people chose which themes they consider essential to their being Jewish. Only the themes in the two left columns of the table—Jewish law and a Jewish community—fit the denominational ordering from ultra-Orthodox to "just Jewish." While the Orthodox give more emphasis to Jewish law and a Jewish community than the other groups, only the ultra-Orthodox give more emphasis to Jewish law than to these other four themes. However, the denominational ordering does not fit responses to the Israel and social justice topics, with the denominations in the middle emphasizing those topics more than either the ultra-Orthodox or the "just Jewish" Jews of no religion. The proportions for the ultra-Orthodox reflect the fact that some ultra-Orthodox sects (especially the Satmar) are anti-Zionist and that some sects have little interest in secular society. Israel is especially important to the Modern Orthodox and the Conservative. The last column of the table shows that the Modern Orthodox most emphasize ethics, but there is not a very consistent pattern on that theme among the other denominations. Comparison between the themes of focusing on Israel and social equality in the third and fourth columns is instructive. The Modern Orthodox focus more on Israel than on social equality, whereas the Reform emphasize social justice concerns more. The "just Jewish" JNR gave the lowest importance rating for all five of these aspects of what being Jewish means to them. They even regard being ethical as less part of their Jewish identity than the other groups, which emphasizes how peripheral their Jewishness is to them.

In any case, a single dimension does not fully suffice for understanding contemporary Jewish identity.[6] Statistical analysis (not shown) of the 2013 Pew data on the several different aspects of being Jewish in table 2.4 reveals a contrast between emphasizing religious/communal themes (including observing Jewish law and being part of a Jewish community) and individualistic/societal topics (e.g., working for justice and equality in society and leading an ethical and moral life).[7] Those two clusters are nearly independent, with only a mild correlation of 0.30 between them, so these two aspects of Judaism are not opposites: some Jews emphasize both, some just one, and some neither. Caring about Israel falls between the two clusters, suggesting that its importance transcends the religious/ethnic distinction. This analysis demonstrates that religious and ethnocultural

TABLE 2.4. Essentials of Jewish Identity by Denomination

Denomination	Observing Jewish law	Being part of a Jewish community	Caring about Israel	Working for justice and equality in society	Leading an ethical and moral life
Ultra-Orthodox	83%	70%	46%	48%	79%
Modern Orthodox	74%	68%	70%	61%	84%
Conservative	24%	40%	58%	59%	69%
Reform	11%	24%	41%	62%	74%
Just Jewish JBR	13%	20%	44%	61%	67%
Just Jewish JNR	5%	8%	19%	46%	55%
All Jews	20%	28%	43%	57%	69%

Source: Analysis of the 2013 Pew Jewish survey, recomputed with noncitizens excluded.

Note: Table 2.4 gives the percentages of survey respondents saying that a topic is an essential part of what being Jewish means to them.

emphases should be considered as separate but not independent foci of contemporary Jewish identity.[8] The Orthodox emphasize religion enough that it could be the basis of their political views, but most Jews' political choices are likely to be based more on their ethnocultural identity than on their religious beliefs.

Conclusions

The focus on Jewish peoplehood described in chapter 1 provides a unifying theme for Jews, but the growth of separate denominations reflects factionalism. While the Orthodox are the most religiously observant, they are the smallest of the organized movements. The non-Orthodox, especially the Reform and the "just Jewish," remain the largest segment of American Jewry. The considerable differences between Orthodox and non-Orthodox Jews suggest that we are moving toward having two somewhat separate Jewries, the Orthodox being more politically conservative and Republican, the non-Orthodox being overwhelmingly liberal and Democratic. However, demographic trends indicate that the Orthodox are likely to keep increasing in relative size, which could shift the political balance among Jews.

A dimension from Orthodox to Reform and "just Jewish" underlies religious observance, but other aspects of Jewish identity, such as emphasis on Israel and on social justice and ethical living, do not follow that ordering. There are some important differences among the non-Orthodox, with the Conservative movement stressing Israel more, the Reform movement putting greater emphasis on social justice, and the "just Jewish" being minimally engaged with Judaism. The implications of denominational differences for Jews' political attitudes and for the possibility of political realignment are discussed further in later chapters.

The findings presented in this chapter and the preceding one suggest that religion per se is not the major source of Jews' predominantly liberal views and Democratic leanings. Instead, their ethnocultural identity as Jews is likely to be more important to their politics. That ethnocultural identity would be transmitted to their politics through the social identity, the values, and the subjective self-interest of Jews, discussed in part II of this book.

PART II

Explanations of Jews' Politics

A wide variety of historical, economic, sociological, political, psychological, personality, and genetic explanations for Jews' liberal and Democratic leanings have been proposed—and criticized—over the years. A group's politics are usually too complicated for any single explanation to suffice. Required instead is a system that explains (1) why the group originally developed its political leanings, (2) why it retains those leanings, and (3) how those leanings are transmitted to the following generations.

The chapters in this part of this book develop an explanatory model covering those aspects and based on three factors that can affect groups' political positions: their self-interest, values, and identity. This model is intended as a general one that can account for the exceptionality of some subgroups, recognize country-specific historical circumstances, and accommodate changing situations. It also calls attention to the situations in which a group's self-interest and values come into conflict, creating the potential for change in their politics.

Chapter 3 presents the importance of Jews' social identity, emphasizing how their political views have been transmitted to newer generations because being liberal and especially being Democratic have become parts of many Jews' understanding of being Jewish. Chapter 4 focuses on two explanations that have fallen out of favor: Jews' self-interest and values. It emphasizes both the role of self-interest in Jews' initial adoption of political views and the role of values in reinforcing those political views. Chapter 5 turns to minority consciousness, as a crucial factor that underlies Jews' self-interest, values, and social identity. This explanatory system provides a basis for examining Jews' political positions in detail in part III of this book.

CHAPTER 3

The Social Identity of American Jews

When I used to ask my aunts and uncles about their politics, their usual answer was something like "I'm a Democrat because Jews are Democrats." By contrast, when I was in a seminar a few years ago with a scholar who specializes in Jews and politics, he insisted that Jews are mostly Republicans. When the rest of us assured him that the data are clear that Jews are mostly Democrats, he insisted that his family and everyone he knows back in his hometown, a city that happens to have an unusually high concentration of Orthodox Jews, are Republican. Both sides of this story emphasize that party identification has become ingrained in many people's Jewish identity, on the Democratic side for most Jews, but on the Republican side for some, especially those coming from Republican families in heavily Orthodox communities.

The key concept here is a person's "social identity," which involves how people think of themselves with respect to societal groups. A group's social identity answers the question "Who are we?" People have multiple identities, from gender, racial, and class identities to nationality, ethnic, and religious identities, and these different identities can be evoked in different situations. This chapter begins by explaining social identity theory and considering the factors that affect Jews' social identity as Jews. The discussion also emphasizes the importance of the corollary question "Who are we not?" It considers how Jews distance their group from relevant out-groups.

Social identities sometimes become politically relevant, in which case they are spoken of as "politicized social identities." The second part of this chapter turns to how social identity becomes politicized. Social identity has become one of the major explanations of why American Jews are predominantly liberal and Democratic. That explanation suggests that being Democratic has become part of the politicized social identity of many American Jews and that this identity is one of the main reasons why their politics is resistant to change. It is as if being Democratic has become ingrained in their DNA as part of their Jewish identity. Having a social identity is not unique to Jews—everyone identifies with some groups. However, politics is not always part of people's religious social identities. In having such an identity, though, Jews are, again, not unique. For example, being Republican has become part of many evangelical Protestants' social identities.

Jews' Social Identity

Early sociopsychological explanations of Jews' politics were based on how Jews related to the general society. Their liberal politics and leftist voting were explained as reactions to their marginality (Lewin 1941; Liebman 1973, 150), alienation from society (Shapiro 2000, 167), status inferiority (Lipset 1963, 256), and status inconsistency in being ascribed low status regardless of their relatively high socioeconomic status (Lenski 1967). As Levey (1996) pointed out, however, the ties between Jews' liberal politics and these conditions were never made clear. In any case, they have little relevance now that Jews are more widely accepted, even if they characterized Jews' positions in society in the mid-20th century. Current theories instead emphasize their in-group relationships and especially their out-group ones.

In-Group Identification. Nowadays social psychologists utilize social identity theory in analyzing group identification. Social identity has been defined (Tajfel 1978) as "that part of an individual's self-concept which derives from his knowledge of his membership of a group (or groups) together with the value and emotional significance attached to that membership." People seem to naturally identify with their social groups, exaggerating the differences between their group and other groups.[1]

Numerous experiments have demonstrated that in-group biases develop even under minimal conditions, known as the *minimal group paradigm*. For example, youngsters who were divided randomly into two groups but were told that their group overestimated the number of dots in a picture and that the other group underestimated the number of dots, consistently favored members of their own group and discriminated against those in the other group. If in-group identification can be created so easily in minimal experimental situations, it can become very strong in real-world settings, as when people grow up thinking of themselves as Jews. Religion is a potent social identity in itself and especially when tied to ethnic identity (Ben-Nun Bloom, Arikan, and Courtemanche 2015). Thus, social identity theory would predict that people who are raised as Jews would develop strong in-group identification.

While there are other possible theoretical explanations of group behavior,[2] social identity theory is particularly relevant here because of how it can relate to the concept of Jewish identity. Of course, people vary in how much they identify with their ethnic and other groups. The strongest political impact would be for people who have high group consciousness (Miller et al. 1981; Barreto and Pedraza 2009), which would be the case for those Jews who interact mainly with other Jews. That 94% of Jews in the Pew survey said they were proud of being Jewish evidences their strong group consciousness (see also A. Campbell et al. 1960, 307–10). As Hertzberg (1989) described, Jewish ethnicity has "a stronger hold than most others, because Jews had been more alien for centuries, as non-Christians, than virtually any other European minority." As a result of Jews' high group consciousness, their Jewish identity may frequently become relevant to their politics.

Out-Groups. The salience of identity to Jews' politics is enhanced by contrast with out-groups. Many explanations of Jews' liberalism focus on the out-group. For example, Fuchs (1955, 399; 1956) referred to Jewish insecurity due to their history as a repressed minority as one factor in their being liberals (see also Levey 1996; Cohen and Liebman 1997; Greenberg and Wald 2001). Sonenshein and Valentino (2000, 361) elaborated on how discrimination can lead to Jews' distinctive politics: "Direct experience of persecution by previous generations does not rapidly dissipate, especially when a group maintains strong cultural and religious bonds." As new generations in a tight ethnoreligious community learn about discrimination against their ancestors, their minority consciousness draws them to the political positions their ancestors developed in response to that discrimination.

Social identity theory emphasizes the role of feelings about out-groups in building loyalty to one's in-group. Being made to feel like a minority can be a factor in establishing stronger identification with one's social group. Even though overt discrimination is less common today than a century ago, Jewish children recognize early that they are part of a minority group—for example, when their families do not celebrate Christmas in the way it is advertised in the general culture. Additionally, as Lipset and Raab (1995, 170) put it, many Jews "are more at ease with the kinds of people they find in the Democratic Party—their fellow ethnics with whom they grew up in America—than with the White Anglo-Saxon Protestants still predominant in the Republican Party." After all, as Achen and Bartels (2016, 266) wrote, "For most people, partisanship is not a carrier of ideology but a reflection of judgments about where 'people like me' belong."

The out-groups that particularly affect Jewish identity are those that would restrict Jews' freedoms, whether because of overt anti-Semitism or because those groups would use the government to create a preference for their own religious views (e.g., using Christian prayers in schools). Thus, when political conservatives and Republicans endorse preferences for Christian views in the public sphere, Jews are likely to see them as part of an out-group (see Wald 2015). The tendency of Republicans to endorse such preferences may similarly explain why most minority religious groups, except for Mormons, identify predominantly with the Democratic Party (Lugo 2008, 206).

Furthermore, when a minority group feels threatened by an out-group, its members come to feel that they have a shared fate, and they therefore become more cohesive. This phenomenon is similar to the "linked fate" concept that Dawson (1994) developed for understanding why middle-class blacks vote Democratic: middle-class blacks feel that the fates of all blacks are intertwined, so they act out of solidarity with less-affluent blacks. Similarly, Jews have developed the belief that their fate is linked to the survival of Jews elsewhere. Anti-Semitic incidents in another state or nation worry American Jews because they realize that the same could happen in their city. Thus, threats from out-groups influence Jews to work together politically.

Politicized Social Identity

Being Democratic has become part of the social identity of many American Jews. Being Jewish is a social identity, and many American Jews incorporate into that identity various common characteristics of Jews, including political characteristics such as being liberals and being Democrats. The result is a politicized social identity.[3] Political characteristics are obviously not essential to being Jewish, but many Jews have come to accept that being Democratic is part of their being Jewish. Importantly, this does not explain why Jews originally began voting Democratic.

The Politicization Process. The social identity argument is that a group can become politicized either from being pulled toward one party or from being pushed away by the other party. Kuo, Malhotra, and Mo (2017) found evidence for the latter cause, explaining that Asian Americans tend to support Democrats as a result of the push of social exclusion, due to feeling that Republicans view them as less "American." A similar logic might hold for many Jews, who may feel pushed away by the conservative social stands of the Republican Party's evangelical religious supporters.

Social identity theorists have come to recognize the importance of group norms that tell people what is expected of them. Norms become "group prototypes" that describe group behavior (Turner 1991), so members come to realize a prototype ("we agree that we are like this") and then behave in conformity to that prototype (see also Hogg 2006, 124). As Jews in the 1930s and 1940s began to consider themselves to be Democrats and liberals, many incorporated those political views into their group prototype and passed them on to subsequent generations.

Thus, many Jews might consider themselves Democrats simply because they have learned to believe that Jews are Democrats. Being Democratic became embedded in the social identity of most American Jews and became part of Jews' "dominant politicized social identity."[4] Sigelman (1991b, 189) was basically referring to that embedded identity when he termed liberalism the "lay religion" of American Jews.

Social networks further reinforce this politicized social identity. When politics comes up in conversations with Jewish friends who are Democrats, the discussion often bolsters Jews' partisan feelings. Even casual partisan remarks made by relatives or friends at the reception after a wedding or bat mitzvah or after Sabbath services can reinforce the group's dominant political direction.

This argument basically suggests that many Jews are Democratic because that political identity has become tradition. As Dawidowicz and Goldstein (1974, 300) describe, it may be a "family group tradition—a habit and custom difficult to shed." This identity is not just due to inertia. Jews are not Democrats today just because their parents or grandparents were decades ago. Their tendency to be Democrats emphasizes, however, that there is considerable stickiness to a group's partisanship. As discussed in chapter 13 in this book, partisanship can change, but it usually takes a fairly dramatic event for large-scale partisan change to occur.

Exceptions. There certainly are exceptions to this dominant social identity. Many Jewish families are Republican, and some Jewish neighborhoods (often in suburban communities) are predominantly Republican. Many Jews grew up in families and communities that were Republican, and they grew up thinking that was part of their being Jewish. That is especially true of people who grew up in tight Orthodox communities. Hence, the politicized social identity of some Jews consists of being Republican and conservative, and they may consider being Republican as essential to their Judaism.

Additionally, Jews who came to the United States after 1950 from Communist and ex-Communist nations are less liberal and Democratic. As shown in table 3.1, the 2000–01 National Jewish Population Survey (NJPS) and the Pew survey find such differences of about 20 to 30 percentage points in the politics of Jews born in the former Soviet Union versus the United States.[5] Consequently, Jews from the former Soviet Union are an exception to the dominant politicized social identity of American Jews. The usual explanation is that they grew up in countries that did not reward individual initiative, so their dissatisfaction with that system led them to be less liberal and hence less Democratic when they came to the United States.

There is also some evidence that Israeli American Jews, defined as Jews who were born in Israel or Palestine or who had a parent born there, comprise another exceptional group here. While there was not much difference between them and U.S.-born Jews in the 2000–01 NJPS survey, con-

TABLE 3.1. Politics of U.S. Jews Born in the Former Soviet Union

	NJPS		Pew	
	Born in former Soviet Union	Born in United States	Born in former Soviet Union	Born in United States
% Democratic	40%	61%	40%	73%
% Liberal	27%	56%	31%	51%
N	163		312	

Source: Analysis of the 2000–01 National Jewish Population Survey and the 2013 Pew Jewish survey.

Note: The data are for Jews who are U.S. citizens.

ducted as Bill Clinton was leaving the presidency, they were considerably less liberal and Democratic than U.S.-born Jews in the 2013 Pew survey, conducted just after President Barack Obama's reelection (table 3.2). This is a small group for statistical analysis, but the survey results imply that the politics of Israeli Americans follows the predominant Israeli view of American politics and therefore turned away from the Democratic Party during the Obama years. Thus, Jews originally from Israel may be another exception to the dominant politicized social identity of American Jews.

Given the importance of parental influence for developing one's social identity, it would be reasonable to expect that children who grew up with two Jewish parents would be more Democratic than those who had intermarried parents. Table 3.3 provides the relevant test on partisanship (see also Abrams and Cohen 2016). Comparing the first two columns, the differences between intermarried respondents who grew up with intermarried versus inmarried parents are trivial.[6] However, one could argue that since moral conservatives are more bound to traditional standards, they are less likely to intermarry, so in-marriage is an effect of conservatism rather than a cause.

TABLE 3.2. Politics of U.S. Jews Born in Israel or Palestine

	NJPS		Pew	
	Israeli heritage	Born in United States	Israeli heritage	Born in United States
% Democratic	58%	61%	43%	73%
% Liberal	51%	56%	25%	52%
N	108		118	

Source: Analysis of the 2000–01 National Jewish Population Survey and the 2013 Pew Jewish survey.

Note: The data are for Jews who are U.S. citizens.

TABLE 3.3. Party Identification by Intermarriage, Non-Orthodox

	Respondent intermarried		Respondent inmarried
Party identification	Parents intermarried	Parents inmarried	Parents inmarried
Republican	13%	15%	23%
Independent	10%	7%	6%
Democrat	76%	78%	71%
Total	99%	100%	100%

Source: Analysis of the 2013 Pew Jewish survey.

Indeed, table 3.3 shows that the in-married respondents in column three are somewhat more likely to be Republican and are correspondingly slightly less likely to be Democratic than the intermarried respondents. These results suggest that partisan differences associated with intermarriage occur because Jews who are bound to traditional social standards (including being conservative and Republican) are less likely to intermarry.

Conclusions

The in-group loyalty of Jews can best be understood as a social identity. This social identity has become politicized, with many Jews viewing being liberal and Democratic as part of their being Jewish. It is as if being liberal and Democratic became part of tradition for many Jews. Indeed, many more Jews are Democratic than perform many of the religious practices that were once considered essential to being Jewish. Some Jews consider being Republican to be part of their being Jewish, but they are the minority; being Democratic has become the dominant politicized social identity of American Jews. Party identification is generally slow to change, but the theory described in this chapter suggests that such change would come even slower for Jews, because liberal politics and Democratic partisanship have become embedded in most Jews' social identity as Jews. Later chapters of this book return to the topic of Republican Jews, as well as to why more Jews are not Republican.

Of course, there are more aspects to people's social identity than their religion and ethnicity, and those aspects can be more relevant in voting decisions. Gender identity, sexual orientation, social class, and occupation are important aspects of people's social identity that, in particular elections, might motivate Jewish voters more than aspects related to being Jewish. These multiple social identities can also be reinforcing, as when Jews' urban residence reinforces their Democratic leanings.

This chapter has begun to describe what can be called Jews' "politics of tradition." Jews are mostly Democratic out of tradition, and that tradition is reinforced when they talk to Jewish friends and relatives. Their social identity is an important aspect of their politics of tradition, in that being Democratic has become part of being Jewish for many Jews. However, there is more to explaining their politics. Chapter 4 turns to two other important ingredients—values and self-interest—and presents an overall model that combines them with identity.

CHAPTER 4

Reinstating Values and Self-Interest Explanations

Most synagogues participate in activities related to Israel, but local community activities in which congregations engage differ between denominations. Reform and Conservative congregations typically encourage social action programs, such as tutoring in inner-city schools or helping in neighborhood food pantries. By contrast, Orthodox synagogues generally limit their social action and charity activities to the Jewish community. This divergence aptly illustrates the different values and self-interest of non-Orthodox and Orthodox Jews, differences that also extend to their political views.

Social psychologists and political scientists consider values and self-interest as fundamental factors affecting people's attitudes, but analysts of Jewish voting have convinced themselves that these factors are not relevant for Jews. Scholars believe they have discredited Lawrence Fuchs' (1956) claim that Judaic values underlie their voting, and "everybody knows" that Jews do not vote their self-interest. This chapter revisits those explanations, arguing that Jews' politics are, above all, based on their values and their generalized self-interest. A group's values spotlight the question "What do we care about?" Its self-interest focuses on the question "What are our basic needs?"

The first section of this chapter applies the contemporary theory of universal values to Jews' politics. The second section broadens the discussion of self-interest to show that Jews' voting is self-interested. The final section proposes an explanatory model that combines Jews' social identity, values, and self-interest. This model emphasizes an important distinction that is usually overlooked, differentiating between factors that initially cause the members of a group to adopt a particular position, factors that lead them to maintain that opinion, and factors that explain why subsequent generations retain that stand. A group's self-interest affects how its members' political views were initially set, and the group's values affect whether members maintain those views so they can become embedded in their social identity.

Values: A Modernized View

When Fuchs wrote his book on Jews' political behavior in the 1950s, he focused on how Judaic values underlie their liberalism (Fuchs 1956, 178–91). Subsequent scholars have dismissed that explanation because today's most observant Jews (i.e., the Orthodox) are the least liberal.[1] However, that fact does not render Jews' values irrelevant to how they vote.

A Universal Theory of Values. The discussion of values that underlie Jews' politics has been sidetracked over the years because it became focused on Judaic values rather than theories of universal human values. Modern theories typically focus on "values priorities," that is, the relative emphasis that people give to a variety of potential values.[2] Different people can prioritize different values, so Orthodox Jews could have a set of values priorities that lead most to be political conservatives, while non-Orthodox Jews could share a different set of values priorities that lead most to be liberals.

Shalom Schwartz's (1994) study of motivational values in several nations revealed 10 universal value priorities that he classified under 4 basic dimensions: self-transcendence (universalism and benevolence), conservation (tradition, conformity, and security), self-enhancement (power, achievement, and hedonism), and openness to change (stimulation and self-direction). Schwartz's analysis located these values along a circle (fig. 4.1), with people who emphasize one value generally also emphasizing others near it on that circle.

Schwartz (1994, 39–40; Feldman 2003, 494–95) noted that these dimensions relate to political ideology. Self-transcendence emphasizes economic egalitarianism, in contrast to the self-enhancement value of protecting existing inequalities in wealth. Openness to change emphasizes

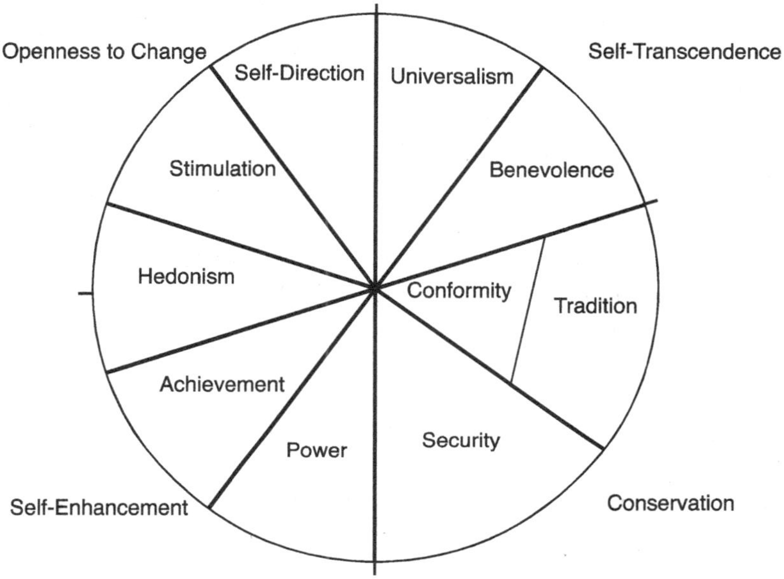

Fig. 4.1. Schwartz's motivational values
(*Source:* Based on Schwartz and Huismans 1995.)

individual freedoms, in contrast to the conservation value of controlling deviations from morality norms. In an analysis of data from 12 noncommunist nations, including Israel and the United States (but not American Jews separately), Schwartz et al. (2014, 921) confirmed that liberal views on civil liberties and equality are most associated with universalism and benevolence values, while issues invoking traditional morality as well as law and order are most associated with tradition, conformity, and security values. Feldman (2003) has provided important perspective on how this focus on values relates to political attitudes, and as described in chapter 8 in the present study, Goren et al. (2016) tested how these value dimensions relate to Americans' positions on political issues.

The Schwartz model has not been studied with respect to American Jews, but Schwartz and Huisman (1995) included a sample of Israeli Jews in their values research. As might be expected, religiosity was most correlated with tradition (defined as "respect, commitment, and acceptance of the customs and ideas that traditional culture or religion provide") and conformity ("restraint of action, inclinations, and impulses likely to upset or harm others and violate social expectations or norms"). Religiosity was negatively correlated with hedonism ("pleasure and sensuous gratification for oneself") and self-direction ("independent thought and action-choosing, creating, exploring").[3] That pattern of correlations means that the most religious Jews emphasized the conservation values of tradition and conformity more than nonreligious Jews, while nonreligious Jews emphasized self-direction more (see also Saroglou, Delpierre, and Dernelle 2004). The values circle suggests some additional patterns, such as a focus on the self-enhancement goals of power and achievement that likely typify many entrepreneurs and business managers.

A common explanation of Jews' liberalism is that they value universalism out of a feeling of kinship to other minorities and feel safer when all minorities are protected, since that protects Jews as well. However, Schwartz's values circle implies that very religious Jews who stress tradition and conformity would instead be particularistic (see Barnett 2016, 7), considering their religion to be the only true religion and rejecting those who do not accept their faith.

Materialist versus Postmaterialist Values. Ronald Inglehart (1977) advanced an important theory of how values develop, positing that values priorities depend on experiences in pre-adult years. Economic deprivation during those years leads to materialist values with an emphasis on economic well-being and maintaining order. If economic deprivation is absent, then postmaterialist values predominate, with an emphasis on self-enhancement (e.g., supporting freedom of speech) and on giving people more say in government decisions.

According to this theory, the generation that began voting during the Great Depression and World War II experienced economic limitations and therefore focused on materialist values. The following generations that grew up and began voting in the more affluent period of the 1960s through the 1990s were more postmaterialist: for example, the Jews of the baby boom generation became involved in the civil rights movement, the free speech movement, and opposition to the Vietnam War. Similarly, the support by Generation X Jews for liberal positions on social and environmental issues exemplifies postmaterialist values.

While not providing specific results, Inglehart's (1977, 90) analysis of early 1970s surveys led him to make a brief side comment that American Jews were predominantly postmaterialist. However, that result may have reflected the preceding tumultuous 1960s. My analysis (not shown) of Jews interviewed from 1992 to 2014 in the World Values Survey finds that they were just 11 percentage points more postmaterialist and 11 points less materialist than the American population as a whole.[4] Whereas fairly equal proportions of the general public were postmaterialist and materialist (21% versus 18%, with 61% being in-between), postmaterialists predominated over materialists among Jews (32% versus 7%).

Another test of the distinctiveness of American Jews' values can be obtained by looking at two series of values questions in the 1992–2012 surveys in the American National Election Studies, on egalitarianism (whether everyone should have an equal chance to succeed) and moral traditionalism (whether traditional family ties should be emphasized more). On an egalitarianism scale ranging from zero to one, with higher scores representing more egalitarian answers, Jews were more egalitarian, with an average of 0.67, versus 0.59 for non-black non-Jews. On a traditionalism scale with higher scores for more traditional answers, Jews were less morally traditional, with an average of 0.44, versus 0.60 for non-Jews.[5] Jews' averages are not very extreme, but Jews are significantly more egalitarian and significantly less favorable to moral traditionalism than non-Jews are.

Judaic Values. While Schwartz searched for universal values, there could also be special values based on Jewish principles. Fuchs (1956, 178–91) argued that three Judaic values underlie Jews' liberalism. Foremost was charity (*tzedakah*), which generalizes to feeling a responsibility to "heal the world" (*tikkun olam*). Second, he pointed to their reverence for the Torah, which results in respect for education. Third was Jews' "nonasceticism," by which Fuchs meant that Jews are not focused on the pleasures of an afterlife (*ha-olam ha-ba*) and are instead receptive to improving society and remaking the environment in this world (*ha-olam ha-zeh*).

The charity argument was stated most forcefully when Lipset (1985, 37) emphasized Jews' charitable giving and focus on community welfare as a factor linking them to liberals and the Democratic Party. He contrasted that link to the one connecting the Protestant ethic's focus on individualism with laissez-faire individualism, conservatives, and the Republican Party. However, Cohen and Liebman's (1997) analysis of the General Social Survey directly refuted Lipset by finding that when compared with non-Jews of similar sociodemographics, Jews are not distinctively liberal as regards sympathy for the poor.

Fuchs' values argument has been viewed as flawed because the most observant Orthodox Jews should be the most liberal if adherence to Judaic values were responsible for American Jews being liberal. Instead, the Orthodox have been more politically conservative than the non-Orthodox since at least the 1970s. It seems difficult to accept Judaic explanations that fit better for less-observant Jews.[6] Furthermore, Liebman and Cohen (1996, 52) argue that Jewish religious values are ethnocentric, rather than universalistic, and hence are not liberal. For example, when Orthodox Jews practice charity, they concentrate on helping other Jews rather than on universal aid.

However, Fuchs is correct in a very important sense: Conservative and especially Reform Judaism emphasize the value of social action to heal the world, and they stress the value of universal charity. Those branches of American Judaism are the two largest, so their Judaic values underpin the liberalism of very large numbers of Jews. Indeed, Judaic values also underlie the political views of Orthodox Jews: they value charity for fellow Jews and the literal teachings of the Torah, basing their political conservatism on their interpretation of those values.

Another Judaic value that has been suggested is concern about the safety of other Jews. Over the centuries, Jews have been victims of the Inquisition, pogroms, and the Holocaust, so it is natural for them to be concerned for their coreligionists in the United States and abroad. This value is sometimes described as concern for the people of Israel (*am Yisrael*), also phrased as all Jews being responsible for one another (*kol Yisrael aravim zeh l'zeh*). It is similar to the notion of "linked fate" discussed in chapter 3, the feeling that the fate of Jews in one place is linked to the survival of Jews elsewhere. This value is widely shared among Jews, though it is not necessarily connected with Jewish liberalism. Today, it underlies American Jews' concern about Israel's security, especially the unconditional support for Israel that is now associated with conservative political positions.[7]

Finally, Cohen and Liebman (1997) cite "argumentative individualism" as a value that could explain Jews' liberalism. Similarly, Walzer (1995, 5) described liberal politics as a Jewish style of questioning and openness to arguments. Levey (1995) adapted that view to claim that a rejection of religious authority is the source of liberal political thinking by American Jews: rejecting religious authority leads to denying moral authority and, therefore, to supporting civil liberties to protect individualism.

Values Summary. Values explanations of Jews' politics have gone out of fashion, largely because of the claim that Judaic values cannot explain Jews' liberalism when the most observant Jews are the least liberal politically. However, the values that inspire Reform and Conservative Jewry help explain their liberalism, whereas the values that underlie the religious beliefs of Orthodox Jews help explain their political conservatism. The Judaic value of concern for the security of other Jews is also relevant. As to Schwartz's universal values, Orthodox Jews would be expected to emphasize tradition and conformity, whereas non-Orthodox Jews would stress self-transcendence values, including universalism, self-direction, autonomy, and egalitarianism.

People do not necessarily think about these values deliberately in making their political choices. Jews develop values as they grow up in a culture. Some values may be picked up by necessity, while others accumulate as they share experiences with other Jews. In any case, their values subconsciously affect their political choices.

Self-Interest: A Broadened View

A group's self-interest is also basic to understanding its political choices. Self-interest is often interpreted in narrow, economic terms, but social groups may have broader interests that are more vital to them than economic ones. That can be especially the case for minority groups. As Fein (1988, 237) said about Jews, "Class interests, however, are not the only interests people have." Cramer (2016, 209) has argued, "When we start to ask why people vote against their interests, we need to acknowledge that interests are subjective. . . . Interests are interpretations that people arrive at through thinking about the world as particular types of people—people with identities."

Applied to Jews, Cramer's insight means that their subjective interests can be based on their identities rather than just on economic status. Historically, American Jews have had four main self-interest motivations: economic, protection of fellow Jews, acceptance, and religious liberty. Those motivations affected their original political decisions, but they also remain important today.

Economic Self-Interest. Discussions of the paradoxical nature of the politics of American Jews generally center on narrowly defined economic self-interest. It seems paradoxical that Jews, being a relatively affluent group, do not vote Republican, instead joining lower socioeconomic status groups in supporting Democratic candidates (e.g., Allinsmith and Allinsmith 1948). As Milton Himmelfarb humorously observed in the 1970s, "Jews earn like Episcopalians and vote like Puerto Ricans."[8] As a result, conservatives often claim that Jews vote irrationally.

However, economic motivations are relevant in explaining how Jews became so liberal and Democratic. Spinrad (1990) saw Jewish liberalism as due to their "socialist heritage," whether from Europe or picked up when they immigrated to the United States. Franklin Delano Roosevelt's success in ending the Great Depression is another economic factor that is commonly cited for why Jews became Democrats. A related economic-based possible explanation is that Jews' particular reliance on public-sector jobs when they faced discrimination in the private sector during and after the Depression led them to become liberal so as to benefit from a large public sector (Ginsberg 1993, 140–43). Another explanation of Jews favoring the Democratic Party during that period is urbanism, as that party's northern wing became more urban in its focus in the 1930s. Jews were primarily urban, so their interests were better satisfied by the political party attuned to urban America's economic problems, such as favoring laws to protect urban workers, rather than by a Republican Party that was still focused on small-town America.[9]

The Depression actually affected different groups of Jews in opposite ways. Many "Russian Jews" (those who immigrated to the United States around the turn of the 20th century) still worked in sweatshop conditions and lived in crowded tenement housing. Neither national party had promised to do much to improve those conditions before the Depression, but the Russian Jews mobilized to the Democratic Party when they saw Roosevelt actively combating the Depression. By contrast, many "German Jews" (those who immigrated in the mid-1800s) were part of the business establishment by the early 20th century and were predominantly Republicans. Their economic interests led many of these German Jews to remain Republican during the Depression.

Economics are also relevant to Jews' voting choices in the contemporary period. Anecdotal accounts suggest that economic self-interest helps explain the conservative political positions of many Jewish professionals, business owners, and corporate managers. Their ideological positions and voting are a prominent exception to the predominant liberal leanings of most American Jews. Furthermore, Sigelman's (1991a) analysis of presidential voting surveys showed that economic assessments affected Jews' voting as much as voting of non-Jews in the 1980s. Improving family financial situations tended to benefit the incumbent party, while worsening assessments served to diminish that party's vote. Income affected Jews' voting no less than voting of non-Jews: higher-income Jews and non-Jews were more likely to vote for Reagan in 1980, while income did not have a significant effect for either Jews or non-Jews in 1984 or 1988. Sigelman concluded that pocketbook-based voting occurs among Jews. As discussed in chapter 12 of the present book, some studies find voting differences between higher-income and lower-income Jews in more recent elections as well, though both groups still vote more Democratic than non-Jews with similar incomes. A broader economic self-interest explanation of Jewish Democratic voting is that Jews have advanced economically under the American economic system as it has developed since Roosevelt's New Deal programs were instituted. As a result, Jews could rationally consider the maintenance of that system to be in their self-interest, rather than risking the uncertain effects of a less-regulated economy.

Protecting Fellow Jews. A second self-interest motivation behind Jewish voting has been to protect fellow Jews. Since the beginning of the American Republic, Jews have wanted to keep immigration open so their relatives would be able to join them in the United States. They also have long been concerned with protecting coreligionists abroad. They petitioned U.S. presidents to express their concern when Jews were persecuted in the Ottoman Empire (the Damascus Affair of 1840), by the Vatican (the Mortara Affair in the late 1850s), in Romania (starting in 1870), and in Russia (peaking with the 1903 Kishinev pogrom). The most serious manifestation came during the Nazi persecution of Jews, when conservatives, particularly the American First Committee, led the opposition to U.S. intervention in the "European war." That isolationism often had "an anti-Jewish flavor" (Solomon 1988, 280), especially reflected by both the German-American Bund and Father Charles Coughlin's anti-Semitic radio broadcasts in the 1930s. Franklin Roosevelt's efforts to help Britain against Germany pleased Jews and reinforced their move toward the Democratic Party, even though Roosevelt did not do more to try to stop the Holocaust after Nazi plans for the "final solution" became known in 1942. In the 1970s and 1980s, American Jews vigorously supported the Soviet Jewry movement that succeeded in getting Soviet leaders to allow the emigration of most of their Jews.

This concern for fellow Jews has evolved into wanting the United States to protect the State of Israel. Medding (1977, 141) described Israel as "a primordial Jewish political interest." While Reform Jewry was originally opposed to establishing a Jewish homeland in Palestine, the Holocaust made American Jews feel that a Jewish state was necessary for self-protection even if they had no interest in moving there themselves. Therefore, most U.S. Jews see self-interest in maintaining Israel's security, even if they disagree with some of its policies (see chapter 9 in the present study).

Acceptance. Minorities have an inherent self-interest in being accepted.[10] Jews had not been accepted in Europe in the 1700s. As Barnett (2016, 8) wrote, "America is different because it did not treat its Jews as different. . . . [They] were allowed to live as both Jews and Americans." Yet Jews were not immediately accepted in the United States. Several of the original U.S. states still had established churches in the early years of the American Republic (Handlin and Handlin 1955), and some maintained limits on Jews' rights. The U.S. Constitution and the First Amendment protected Jews against the federal government but not against the states. Jews could vote in all the states (Chyet 1958; Marcus 1989, 512), but as of 1792, only New York, Virginia, Georgia, Pennsylvania, South Carolina, Delaware, and Vermont allowed Jews to hold public office. The other six original states slowly extended full rights to Jews between 1826 and 1877.

While early presidents preached tolerance, there were anti-Semitic incidents, as when James Monroe, as secretary of state, initially claimed that the recall of Mordecai Manual Noah as consul to Tunis occurred because it had become known that Noah was a Jew. Most notably, in dealing with a smuggling problem during the Civil War, General Ulysses S. Grant issued General Order No. 11 to expel Jews from the Department of Tennessee (the state of Mississippi along with parts of Tennessee and Kentucky), though that order was repealed as soon as President Lincoln was apprised of it (Sarna 2012). The German Jews who came to the United States in the mid-1800s were well accepted, but active discrimination against them began with the large infusion of Russian Jews. For example, banker Joseph Seligman and his family were refused their usual summer hotel room in Saratoga Springs, New York, in 1877, when the owner, Henry Hilton, instituted a policy of no longer accepting Jewish guests.

The Russian Jewish immigrants originally wanted to assimilate and become "Americans." When they encountered discrimination, Jews' focus became joining with other minorities to root out prejudice. That included working with the National Conference of Christians and Jews to ease interfaith divisions, joining the National Association for the Advancement of Colored People to fight racial discrimination, founding B'nai B'rith's Anti-Defamation League to combat anti-Semitism, and joining American Civil Liberties Union litigation to preserve individual rights. In these instances, Jewish groups worked with liberal forces against conservative elements.

Religious Liberty. An important self-interest of every religious minority is to practice its religion freely. Werner Cohn (1958) posed this self-interest as a historical explanation of Jewish liberalism, going back to when Jews became politically emancipated during the French Revolution. Jews gravitated toward the political left because the political right, which remained opposed to equality, was tied to Christianity. As Fein (1988, 226) put it, Jews "preferred the left not only because of what it promised to do *for* them but also because of what the right had done *to* them" (emphasis in original). The minority status of American Jews has traditionally meant desiring a strict separation of church and state. Most oppose conservative parties that favor a greater role for religion in the public sphere, which would allow the state to favor the majority religion. Accordingly, Cohn (1958, 626) described "American Jewish Liberalism as the expression of what American Jews feel is their insecure place in the worldwide Gentile environment."

Wald (2015) insightfully argues that what is critical to American Jews is that they have prospered under the liberal political system. He particularly stresses the clause in the U.S. Constitution that bars religious tests for holding federal office. Wald contends, "Jewish political behavior seems consistent with a overriding concern to defend the liberal citizenship regime" (14). More generally, this could be read as self-interest in maintaining American democracy. Several writers have stressed this value. Fein (1988) underscored American Jews' self-interest in the continuation of pluralism. Similarly, in explaining why Jews have continued to be liberal and Democratic, Ginsberg (2001, 15) emphasized "the benefits they have derived from membership in the liberal Democratic coalition." Himmelfarb (1978, 303) encapsulated this argument by writing, "We may conclude that liberalism itself was the Jewish self-interest."

Medding (1977) added an important consideration to the theory that Jews' votes are based on their self-interest in feeling secure. He pointed out that they could be reacting to perceived threats from either of two opposite directions: from dominant groups (usually ones on the political right) or from disadvantaged groups (normally ones on the political left). Wald (2015) speaks of these as two possible threats to the American "regime." Furthermore, Medding recognized that different sets of Jews might be most sensitive to those two types of threats. His example (1977, 136–37) was based on the 1972 U.S. presidential campaign, when Richard Nixon won reelection against Democratic Senator George McGovern. Medding claimed that less affluent, urban Jews voted more Republican than usual that year because they felt threatened by blacks' demands for affirmative action (a threat "from below"). That same year, more affluent, suburban Jews, whose socioeconomic status insulated them from that threat, voted more Democratic than usual because they felt threatened by dominant forces seeking to maintain social order in an era of political protest (a threat "from above"). The larger point is that different groups of Jews can be sensitive to different perceived threats to their security.

Self-Interest Summary. American Jews are more liberal politically than would be expected given their economic position. Yet it would be arrogant to claim that they do not understand their own self-interest, especially since their high level of education makes them fully competent to assess self-interest. Indeed, people always follow what they consider to be their self-interest.

Economic aspects play a part in Jews' liberalism and their support for the Democratic Party, but noneconomic factors may dominate Jews' view of their self-interest. Their concerns with acceptance, protecting fellow Jews, and religious liberty add additional self-interest dimensions. Their success in achieving widespread acceptance, decreasing overt anti-Semitism, winning equal civil rights for minorities, getting the Soviet Union to let its Jews emigrate, and insuring that Israel is strong enough to protect itself means that many of their original missions have been satisfied, leaving less of a collective agenda for Jews today. Still, they may feel that their self-interest is in protecting the liberal economy and pluralistic democracy that have allowed them to prosper in the United States. Furthermore, different types of Jews can vary in their self-interest concerns. For example, some may be more concerned with economic interests, while others may be more concerned with noneconomic matters.

Like values, self-interest motivations are generally nonconscious. It is unlikely that Jews think they should have particular self-interest motivations because they are Jews and then apply those motivations to their politics. It is more likely that most Jews share a set of self-interest needs, such as protecting their security and religious liberty, and that those needs affect how they intuitively think about politics.

The SVI Model of Jews' Political Positions

This chapter and the previous chapter considered three important factors that can affect groups' political positions: their self-interest, values, and identity (SVI). Social scientists have emphasized the social identity explanation of group politics in recent years, but self-interest and values are also relevant for Jews' politics, particularly when non-Judaic values are considered and when self-interest is viewed more broadly than just through narrow economic calculations.

The SVI model proceeds in three stages. First, a group's self-interest matters for their initial adoption of political views. For example, self-interest led most Jews to be attracted to the economic programs and urban character of the northern Democratic Party in the 1930s, though a minority of well-off Jews remained Republicans. Second, the group's values can help reinforce their political views. Thus, when Jews became less religiously observant, they favored individual autonomy over following traditional moral strictures, and their inclination fit with the Democratic Party's positions on social/cultural issues. If a group's values conflict with its initial political views, the group is likely to split between the parties rather than stay with its original party, as happened when other social groups defected from the New Deal coalition.

The third part of the SVI model is that members' social identity helps maintain the group's views, particularly across generations. Liberal and Democratic predispositions became ingrained in Jews' social identity in a manner that is reminiscent of the title of the opening song of the 1964 Broadway musical *Fiddler on the Roof*, about the life of Jews in early 1900s Russia: "Tradition, Tradition!" Most Jews identified with the Democratic Party in the 1930s and 1940s and eventually viewed it as part of their being Jewish, and they transmitted that view to their children. Meanwhile, the Republican Party was becoming more conservative on social issues, which turned off younger, postmaterialist Jews who might otherwise have been ready to abandon their grandparents' party by the 1990s.

Sonenshein and Valentino (2000, 379) captured the essence of this model when they wrote about Jews, "Long-standing values and beliefs, passed down from generation to generation, serve as an anchor for group members. *As long as the group ties remain* [emphasis mine], so will the political orientations that derive from them." A politics of tradition is created when a group's values and self-interest are transmitted to subsequent generations, yielding a politicized social identity, as long as people feel attached to the group. The SVI model is intended to be general enough to apply to other groups as well. For example, a combination of conservation values (tradition, conformity, and security) and subjective self-interest (in religious liberty and in protecting their place in society against new groups) led evangelical Protestants to become Republicans, and that has become ingrained enough in their social identity since the 1980s to become part of their voting tradition.

In exploring Jews' values and self-interest in this chapter, it has become clear that there are differences in the American Jewish community as to which values to emphasize and how to define their self-interest. These differences play out directly in the political choices that Jews have been making in recent years. Thus, a minority of Jews whose self-interest was different in New Deal days did not become Democrats. Their values reinforced their Republicanism, and their social identity kept them Republican.

The explanatory SVI model has the advantage of being general enough to account for why some subgroups are exceptions, including why Orthodox Jews, business-oriented professionals, and immigrants from the former Soviet Union are more conservative and Republican. It also can accommodate change, recognizing that changing situations can alter values and self-interest calculations, as when some Jews feel that the Democrats are no longer sufficiently supportive of Israel or when decreasing job opportunities make Jewish young adults become more materialist. Additionally, this explanatory model accepts that self-interest and values can be linked to country-specific historical circumstances, so it should satisfy those (e.g., Medding 1977) who want explanations to hold universally, including for Jews outside the United States.

The most challenging situation is when a group's self-interest and values conflict, which could lead to the group becoming less politically cohesive. A conflict could occur for Jews, for example, if their economic self-interest favors one party while their postmaterialist values are more in accord with the opposite party. Litt (1960) made such an argument in explaining Jews' partisanship in the 1950s: the lower-middle class stayed Democratic because of their economic self-interest, and the upper class remained Democratic because of their value of social justice, but the ties of upper-middle-class Jews to the Democratic Party weakened because they shared neither the social justice value nor that economic self-interest. We may be seeing such a conflict in the 2010s, when some Jews feel that Republican positions on security for Israel better satisfy their self-interest in protection of fellow Jews, while others find that Democratic positions on social issues correspond closer to their values.

What is the relative importance of these different elements in any specific election? The argument is that social identity would matter the most in Jews' voting, which fits with the primary importance of party identification in voting. Values and self-interest would also matter, though, in evaluating the issues and candidates of the given election. Jews can deviate from their politicized social identity when their party's candidate takes stands that do not fit with their values or that violate their subjective self-interest, but such deviation has become rare in this era of increased partisan polarization.

In any case, self-interest, values, and social identity have all played a role in most Jews being liberal and Democratic. These factors are bolstered by Jews' feeling of being a minority and by their perception of threat from out-groups. Over the centuries, defense against anti-Semitism has served to buttress Jews' group solidarity. Thus, it is important to emphasize one further factor in explaining Jews' political positions, the status of Jews as a minority.

CHAPTER 5

Minority Consciousness

The day after the 2016 presidential election, the young grandson of one of our congregants was devastated when his school soccer teammates called him "Jew boy" and gave him a Nazi salute. That anti-Semitic incident was not isolated. Other, similar stories were shared in our congregation, and comparable episodes occurred in many communities in the wake of Trump's surprise victory. Over 150 bomb threats were made to Jewish community centers across the nation in the opening months of 2017, and they were capped off with the march of neo-Nazis through Charlottesville that August and the Pittsburgh synagogue shooting the following October. The level of actual violence against Jews in the United States had been low, but such incidents remind Jews of an ever-present undercurrent of anti-Semitism among a small number of Americans and thereby undermine their sense of security.

Historically, Jews have been concerned about discrimination against their religion and against them personally. America has accorded them unprecedented freedom to exercise their religion, but they are very sensitive to threats to the church-state separation that has facilitated that freedom. The immigration of millions of Eastern European working-class Jews starting in the late 1800s led to considerable anti-Semitism, along with discrimination in businesses and universities. The extent of prejudice has considerably diminished since World War II, with Jews now being widely accepted. Still, there are anti-Semitic groups and incidents in the United States today, with the unanticipated uptick after the 2016 election being of serious concern to the Jewish community.

Jews have experienced so much persecution over the centuries that they still treat their position in the United States as if it were precarious. After all, they had achieved considerable acceptance in Moorish Spain before their expulsion when the Christians conquered Spain, they mostly got along with their Russian neighbors before the pogroms, and they had largely assimilated in Germany before the Nazis took power. Therefore, American Jews seek to protect the rights they have obtained, while still fearing that their security is vulnerable and that discrimination against them could be resumed. This leads to what Lipset and Raab (1995, 151) describe as a "defense impulse," with Jewish liberalism being "dominated by its reference to freedom" (162).

Jews' minority status directly affects their social identity, values, and subjective self-interest. After all, members of minorities that are sometimes threatened have a greater need for group identification than majority groups have. Being a minority also increases the extent to which members value security. Self-interest is especially important in relations with other social groups, where it is manifested in competition with some groups and in fear of other groups. History has made Jews particularly wary of potential threats from other social groups, including some groups with which they share some common interests, such as African Americans and evangelical Christians. This paradoxical caution toward would-be allies is understandable for a people who have learned over the centuries how easily societies can turn against them, but it also has political consequences for Jews' politics in a party system based on coalitions of disparate social groups.

This chapter examines how their "defense impulse" affects both Jews' attitudes toward other social groups and their politics. Two potential threats that worry many Jews are described: the threat to church-state separation and the threat of anti-Semitism. That examination is followed by analysis of the relations of Jews with African Americans and with other religious groups.

The Threat to Church-State Separation

Jews historically lived in European nations that had established religions. They were not accepted as citizens in those countries until the French Revolution, with its emphasis on equality. This history makes them particularly appreciative of the U.S. Bill of Rights prohibition against Congress making any law respecting an establishment of religion. That Jews see such church-state separation as a major reason for their prospering in the United States provides an important impetus for their liberal political views.

Jews' concern about church-state separation is not entirely hypothetical. There was a movement in the second half of the 19th century to add a Christian amendment to the U.S. Constitution. In the mid-20th century, the U.S. Senate Committee on the Judiciary held hearings on a proposal, favored by the National Association of Evangelicals, to add to the Constitution recognition of "the authority and law of Jesus Christ, Savior and Ruler of Nations." A 2013 HuffPost/YouGov poll found that one-third of the public favored a constitutional amendment making Christianity the "official religion" of the United States (Swanson 2013), with Republicans narrowly supportive (by a margin of 46% to 38%) and most Democrats opposed (26% to 54%).

Jews have viewed the recital of prayers in public schools as imposing religious beliefs on them, in violation of church-state separation. In the early 1960s, the Supreme Court ruled that such school prayers violated the First Amendment prohibition of any law respecting an establishment of a religion. That ruling was controversial and was followed by attempts to amend the Constitution to permit prayers in public schools. In a 2000 poll, Greenberg and Wald (2001, 180) found that only 14% of Jews were favorable to such an amendment, while 70% of non-Jews were in favor. When the American National Election Studies (ANES) asked in the 1980s and 1990s whether school prayer should be permitted, Jews were significantly more opposed than the public at large. The General Social Survey (GSS) continues to ask views on the U.S. Supreme Court ruling "that no state or local government may require the reading of the Lord's Prayer or Bible verses in public schools." Jews are supportive of the ruling, whereas a majority of the public has consistently registered disapproval. As shown in table 5.1, there is a difference between Jews and non-Jews of about 40 percentage points in the GSS data and 50 in the ANES. The distinctiveness scores on the right in the table (which are explained more in chapter 8) show that these differences remain significant even when comparing Jews and non-Jews with similar social demographics and similar self-identified liberal/conservative ideology. As will become evident in later chapters of this book, this is one of Jews' most distinctive opinions.

Jews' emphasis on separation extends to opposing government protections of morality, which they see as the domain of religion rather than government. Pew's 2007 Religious Landscape Study asked whether the government should do more to protect morality in society or if the government is getting too involved in that issue. Whereas 40% of the public at large wanted a greater government role, only 22% of Jews agreed. Of the 12 religious faiths that the report tabulated, Jews gave the least support to the idea that government should have a greater role in this respect (Lugo 2008, 127). Yet Jews are not totally doctrinaire on church-state separation. The 2003 AJC Annual Survey of American Jewish Opinion found, for example, that only 31% of Jews felt that the phrase "under God" should be removed from the U.S. Pledge of Allegiance.

In line with their support for church-state separation, Jews have traditionally opposed the provision of government tax money to parochial schools. For example, the 2004 AJC survey found that 72% of Jews at that time were opposed to government aid to parochial or religious schools. That opposition has likely lessened, though, as a result of the considerable growth in Jewish day schools (Wertheimer 2002).

Since the 2015 Supreme Court ruling that there is a fundamental right to marry that includes same-sex couples, one question that has arisen is whether religious liberty extends to allowing individuals and businesses to decline service to customers for religious reasons. This question has been raised with respect to whether bakers can refuse to sell wedding cakes for same-sex weddings, though it would also apply to whether scribes can follow Jewish law in refusing to sell a Torah scroll to a non-Jew. A brief submitted to the Supreme Court by Orthodox Jewish groups has argued that not permitting such refusal would constitute a danger to free exercise of

TABLE 5.1. Jews' Distinctiveness on School Prayer

			Liberal answers		Distinctiveness scores	
Survey	Variable	Question	Jews	Non-Jews[a]	Control on demographics	Also control on ideology
GSS	prayer	Disapprove of Bible prayer in public schools	81%	43%	32***	27***
ANES	vcf9043	Prayer should not be allowed in schools	62%	12%	49***	44***

Source: Analysis of the General Social Survey data for 1992–2016 (including 352 Jews) and the 1992–98 surveys of the American National Election Studies (including 113 Jews).

[a]Comparison is with nonblack non-Jews.

***significant at the .001 level; **significant at .01; *significant at .05.

Orthodox observance, while a brief submitted on behalf of several non-Orthodox Jewish organizations argued that personal religious views should not provide a license to disregard antidiscrimination protections.

The Threat of Anti-Semitism

Jews have long been "a people apart" from the general populace (Ginsberg 2001, 18–19), a minority group with its own religion, language, dietary restrictions, and customs. As a result, the general populace in earlier eras did not understand Jews, and Christian religious authorities attacked their rejection of Jesus. It was easy to scapegoat Jews whenever there was a problem in a community. Over the centuries, they faced prejudice, discrimination, possible forced baptisms, and frequent massacres, and they were required to live in separate ghettoes in many medieval cities. Many Western European Jews assimilated during a period of Enlightenment (*Haskalah*) in the 1800s, though both considerable anti-Semitism and pogroms occurred in Russia and other Eastern European countries.

When Jews immigrated to the United States, they wanted to be accepted as Jews, without being faced with the prejudice that they had experienced in Europe. However, Jewish immigrants of the turn of the 20th century found that they, along with Irish and Italian immigrants, were not considered to be whites (Brodkin 1998). Jews were classified as of the Hebrew race (Goldstein 2008) and experienced prejudice and discrimination.

Decreased Prejudice. The organized Jewish community partnered with other minority groups to end discrimination, "on the assumption that Jews would only be secure if all groups in American society were secure" (Chanes 2001, 100). The National Conference of Christians and Jews (now the National Conference for Community and Justice) was founded in 1927 to address interfaith divisions. By the 1950s, it was a major force in combating anti-Semitism. In that decade, a new threat developed when American Jews who supported Israel had to defend themselves against charges of disloyalty, so they worked to achieve a broad consensus across religions on American support for Israel. In 1965, century-old conflicts between Catholics and Jews at the organizational level were eased when Vatican II adopted the *Nostra Aetate*, a declaration that absolved Jews for responsibility for the death of Jesus and decried anti-Semitism. Such orga-

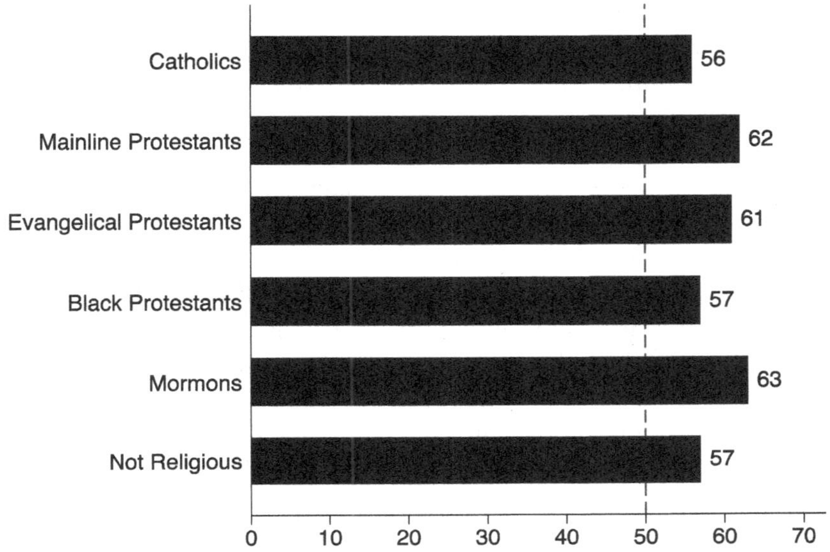

Fig. 5.1. Average ratings of Jews by members of other religious traditions (*Source:* Analysis of 2006 Faith Matters Survey.)

nizational steps toward religious tolerance never completely eradicate prejudice, but they have helped to decrease overt anti-Semitism in America.

In sharp contrast to the centuries of anti-Semitism and discrimination that they suffered, the 2006 Faith Matters survey (Putnam and Campbell 2010, 506–8) found that Jews were as positively viewed as any religious group in the country. That finding was based on respondents' ratings of how warm they felt about members of several religions, using a thermometer scale from 0 to 100. The average rating given to Jews by members of other religious groups was 59, which was comparable to the scores of 58 given to mainline Protestants and Catholics.[1] The average ratings that members of all religious traditions gave to Jews were positive (fig. 5.1) and very close to the highest those groups gave to any religion other than their own. The Pew Research Center (2017) obtained even more positive results in early 2017, with a mean of 67 for Jews, again as high as for any religious group.[2] These results confirm the considerable acceptance that Jews have achieved in the United States and emphasize the extent to which Jews are now integrated into American society.[3]

The Anti-Defamation League (ADL) has conducted a series of nationwide polls to monitor trends in anti-Semitic feelings in the general population. Its October 2016 poll found that only 14% of Americans have "anti-Semitic propensities" (ADL 2017, 4), measured by agreement with at least 6 of 11 prejudiced statements about Jews. While that is half the 29% level that the ADL found in 1964, it shows that anti-Semitism is not rare. The proportion of Americans who are "essentially free of anti-Semitic views" went up to 58%, which leaves 28% in the middle category who exhibit some prejudice. While those figures show much less anti-Semitism than at mid-20th century, about a quarter of the public still believe that Jews are more loyal to Israel than to America, hold that Jews were responsible for the death of Christ, and/or feel that Jews talk too much about what happened to them in the Holocaust.[4]

Most Americans considerably overestimate the size of the Jewish population, which could be a mark of anti-Semitism. Herda's (2013) analysis of the 2000 GSS found that the average American thinks that 18% of Americans are Jewish, while the actual percentage is just under 2%. That overestimation was not more common among people who have negative perceptions of Jews or who would not want to live in a Jewish neighborhood, which suggests that this error was not due to anti-Semitism. Instead, the inaccuracy seems mainly due to the difficulty that most people have in estimating percentages (see also Nadeau, Niemi, and Levine 1993).

Threats to Jews. There has been a history of violence against Jews in America. The most notorious incident was the 1915 lynching of Leo Frank in Georgia after the state's governor commuted his sentence to lifetime imprisonment for lack of sufficient evidence of his having killed a young girl. In 1957–58 there was a series of bombings and attempted bombings of Jewish religious institutions in the South, capped by the explosion of a bomb in The Temple in Atlanta; five members of the National States Rights Party were arrested, but trials ended after one was acquitted after an Imperial Wizard of the Klan served as a character witness for him.

While the evidence is that Jews have since attained considerable acceptance in the United States, violent incidents against American Jews and media reports of them naturally increase Jews' concern about anti-Semitism. That was especially the case in 2018 after the killing of 11 Jews at a Pittsburgh synagogue by a shooter who allegedly told a SWAT officer that he wanted all Jews to die. Jews' sense of vulnerability is also increased by serious incidents outside the United States, particularly the 2015 attack at a Paris kosher supermarket. Such widely publicized incidents remind American Jews of the threat of anti-Semitic attacks and highlight the need for security at community establishments and events.

Organized movements targeting Israel and/or Jews are another source of concern. The Boycott, Divestment, Sanctions (BDS) movement was formed to protest Israel's continued control of and settlements in the West Bank. While its proponents describe the BDS movement as parallel to the successful antiapartheid sanctions against South Africa, American Jewish organizations view the movement as both seeking to delegitimize Israel and promoting anti-Semitism. The BDS movement is often seen as an instance of anti-Semitism by the political left, in contrast to the usual anti-Semitism by the political right. Anti-Semitism by the left has also been manifested on some college campuses by intimidation of Jewish students who are supportive of Israel.

The growth in the mid-2010s of the alt-right movement (a loosely organized white supremacist movement that is tolerant of anti-Semitism) led to an increase in anti-Jewish comments on the Internet, as well as a spike in anti-Semitic incidents in the aftermath of Donald Trump's 2016 election victory. The annual ADL report in 2018 documented that such incidents increased by 57% in 2017 over 2016. A total of 1,986 anti-Semitic incidents reported across the United States consisted of 163 bomb threats against Jewish institutions, 852 other incidents of harassment, 952 incidents of vandalism, and 19 physical assaults.[5]

Jews' Perceptions of Anti-Semitism. The greater acceptance of Jews does not necessarily translate into their feeling accepted. In the 2013 Pew report, 43% of the Jewish survey respondents answered that Jews face a lot of discrimination, and 16% said that they had been called offensive names and/or been snubbed in social settings in the previous year (Pew Research Center 2013, 105). Orthodox Jews, whose clothing often makes them conspicuous, were particularly vulnerable to such incidents, with 24% reporting that they had experienced anti-Semitism.[6] That American Jews still feel like a people apart should not be surprising in an era in which even many Christian groups feel discriminated against.[7]

The upsurge of anti-Semitism during the 2016 presidential campaign and subsequent events through 2017 and 2018 further increased Jews' feeling of being vulnerable. The proportion of Jews who viewed anti-Semitism as a very serious problem in the United States doubled from 19% to 41%

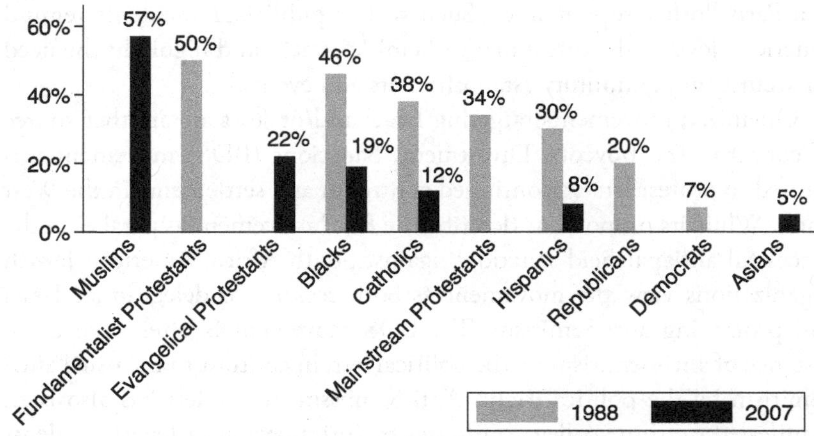

Fig. 5.2. Proportion of Jews perceiving groups as anti-Semitic
(*Note:* Data from my analysis of American Jewish Committee surveys. Data shown is the percent of Jews who saw most or many of the people in these groups as anti-Semitic. Some groups were asked about in only one year rather than both.)

between surveys taken by the American Jewish Committee in 2016 and 2017, with 84% of respondents in 2017 viewing it as at least a serious problem. Instead of asking about anti-Semitism, an April–May 2018 AJC poll asked whether, compared to a year earlier, the status of Jews in the United States is more or less secure: 55% of Jews saw it as less secure, 24% as about the same, and 18% as more secure. The October 2018 Pittsburgh synagogue shootings further diminished Jews' feelings of security, though they were heartened by considerable outpouring of sympathy from non-Jews. Chapter 14 in the present study discusses this increased concern with anti-Semitism and its effects on Jews' political views.

Figure 5.2 compares the 1988 and 2007 AJC surveys of American Jews (S. Cohen 1989, 41), showing a decrease in Jews' perceptions of most religious and ethnic groups as anti-Semitic. For example, the number of Jews who saw Catholics and Hispanics as anti-Semitic in 2007 was one-third the number from 1988. While fewer Jews saw fundamentalist/evangelical Protestants and blacks as anti-Semitic in 2007 than in 1988, those groups were still regarded, along with Muslims, as among the most anti-Semitic. The following sections of this chapter focus on Jews' relations with these groups.

Jews and African Americans

The Jewish community has shared with African Americans a strong commitment to protection of the rights of minorities. Jews were historically very active in the National Association for the Advancement of Colored People, and some held key NAACP leadership positions. Jews participated in many of the well-known civil rights demonstrations of the 1960s. Two of the three civil rights workers murdered in the 1964 Mississippi Freedom Summer were Jewish.

Points of Conflict. Notwithstanding Jews' support of African Americans' rights, tension between the two groups has boiled over several times. The 1960s urban riots by blacks in New York, Detroit, Los Angeles, and other cities torched many Jewish-owned businesses in black neighborhoods. These tensions were further exacerbated by the riots following Martin Luther King's assassination in 1968. The rise of the Black Power movement in the late 1960s particularly alarmed many Jews. The 1991 Crown Heights riot in Brooklyn was the most serious direct clash. A car in the motorcade of a Lubavitcher-Hasidic community leader hit another car and then went onto a sidewalk, where it hit two black children. A riot by blacks against Jews ensued for the next three days after one of the children died at the hospital.

Tensions related more directly to government and politics have developed as well. In 1979, Jewish and black leaders blamed each other when civil rights icon Andrew Young resigned, under pressure, as American ambassador to the United Nations. He had met with a Palestinian Liberation Organization representative to urge postponement of a UN vote on a resolution for Palestinian statehood, in contravention to U.S. policy against meeting directly with the PLO. When black activist Rev. Jesse Jackson ran for the Democratic presidential nomination in 1984, he referred to New York as "Hymie Town." After initial denials, Jackson admitted having used the term, but he refused to renounce the Nation of Islam leader Rev. Louis Farrakhan for threatening the life of the reporter who had reported the anti-Semitic slur. That incident led to some Jewish disaffection from the political party in which Jackson was a leader.[8]

Intergroup Attitudes. The specific incidents mentioned in the preceding section are now old, but the relations between Jews and African Americans are still not as warm as they once were. Jews who lived near the riot sites understandably have long memories of the danger. Most Jews likely sympathized with blacks' reactions to the spate of police killings of unarmed blacks in the mid-2010s, but many were probably less supportive of the subsequent protests by the Black Lives Matter movement. Additionally, black activists tend to be negative toward Israeli policies in the West Bank, sometimes to the extent of supporting the BDS movement, which irritates Jews who feel that blacks are not giving them the degree of support that Jews gave blacks during the civil rights era.

The level of anti-Semitism among blacks also concerns Jews. The 2016 ADL survey on attitudes toward Jews (ADL 2017, 16) found that anti-Semitism among African Americans was at 23%. That was a drop from the levels of 28% and 29% in the 2009 and 2011 ADL surveys, but it was still much higher than the 14% rate among the general population.

The greater tension between Jews and blacks is often used as an explanation of a decline in Jews' votes for Democratic presidential candidates in the 1970s and 1980s (JTA 1972; Wald 2015; cf. Himmelfarb 1978). The common claim is that some Jews felt that voting Democratic was against their self-interest because the Democratic Party was increasing its support for the political interests of blacks. It is not possible to prove whether this was the cause of the drop in Jews' Democratic voting. In any case, Jewish support for the Democrats went back up starting in 1992. Any tension that may have remained did not stop Jews from providing a large vote for both Barack Obama's election as the nation's first African American president in 2008 and his reelection four years later.

Jewish support for voting rights legislation remains strong, but as discussed in chapter 8 of this book, most Jews are opposed to affirmative action because of their own history of being discriminated against by quota systems. Their opposition is sometimes interpreted as protecting their own status; it also can be seen as Jews having become wary of black political demands.

Jews and Other Religions

As Christians have become more acceptant of Jews, American Jews have developed warmer feelings toward them. Figure 5.3 portrays the attitudes of Jews when the 2006 and 2011 Faith Matters surveys asked them to rate

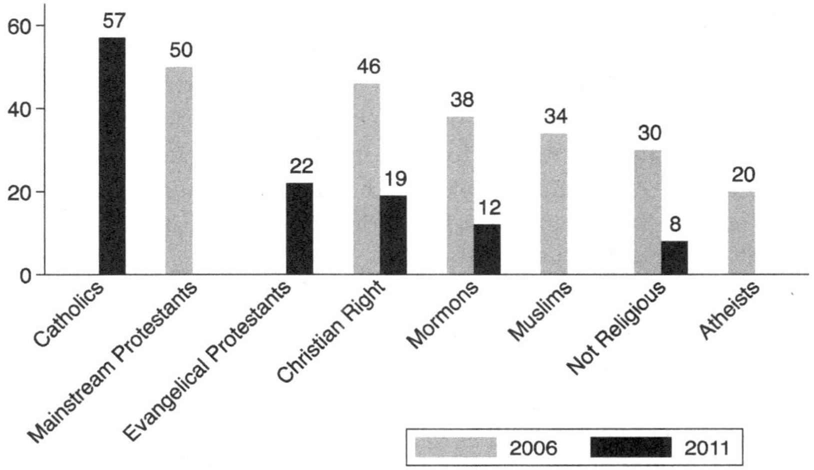

Fig. 5.3. Average ratings by Jews of other religious groups
(*Source:* Analysis of 2006 Faith Matters surveys. Some groups were not asked about in the 2006 survey.)

religions on the 100-degree thermometer scale. Regardless of centuries of distrust between Jews and Christians, Jews, on average, gave positive ratings to Christians. Jews' regard is more positive for Catholics than for other religious groups, which fits with the large decrease shown in figure 5.2 in the perception by Jews that Catholics are anti-Semitic. By contrast, Jews are negative toward evangelicals and especially toward the Christian right.

The Christian Right. Several factors account for the negative feelings of most Jews toward the Christian right. First, as shown in figure 5.2 above, many Jews consider fundamentalists and evangelicals to be anti-Semitic. Southern Baptists, the largest fundamentalist Protestant denomination in the United States, were prominent in the early 20th century Ku Klux Klan, which vilified Jews as well as blacks and Catholics. The Southern Baptist Convention went on record in 1972 in opposition to anti-Semitism but passed a resolution in 1996 stating that Jews have to come to Jesus to be saved, restating Southern Baptists' emphasis on "the proclamation of the gospel to the Jewish people." The resolution emphasized that Jews are beloved, but Jewish organizations regarded its encouragement of prayers for their conversion as offensive (Stammer 1996). Fundamentalists have historically given anti-Semitic answers to survey questions, though that has lessened considerably in recent surveys (Uslaner 2013).

Second, anti-Semitic comments by some prominent fundamentalist leaders have made Jews suspicious about fundamentalists' motives. For example, William Bell Riley, a founder in 1919 of the World's Christian Fundamentals Association, spoke of a Jewish-Communist conspiracy (Fitzgerald 2017, 144–45). Moral Majority leader Jerry Falwell stated that the anti-Christ will be Jewish. Even Rev. Billy Graham, a leading speaker for the evangelical movement in the second half of the 20th century, made anti-Semitic comments that became public when President Nixon's taped conversations with him were released (Firestone 2002).

Third, while the strong support of fundamentalists for the State of Israel might seem like a factor that would lead to positive relationships with Jews, Jews do not appreciate part of the reasoning behind that support. Fundamentalists see the establishment of Israel as a key step in a biblical prophecy essential to the Second Coming of Jesus, a prophecy that entails the destruction of Jews. Nonfundamentalist evangelicals are equally strong supporters of Israel, but, significantly, without considering the destruction of Jews as a necessary step toward Armageddon.

Fourth, Jews view fundamentalist and evangelical groups as devoted to eliminating the separation of church and state, which Jews consider essential to their free exercise of religion. Nonfundamentalist evangelicals are less focused on conversion of Jews than are fundamentalists, but the National Association of Evangelicals lobbied in the late 1940s and early 1950s for passage of a Christian amendment to the Constitution. Jews consider such an amendment a serious threat to their religious freedom.

Fifth, most Jews oppose many fundamentalist and evangelical positions on social issues, such as attempting to put prayer back in the public schools, fighting the Equal Rights Amendment, trying to outlaw abortion, and resisting gay rights. Jews feel that evangelicals seek government acceptance of their religious positions on social issues to impose Christian religious beliefs on non-Christians. As Wald and Sigelman (1997, 141) wrote, "Many of the policies most ardently embraced by Christian conservatives . . . are perceived by Jews as instruments of Christianization."

Most Jews do not distinguish between fundamentalists and evangelicals. Fundamentalists are a subset of evangelicals; both view the Bible as inerrant, but fundamentalists read it literally, while other evangelicals read parts as metaphor. Fundamentalists practice separation from people who do not accept their doctrines, but other evangelicals are generally more acceptant of those who do not agree with them theologically. However, both Jews and non-Jews link them together: thermometer ratings of fundamentalists and evangelicals in the 1988 survey in the American National Election Studies were correlated at 0.56 for Jews and 0.54 for non-Jews (Uslaner and Lichbach 2009, 403), which are fairly high correlations.

The extremely negative feelings of most Jews toward the Christian right are exemplified by the average thermometer rating of just 21 given to them in the 2012 PRRI Jewish Values Survey, with a modal rating of zero.[9] Similarly, a 2014 survey found that Jews' average thermometer rating of evangelical Christians was only 34 (Pew Research Center 2014, 4), though a comparable study in 2017 found that their rating had increased to 59 (Pew Research Center 2017, 8). At the same time, many Orthodox Jews share some interests with the Christian right on social issues as well as on aid to parochial schools and uncritical support for Israel. Accordingly, Orthodox Jews rated the Christian right more favorably than Jews as a whole, though the average score they gave them in the PRRI survey was still just 37. Since the Christian right is seen as active in politics on the conservative Republican side, one would also expect ideological and partisan differences in reactions. Indeed, Jewish political conservatives gave the Christian right a much higher average rating (44) than liberals (11), as did Jewish Republicans (39) versus Democrats (15), though these averages were all below the neutral value of 50.

Negativism toward the Christian right is often cited as an explanation of the increase in Jews' votes for Democratic presidential candidates in the 1990s and the first decade of the 2000s. The timing coincides with Pat Buchanan's provocative "Culture War" speech to the 1992 Republican National Convention, in which he spoke of "a religious war going on in our country for the soul of America" and attacked the positions of Bill and Hillary Clinton on "radical feminism," abortion, homosexuals' rights, and religion in the schools. It is not possible to test the effect of Buchanan's speech on Jews' move away from the Republicans, but Jews' increased Democratic voting occurred as the Republican Party became more associated with the Christian right and moved further right on social issues. The use of explicitly Christian language in the 2016 presidential nomination campaigns of Ben Carson and Ted Cruz may have further bolstered Jews' association of the Republican Party with the Christian right.

That a 2004 National Jewish Democratic Council (NJDC) survey and the 2012 PRRI survey asked Jews to rate evangelicals (NJDC) and the Christian right (PRRI) on feeling thermometers allows a test of the importance of attitudes on the Christian right in Jews' political thinking. Both surveys also included questions on social issues that allow for testing the relative importance of attitudes on the Christian right versus a social issue. Jews are so strongly pro-choice that there is not sufficient variance to consider the abortion item informative here, but both surveys included questions on gay rights that are: a question about allowing civil unions for same-gender couples in the NJDC survey and one about gay marriage in the PRRI survey.

Figure 5.4 shows the importance of different predictors of Jews' party identification in the NJDC and PRRI surveys. The longer the line in the figure is, the larger the effect on party identification is, with the other predictors controlled; significant effects are marked with asterisks. Jews who are less favorable to the Christian right are much more likely to be Democratic, even when controlling for their political ideology and other factors. Indeed, attitudes toward the Christian right are second in importance only to ideology and are much more important than sociodemographic variables. Denominational differences are not significant predictors of partisanship. Attitudes on civil unions were significant in the NJDC survey, though attitudes on gay marriage were not significant in the more recent, PRRI survey. This analysis affirms the importance of attitudes toward the Christian right in relating to Jews' party identification but is equivocal as to whether social attitudes (specifically gay rights) have an additional effect or are subsumed by the other predictors.

The Tea Party. The Tea Party movement of the early 2010s is sometimes treated as an adjunct of the Christian right, though academic studies (Skocpol and Williamson 2012, 35–40) and surveys (Pew Research Center 2011) emphasize the distinction between them. Tea Party supporters viewed it as a movement to take back their government from an elite that does not follow the Constitution. Studies found that its members were concerned more with economic issues than with social ones (Skocpol and Williamson 2012), though the politicians most associated with the movement were also conservative on social issues.

Jews tended to view the Christian right and the Tea Party similarly, with a correlation of 0.72 between ratings of the two groups in the 2012 PRRI survey, one of the largest correlations in any analysis of group thermometer

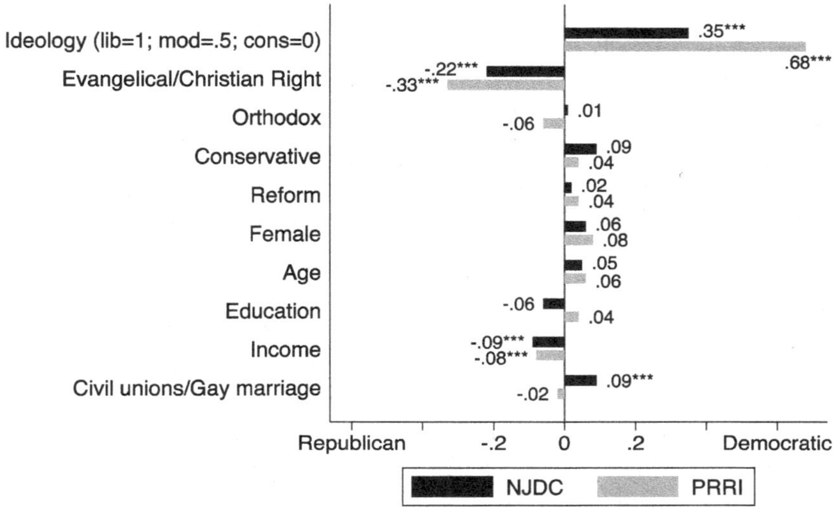

Fig. 5.4. Regression analysis of Jews' party identification
(*Source:* Analysis of 2004 NJDC and 2012 PRRI surveys. "Just Jewish" is the baseline category.)

ratings. Uslaner (2015) interpreted that high correlation as indicative that Jews regarded the Tea Party as a movement of the Christian right, though the correlation may instead be largely due to Jews recognizing that both the Tea Party and the Christian right are closely allied with the Republican Party. The average thermometer scores given to the Tea Party by Jews was just 26, but much higher ratings were given by Republican Jews (58) and politically conservative Jews (65), showing that many perceived the Tea Party as a conservative Republican movement.

Jews and Other Minority Groups

The data on anti-Semitism suggests that there is a potential for conflicts between Jews and some other minority groups, such as Hispanics and Muslims. However, there have been few direct conflicts with those groups. The 2016 ADL Report (ADL 2017, 17) found that the rate of anti-Semitism among U.S.-born Hispanics in 2016 was 19%, versus a rate of only 10% among whites. The rate is sharply higher (31%) among foreign-born Hispanics, which is usually explained as resulting from Catholic anti-Semitism in Latin America. Still, there is little indication of tension between the Jewish and Hispanic communities. Indeed, the 2007 AJC survey (fig. 5.2) found that less than one-tenth of Jews thought that many or most Hispanics were anti-Semitic. As discussed in chapter 8 of the present study, Jewish views on immigration are not very distinctive, which suggests that there is not tension between Jews and Hispanics due to anti-Semitism.

By contrast, the 2007 AJC survey found that most Jews considered Muslims to be anti-Semitic, probably reflecting the Middle East conflict. Jewish organizations work with Muslim groups in many American cities to campaign against religious-directed violence, but direct contacts between individual Jews and Muslims are limited in most communities. Figure 5.3 shows that Jews gave them average thermometer ratings slightly below 50 in 2006 and 2011. That average fell to 41 in the 2012 PRRI survey. Yet two-thirds of Jews in that PRRI survey agreed that Muslims are an important part of the U.S. religious community (66%), with only 22% thinking that American Muslims want to establish Sharia, or Islamic law, in the United States. There were partisan differences, however, with a majority (57%) of Jewish Republicans disagreeing that Muslims are an important part of the religious community and with one-third believing that Muslims want to establish Sharia. Thus, the reaction of Jews to Muslims is very mixed, with the former viewing the latter with suspicion but many Jews still respecting Muslims' role in a religiously diverse country.

Conclusions

Cohen and Liebman (1997, 425) provided an important answer as to why Jews are as Democratic as they are. They wrote, "Jews have historically seen themselves as a *vulnerable* [emphasis mine] minority group and have seen the Democratic party as the party more favorable to their group interests." The present chapter supports that argument. Over the centuries, minority consciousness has served to buttress Jews' group solidarity. Jews currently experience considerably less overt discrimination than previous generations did, but anti-Semitism and anti-Semitic violence have reemerged as very serious concerns to them.

Jews' minority consciousness has two important political effects. First, it underlies most explanations of Jews' politics. Their social identity, their values, and their self-interest are all based on their reactions to being a minority that has been discriminated against over the years. While some analysts dismiss the importance of minority consciousness, it underlies many alternative explanatory systems, such as Wald's (2015) emphasis on Jews' citizenship, which is based on their recognition that the United States is the first country that gave them full citizenship rights instead of discriminating against them as a minority.

Second, Jews' minority consciousness affects their relations with other social groups. Group solidarity can be based on competition with and/or fear of relevant out-groups, seen through the lens of the group's self-interest. These different motivations are apparent in how American Jews react to other social groups. While Jews and African Americans are very different in socioeconomic terms, they have been competitors in the nation's urban centers and rivals in the Democratic Party. After working with black groups in the fight against discrimination, many Jews felt threatened by blacks. While there are claims that attitudes toward blacks were responsible for Jews' lessening Democratic support in the 1970s and 1980s, Jews increased their Democratic voting after the 1980s.

The other social group that has affected Jews' politics is the Christian right. Many Jews see evangelicals as attempting to erase the separation of church and state, under which American Jews have flourished, and as attempting to legislate its view of morality through the Republican Party. In recent decades, evangelicals have said positive things about Jews and especially about Israel, but by the 1990s, the main perceived threat for Jews was from the Christian right. That may be one reason why the Jewish vote for Democrats increased again at that time, with the exception of Orthodox Jews who support the Christian right's political stands on social issues and aid to parochial schools. A defensive reaction against the Christian right has become one of the pillars undergirding Jews' political choices. Not surprisingly, most Jews see the Christian right's claims that America is a "Christian nation" as defining Jews out of the nation. The relationship between Jews' partisanship and their attitudes toward the Christian right is more than an ideological effect; positions on separation of church and state are likely to keep the groups apart politically.

Jews' wariness of potential allies will continue to affect their politics, adding an extra dimension to the effects of their minority consciousness. That consciousness underlays Jews' self-interest, their values, and, ultimately, their social identity. It provides a continuing basis for their political attitudes and behavior that are discussed in part III of this study.

PART III

The Distinctiveness of Jews' Politics

Jews are usually depicted as having very high political participation as well as being liberal and Democratic in their political leanings. However, what matters is not just the level of participation or the direction of their political leanings but how distinctive those factors are. Assessing distinctiveness is a matter of comparing Jews with comparable non-Jews, because their religion, values, and self-interest are not especially relevant if their political attitudes and behavior are at the same levels as non-Jews.

The chapters comprising this part of this study document the current-day politics of American Jews, along with tests of how distinctive their politics are. Chapter 6 determines that Jews' political participation is at a level that fits with their socioeconomic status, so they are only slightly distinctive in their participation. By contrast, chapter 7 establishes that they are very distinctive in being Democratic and liberal and are more distinctively Democratic than liberal. An examination of domestic issues in chapter 8 demonstrates that Jews are distinctively liberal on social and science issues but are no longer especially liberal on economic issues. The analysis of Jews' attitudes on Israel in chapter 9 emphasizes how those attitudes have become politicized.

Chapter 10 discovers that many Jewish political conservatives are not Republicans and that their social issue positions are distinctive as compared to those of non-Jewish conservatives. Chapter 11 determines that the usual liberal/conservative distinction does not fit well for Jews, because many are small-government social liberals. Many non-Jews are also are small-government social liberals, but Jews are distinctive in that many more of them are large-government social liberals, while many fewer are small-government social conservatives. In part IV of this book, these several separate aspects of Jews' political distinctiveness are assembled together for an analysis of Jewish voting.

CHAPTER 6

Resourced Participants

Presidential election turnout among Jews was an astonishing 96% according to the 1992–2012 surveys of the American National Election Studies (ANES), as if the 11th commandment for Jews[1] were "Thou shalt vote!" That percentage must assuredly be an overestimate, since people who do not vote are less likely to agree to participate in election surveys. Yet Jews do have a higher proclivity to vote in elections than do non-Jews. Jews also have an unusually high propensity to participate in politics, contribute to campaigns, and lobby. One question that arises is whether Jewish voting turnout and general political participation are remarkably high, or whether Jews' participation in politics is not very different from that of other Americans with similar levels of education and income.

A second question that presents itself is whether the high turnout of Jews is rational. After all, the outcomes of nearly all elections would be the same if you had not voted. The paradox of Jews' high political participation is that it is higher than may seem rational. This chapter begins the analysis of Jews' politics by diagnosing this paradox and showing that Jews' high participation is not irrational but is in their self-interest, as a means of protecting the democratic system under which they have prospered. This chapter's analysis then shows that their turnout level is only marginally above that of comparable non-Jews.

After examining voting turnout, this chapter examines Jews' political participation more generally and their political contributions, considering how rational these forms of participation are, along with what factors make people more likely to engage in these activities. Comparison of the levels of participation by Jews and non-Jews finds that Jews' participation is mainly what should be expected from their sociodemographic characteristics. Communal activity can be particularly effective, so this chapter ends with a review of political lobbying efforts by Jewish organizations.

Voting Turnout

The Rationality of Voting. Jews' voting turnout is higher than that of non-Jews, but is Jews' turnout rate rational? Voting is considered essential for democracy, but cost-benefit analysis suggests that it may not be rational for people to vote. Voting is not costless. One cost of voting is the time it takes to register and to go to the polls or to request and fill out an absentee ballot. It also takes time to become informed about candidates and issues, time that could be spent on other activities.

Voting is rational only if benefits expected to come from voting outweigh those costs. The expected benefits are the gains from getting your preferred candidate elected. However, your preferred candidate may be elected even if you do not bother to vote, so the benefits must be discounted by the chance that your vote will be the vote that puts your candidate into office.[2] Of course, with a large electorate, the chances are tiny that your vote will be pivotal, so the costs of voting always exceed the expected benefits. From this perspective, it would not be rational to vote (Riker and Ordeshook 1968). Jews vote at unusually high levels, even though they should be expected to recognize that the cost of voting exceeds its expected benefits. So, why do so many bother to vote? Is their voting an instance of their paradoxical political behavior? Or are there other rational reasons that Jews vote?

There are three respects in which voting might be particularly important to Jews. First, voting is rational when members of a minority social group feel that their collective votes can affect the election outcome, even if no individual's vote is likely to be pivotal by itself (Uhlaner 1989). That rationale is reinforced by close elections, as when the 2000 presidential election was decided by Florida going for George W. Bush by only a 537-vote margin.[3] Thus, the collectivity of Jewish voices in an election can be effective. However, this collective voting argument seems unlikely to hold for Jews, since most of them think individually about their politics, as they do about their Judaism.

Second, cost-benefit analysis may not be the appropriate approach for analyzing the rationality of low-cost behavior such as voting. An alternative, "minimax regret" theory is that people vote so they do not feel responsible if their not voting allows their least-favored candidate to win. Ferejohn and Fiorina (1974, 535) verbalize this rationale as "My God, what if I didn't vote and my preferred candidate lost by one vote? I'd feel like killing myself." Jews have had experience with election adversity, as when German president Paul von Hindenburg's 49.6% in the first round of presidential voting in 1932 narrowly missed getting the required majority, providing the opportunity for Adolf Hitler to be a strong enough challenger in the second round that he was ultimately appointed chancellor. American Jews can afford the slight cost that voting entails, so they could rationally feel that it is best to vote to forestall an outcome that they strongly oppose.[4]

Third, Jews may gain a psychological benefit from feeling that they have satisfied their citizen duty to vote (Riker and Ordeshook 1968).[5] High levels of civic duty can be instilled in groups through their social networks, as when one's family, friends, and work colleagues talk about an upcoming election. That effect can lead to high participation in homogeneous communities (D. Campbell 2006), which is especially applicable to Jews because of their strong in-group social networks. This is probably the best explanation of Jews' high voting level: Jews feel that living in American democracy is in their self-interest, so they consider it their duty to vote to keep turnout high enough to preserve the legitimacy of our elections.

The Impact of the Jewish Vote. The impact of the Jewish vote varies geographically because the percentage of Jews is uneven across the states, as shown in figure 6.1. States that are unshaded in the figure have a Jewish population of less than half of 1%. The darkest shading indicates states with the highest percentage of Jewish population: New York (9%), followed by New Jersey (6%) and then Massachusetts, Maryland, and the District of Columbia (4% each).

This distribution across states does not give Jews as much voting power as it did in the mid-20th century, when the large Jewish population in New York and a few other urban states with many electoral votes was seen as making Jews' votes especially pivotal (cf. El Azhary 1980). In the beginning of the 21st century, the polarization of American politics means that most of those urban states are reliably Democratic, so the Jewish vote is less consequential in presidential elections. The Jewish population is relatively small in the quintessential battleground states of Florida (3%

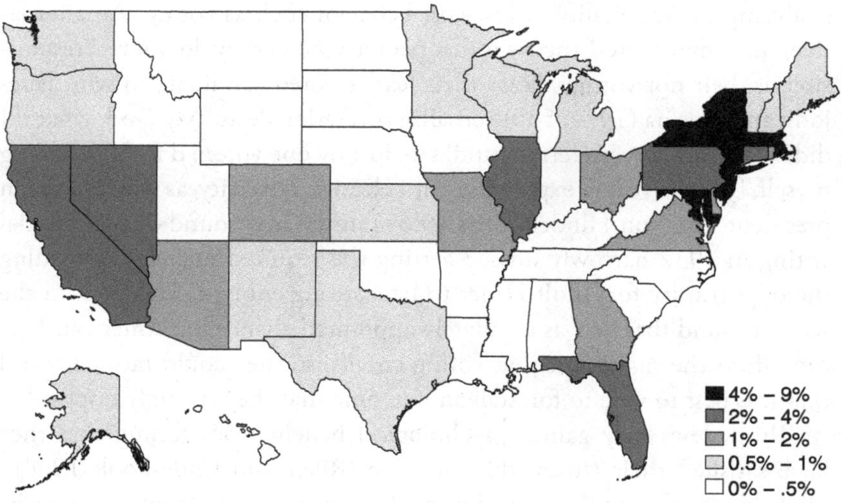

Fig. 6.1. Jewish population percentage by state
(*Note:* Percentages are from Sheskin and Dashefsky 2018, 192–93.)

of the population) and Ohio (1.3%), but it is still large enough to swing a close election, especially since the Jews' vote is magnified by their high turnout. In the states and cities where it is concentrated, their vote can be especially consequential when Jewish turnout is high in primaries and nonpresidential-year elections. While the Jewish vote is no longer concentrated in battleground states, the decline in anti-Semitism has meant that Jews have been able to win high elective offices even in some states with small Jewish populations. For example, Jews have been elected to the U.S. Senate from such states as Alaska, Hawaii, Minnesota, Nebraska, New Hampshire, Oregon, and Vermont.

Jews have become a largely urban and suburban population. There never have been a large number of Jews in rural areas, but there was a significant Jewish presence in small-town America. That presence has been disappearing as college-educated young adults have moved to jobs in large cities. The urban character of American Jews leads them to be very sensitive to the problems of cities and the needs of urban dwellers. American cities are generally more liberal and more Democratic than small towns and rural areas, and Jews follow that pattern.

Jewish population surveys that have been conducted in some cities reveal inevitable variation in demographics and politics. Jews generally constitute no more than 6% of the population of most large metropolitan areas, with the exceptions of New York (11%) and Miami (9%). The Jewish population in south Florida is much older than in most other cities. One-fifth of the Jews in New York City and Baltimore are Orthodox. As to politics, 88% of Jews in New York City are registered to vote, with upwards of 90% registered in many other cities. The Democratic lead over the Republicans in surveys of a dozen cities ranges from 31 percentage points to 58, with the significant exception of Houston, where the Democrats have a narrow 10-point lead (Sheskin 2016; Sheskin 2017, 15–17).

Is Voting Turnout by Jews Unusually High? While the estimate by the American National Election Studies that 96% of Jews turned out for the 1992–2012 presidential elections might be exaggerated, there is no reason to expect it to be more exaggerated than the 75% turnout reported for nonwhite non-Jews. But is Jewish turnout really unusually high, or is it just due to their sociodemographics? They do have sociodemographic characteristics that are associated with high voting rates. First, they are an older group, and older people vote at higher rates than younger people. Second, voting turnout is higher among people with higher socioeconomic status. The 2013 Pew survey found that 58% of Jews were college graduates, compared to 29% of the general public, and only 31% had family incomes below $50,000, versus 56% of the public at large.[6] Of course, there are socioeconomic differences in the Jewish community (see especially Kotler-Berkowitz 2014), and the ultra-Orthodox are significant exceptions in these regards, with 38% not having college education (versus 17% for other Jews) and with 43% having incomes below $50,000. Still, Jews' turnout level could mainly reflect their educational and socioeconomic levels.

Comparing levels of voting and nonvoting among Jews and non-Jews requires analyzing surveys of the general electorate. The American National Election Studies (ANES) and General Social Survey (GSS) show that compared to non-Jews, the rate at which Jews voted in national elections was about 20 percentage points higher.[7] Statistical analysis of voting turnout was conducted, with controls on several sociodemographic characteristics, starting with education, then adding in age, gender, and living in the South. Additional analysis also controlled statistically for income differences, though many survey respondents do not answer the income question.

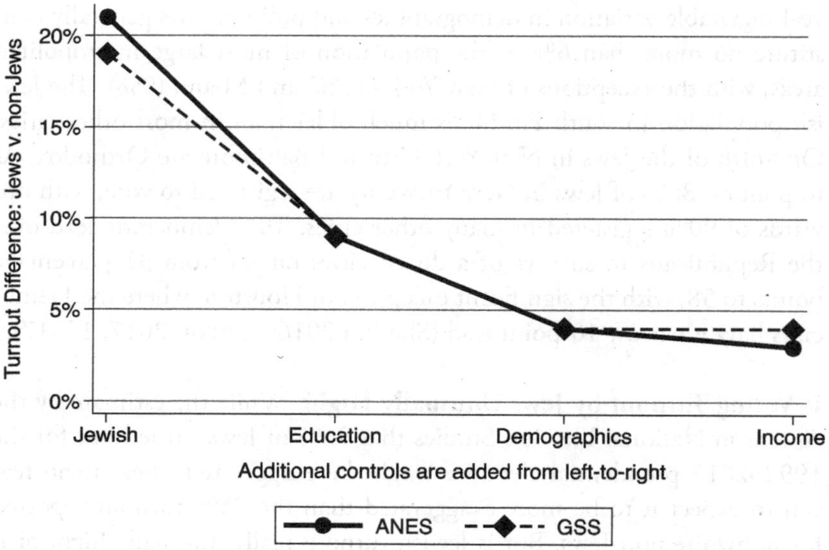

Fig. 6.2. Distinctiveness of Jews' presidential election turnout, 1992–2012 (*Source:* Analysis of American National Election Studies and General Social Survey.)

Figure 6.2 displays the results. The height of each line at the left side of the graph shows the approximate 20% difference in voting turnout rates between Jews and non-Jews before statistical controls. As one moves to the right, the line's height shows the effect of adding additional sociodemographic controls.[8] Education is known to be a strong correlate of voting, so the first test is whether the turnout difference remains when looking at Jews and non-Jews of the same education level. The turnout difference between Jews and non-Jews drops by half when controlling on education. It falls further when other sociodemographic controls are included along with education, and it ends up at no more than four points (and not significant in the ANES analysis) when income is also controlled. Thus, the turnout difference between Jews and non-Jews is considerably decreased when sociodemographic characteristics are considered.

This analysis demonstrates that the high voting rate of Jews is mostly due to their sociodemographics. Jews and non-Jews with similar sociodemographic characteristics vote at about the same rates. Jews' turnout may still be slightly higher than that of comparable non-Jews, but the difference is just a fraction of the raw difference in their turnout rates.

That does not mean that the higher Jewish voting turnout is fallacious. Jews' voting turnout level is indeed high, but that high turnout is typical for people with comparable sociodemographics, rather than just due to being Jewish.[9]

Still, Jews have a turnout advantage. As an older population, a higher percentage are of voting age, their registration rate is very high, and their turnout rate is high (Sheskin 2013, 42). Because they vote at high levels, politicians seeking to maximize their votes should try to appeal to Jews. But they should also appeal to non-Jews who fit the sociodemographic profile and especially the education level of Jews, because those non-Jews also vote at high rates.

Political Participation More Generally

Jews are also thought to participate in politics at a high rate. But is that rate again mainly due to higher levels of education and income among Jews and to other sociodemographics? Understanding their participation involves considering what factors lead people to participate in politics.

Voluntary Civic Activity. Political participation is a form of voluntary participation in civic activities. Verba, Schlozman, and Brady (1995) developed a three-factor model to explain why some people participate in such activities more than other people do. Their framework helps focus attention on advantages that Jews have in political participation.

First, people must have resources to be able to participate. Monetary resources and time are essential resources for civic activity. These activities take time, and one must be able to afford to take time away from money-earning activities. "Civic skills" are another necessary resource. Important civic skills beyond the basic ones of education and language competency include experience in attending decision-making meetings, planning such meetings, writing letters, and making speeches. These skills can be learned on the job or in nonpolitical organizations, and there are many Jewish institutions that provide such opportunities. Second, people must be civically engaged. Being exposed to politics at home while growing up can make people want to become civically engaged. Developing interest in politics and acquiring political information further increase one's engagement potential. Third, recruitment to participate is important. Recruitment occurs when other members of organizations, such as clubs, unions, and religious institutions, ask people to help out.

Participation increases when people possess resources, become engaged, and get recruited, and American Jews stack up very well in these regards. Their education level is high. Their socioeconomic status is high enough that most would have time for voluntary activities. Many have gone to college, where they would have had opportunities to develop civic skills such as giving speeches and attending meetings. Surveys find that most Jews are interested in politics, so exposure to politics at home is common. They belong to many organizations that may recruit them to become active participants. Indeed, Jewish organizations often have programs in leadership training to groom future leaders. From this perspective, a large number of Jews possess characteristics that facilitate civic participation.

But is political participation rational for individuals? Rational choice theory applies to types of political participation beyond voting, except that the costs and expected benefits calculations vary between different forms of participation. Campaign participation is usually considered to be rational. Even though it entails greater time costs, working on a campaign can offer larger expected benefits than voting turnout can. It permits a greater impact on a candidate's chance of winning than a single vote does, and it provides the social benefits of meeting like-minded people.

Is Political Participation by Jews Unusually High? Jews are thought to have high levels of political participation. But whether their participation level is distinctively high is again a matter of whether it is greater than other Americans with similar sociodemographic characteristics. Greeley's (1974) analysis of a 1967 survey on political participation concluded that Jews' high level of participation was due to social class, though, surprisingly, they had the lowest activity level of all the groups analyzed when a full range of sociodemographics were controlled.

Kenneth Wald (2016) has pursued this topic further, looking at whether Jews are hyperactive in their political participation when matched with comparable non-Jews. He analyzed a series of 35 monthly polls taken by the Roper Organization from 1989 through 1992, employing a sophisticated "matching" technique to compare each Jew in the sample with the non-Jew in the sample who had the most similar sociodemographics. Respondents were asked about a dozen political activities that they might have performed within the past year, such as writing their member of Congress and going to public town meetings. Wald's results are striking: Jews are not hyperactive politically. Their seemingly high participation levels are similar to those of non-Jews with comparable sociodemographic characteristics. Indeed, like Greeley, Wald found that Jews participated less than those with whom they were matched. The finding that education, income, race, age, and labor union affiliation all matter for participation emphasizes the importance of social stratification.

This topic can also be analyzed via the 1992–2012 ANES surveys used for analysis above. Those surveys asked whether the person tried to influence someone's vote, attended a campaign rally, and did party work. At least one of these three acts were performed by 53% of Jews, versus 37% of non-Jews. That difference is cut to 10 percentage points when socioeconomic controls are introduced. The largest effect is due to education, with income and gender (men participate more) also mattering more than whether the person is Jewish.

Thus, the story for participation is similar to that for voting turnout: Jews are very active political participants, but a high level of participation also holds for demographically similar non-Jews. Education is a key factor, with much of the difference between Jews and non-Jews being due to educational differences. Thus, for their political participation, the resources that Jews bring to the table matter more than their religion. Social stratification dominates over religion and ethnicity.

Furthermore, Kotler-Berkowitz (2005) found differences among Jews on political participation. The 2000–01 National Jewish Population Survey asked respondents if they had attended a political meeting, contributed money to a candidate, or contacted a government official in the past year. The Orthodox were low participants on these criteria. Education and income correlated with greater participation, as the resource model would predict. Those who scored high on "structural ethnicity" (e.g., belonging to a Jewish organization, volunteering for one, and living in the same household as a Jew) participated more, while those who scored high on "cultural ethnicity" (e.g., attending services, going to a seder, fasting on Yom Kippur, and believing in God) participated slightly less.

Campaign Contributions

There are many stories of Jews making large monetary contributions to political candidates. Is this just another case where the differences are less real than they seem? Does the high level of political contributions by Jews simply reflect their income levels?

Contributing money to a political candidate is considered rational political activity. It has direct monetary costs, but its expected benefits are higher than those of just voting, since contributions enable a candidate to conduct more campaigning and thus increase the likelihood of victory. Larger contributions can actually be more rational, since they may increase the chances that a candidate, if elected, will pay attention to the contributors' needs and policy preferences.

Few people make political contributions, but older people, those with more education, and, naturally, those with higher income are most likely to contribute. Those characteristics fit the profile of many American Jews. Furthermore, Jews are used to contributing money for causes (Gerstein, Cohen, and Landres 2013), including synagogue dues and Jewish as well as non-Jewish charities, so they should be able to extend their financial contributions to political candidates.

Both parties have sought large contributors in the last several presidential elections, and Jews have been among those large contributors. While we tend to think of Jews as giving large contributions to Democratic candidates, the largest contributor to Republican Mitt Romney's 2012 campaign was Jewish billionaire casino operator Sheldon Adelson, and the only other Jew who gave $10 million or more that year to candidates was New York's mayor Michael Bloomberg, who gave as an Independent (Center for Public Integrity 2012). Jews were among the large contributors to some Republicans who ran for their party's 2016 presidential nomination. However, federal campaign contribution records released shortly before Election Day showed that fewer than one-fifth of the Republican Jewish Coalition's 55-member board of directors had contributed to Donald Trump's campaign (Sales 2016), reflecting the limited support of prominent Jewish Republicans for his candidacy. The top contributors to Democrat Hillary Clinton in 2016 included several Jews (Gold and Narayanswamy 2016).

The ANES surveys ask whether the respondent has made a campaign donation. While Jews answered yes at a higher rate than non-Jews, with a difference of 10 percentage points from 1992 through 2012, that difference falls to a nonsignificant 4 points once socioeconomic differences are controlled. As expected, older people, the more educated, and, those with higher income were more likely to donate. The ANES surveys also ask separate questions about political contributions to candidates, political action committees, and parties. More Jews than non-Jews contributed to at least one of them during this period, with a difference of 12 percentage points, but that difference falls to a nonsignificant 5 points when comparing Jews and non-Jews with similar socioeconomic characteristics. On political contributions, education, age, income, and gender (men are more likely to contribute) had much larger effects than whether the person is Jewish.[10]

Surveys of campaign contributors find that Jews constitute a disproportionate share of contributors. A survey of contributors to presidential nomination campaigns in 1992 found that Jews were significantly more likely to be solicited for campaign contributions, possibly because they were known to be contributors in the past (Brown, Powell, and Wilcox 1995, 117–19). A survey of congressional campaign donors in 1996 found that Jews were disproportionately in friendship networks that motivated them to contribute (Francia et al. 2003, 56–57). As could be expected, surveys have found that Jews disproportionately contribute to Democratic candidates (Brown, Powell, and Wilcox 1995, 44–45; Francia et al. 2005, 12–13). Although corporate executives generally contribute more to Republican candidates, Jewish corporate executives were significantly more likely to contribute to Democratic candidates (Burris 2001).

In summary, some large contributors are Jewish, but many more are not. Most Jews are Democrats, so it is not surprising that Jews make more contributions to Democratic candidates than to Republicans. Still, some of the large contributors to the Republican Party are Jewish. Survey data show that Jews are more likely than non-Jews to contribute to political campaigns, but that difference seems to be mainly a matter of sociodemographics, especially income and education. However, it is still possible that there is a hyperactive subset of Jews who are so interested in politics that they vote, participate actively in campaigns, and make campaign contributions.

Political Lobbying

Working together as a group is a rational means to influence political outcomes, since it can be more effective than individual efforts. Political lobbying costs both time and money, but it can have very direct policy benefits. Many Jewish groups try to affect government policies, and Jews also support the lobbying work of non-Jewish organizations such as the American Civil Liberties Union and the Sierra Club.

Jewish organizations are very involved in political lobbying. The first Jewish lobbying organizations were "defense" agencies, including the American Jewish Committee, which was established to lobby on behalf of threats to Jews overseas, and the Anti-Defamation League, which was formed to counter domestic anti-Semitism and discrimination. A very large number of organizations now conduct Jewish advocacy activities at the local, state, national, and international levels. Chanes (2001, 117) appropriately summarized, "No self-identifying group in the United States offers as many institutions that provide opportunities for advocacy as does the American Jewish community."

The Israel lobby has received particular notice. In Paul and Paul's (2009, 137) survey of Washington insiders, the American Israel Public Affairs Committee (AIPAC) was ranked as having the most influence of any ethnic lobby, making it "the gold standard of an effective lobbying organization." Moreover, the influence of pro-Israel groups is enhanced by the strong support for Israel by non-Jews, especially evangelical Christian groups. Pastor John Hagee's Christians United for Israel is the largest pro-Israel organization, claiming more than 2.5 million members. The pro-Israel lobby has been particularly effective in gaining military arms and foreign aid for Israel. AIPAC is able to mobilize a large number of grassroots members devoted to Israel. It contributes to congressional reelection campaigns of members of Congress who have been longtime supporters of Israel, and it has been successful in the occasional instances when it has supported a challenger running against an incumbent who took positions it deemed to be anti-Israel (Paul and Paul 2009, 49–50). Yet the size of the pro-Israel lobbying should not be exaggerated. Their spending constitutes only a minor part of total donations to political action committees. For example, figures from the Center for Responsible Politics show that even with the motivation of the Iran accord dispute in 2015, the $3.3 million AIPAC spent on lobbying that year was less than one-tenth of the $37.7 million spent by the National Association of Realtors.

Mearsheimer and Walt's (2007) book *The Israel Lobby and U.S. Foreign Policy* provocatively argued that the pro-Israel lobby has had too much influence on U.S. policy in the Middle East. However, the broad American consensus on the importance of Israel's security implies that U.S. policy might be similar to what it has been even without that lobby. There are limits to the Israel lobby's effectiveness, especially when it has fought American presidents. As Steven Spiegel (1982–83, 245) wrote, "Activities of Jews and their allies . . . have been successful in creating a positive atmosphere toward Israel on Capitol Hill. . . . Yet, broad pro-Israeli statements by congressmen have not prevented every administration from engaging in bitter disputes with the Israelis." For example, AIPAC lost high-profile fights against Jimmy Carter's 1978 sale of bombers to Saudi Arabia and Egypt and against Ronald Reagan's 1981 sale of AWACS surveillance planes to Saudi Arabia. Similarly, attempts to get George H. W. Bush to give a loan guarantee to Israel without assurances that new settlements would not be constructed in the West Bank and Gaza failed after Bush stated at a 1991 public press conference, "We are up against very strong and effective groups [AIPAC] that go up to the [Capitol] Hill." Not only did Bush prevail, but the Israeli prime minister was replaced at Israel's next general election, and his successor lectured the members of AIPAC that they "had done more harm than good, 'waging battles that were lost in advance'" (Rubin 2012, 48; see also Ross 2015, 250–54).

A fracture developed in Jewish lobbying when J Street was founded in 2008 as an alternative to AIPAC. J Street is a "pro-Israel, pro-peace" organization favoring a two-state solution to the Israeli-Palestinian conflict. It lobbies in support of diplomatic solutions to Middle East conflicts involving Israel. J Street contends that it is more in accord with the views of younger Jews than AIPAC is. The divergence of J Street from the old guard became most evident in April 2014, when its membership application to the Conference of Presidents of Major American Jewish Organizations was voted down, even though it had the support of the large Reform and Conservative Judaism organizations. That vote underlines the fissures that have developed in the Jewish community with respect to Israel, which are discussed further in chapter 9.

AIPAC lobbied Congress to stop Barack Obama's 2015 agreement with Iran that would limit its nuclear activities. That effort failed when it became politicized because the Republican Speaker of the House, John Boehner, did not inform Obama in advance before inviting the Israeli prime minister, Benjamin Netanyahu, to speak to Congress. The House voted, largely along party lines, to block the accord, but it went into effect without a direct Senate vote, when Senate Democrats defeated a procedural motion. One could reasonably contend that a powerful lobbying group could work behind the scenes to get what it wants rather than publicly challenging a president in these ways. From that perspective, AIPAC's fight against the 2015 nuclear agreement with Iran could be seen as revealing its weakness rather than its influence. Yet AIPAC may have been playing a long game, recognizing that it would lose but showing how hard it was willing to fight, so that members of Congress would follow its lead on lower-profile matters. In retrospect, AIPAC's determined fight may have been a factor when President Trump disavowed the Iran accord. A critical part of AIPAC's reputation has been that its influence over the years has been bipartisan, but the partisan differences in the battle over the Iran agreement suggest that its bipartisan influence may diminish. J Street lobbied in favor of the 2015 Iran accord. Its goals were in line with those of the Obama presidency, but its influence waned when Donald Trump was elected president.

In addition to lobbying, Jewish organizations have sought to influence public policy through litigation strategies. In a sense, that method can be traced back to Louis Brandeis and his legal briefs on behalf of workers' rights in the early 20th century. It was advanced in the civil rights struggle in the middle of that century and in the continuing litigation on issues involved in church-state separation.

Conclusions

Jews are commonly said to be unusually politically active, in terms of voting turnout, campaign participation, political donations, and lobbying. Jews are indeed more active than non-Jews, but this is largely because of higher levels of education and income among Jews as well as to general sociodemographics. Close analysis reveals that Jews' voting turnout is only a few percentage points higher than that of comparable non-Jews, and that is true for other forms of campaign participation as well. The higher turnout and campaign activity of Jews makes them appropriate targets for election appeals, but so are non-Jews with similar sociodemographic characteristics.

Rational choice theory implies that it may not be rational for individuals to vote. But participation in politics is in the self-interest of a minority that wants to be protected. Thus, the high turnout of Jews is rational because high turnout helps maintain the legitimacy of elections and, thereby, the American democratic system under which Jews have thrived.

Studies of civic voluntarism show that participation in voluntary civic events depends on people's resources, sense of civic engagement, and recruitment to participate. Jews stack up high in these regards. Their education and income provide important resources, their high level of interest in politics makes them civically engaged, and membership in synagogues and other organizations help recruit them into volunteering activity.

Jews are less cohesive than they used to be in both campaign contributions and lobbying efforts. There are some major Jewish contributors to national Republican campaigns, and Jewish lobbying on Israel is now split into two factions. Both of these trends are likely to continue and to accelerate.

Isaacs (1974, 15) described fear as "undoubtedly . . . the greatest single factor accounting for Jews' high level of political activity." That may explain why there are so many Jewish defense organizations, but it does not explain the political activity of individual Jews. While there are many paradoxes relating to Jews' politics, there is nothing paradoxical about their political activity. It is at the high level that should be expected given their social demographics.

This chapter has shown that the myth that Jews are unusually politically active is not true. They are only marginally more active than other educated and affluent Americans. But, as the next chapter makes clear, that does not mean that Jews' political views are similar to those of other comparably situated Americans.

CHAPTER 7

More Democratic than Liberal

"Ask two Jews, get three opinions" is one of the oldest quips that Jews say about themselves. Jews recognize that they do not agree on everything and that they enjoy disagreeing. A more extended version of the joke involves two Jews who were shipwrecked on a desert island. They built three synagogues on it, one of which was for the Orthodox Jew and one of which was for the Reform Jew. When their rescuers asked about the third synagogue, the two Jews replied in unison, "No one would ever step foot in that one!" Even on a desert island, they could not agree enough to pray together. This joke suggests that Jews inevitably separate into factions. Some Jews claim that Jewish unity (*achdut Yisrael*) is essential, but there have always been disagreements among Jews, from when there were two separate Jewish kingdoms in ancient Israel to when there were warring factions in the early-20th century Zionism movement. There is no reason to expect political unity of Jewish American voters. There is considerable cohesion to Jews' politics, but some division is inevitable.

Fein (1988, 224) wrote of Jews, "Politics is our religion; our preferred political denomination is liberalism." But the claim that Jews are all liberal Democrats is a false stereotype. While 90% of Jews evidently voted for Franklin Roosevelt's reelection in the 1930s and 1940s, Jews are not that politically united today. The 2013 Pew data show that just under half are liberal Democrats, and even that is a high estimate. Many are conservatives, and many are Republicans. Just like other Americans, individual Jews consider a wide variety of matters when deciding how to align politically, and they do not come out with identical decisions.

This chapter begins by comparing the partisanship and ideology of

Jews and examining how distinctive their politics are. While their high participation level is mainly a matter of their sociodemographics, that is not the case for their Democratic and liberal self-identifications. However, Jews are not monolithic in their politics, so important differences among them are described below. Finally, this chapter's assessment of the stability of Jewish partisanship and ideology over time finds some change but considerable stability. As argued in chapter 3, the dominant politicized social identity of Jews includes being Democratic and being liberal; their politicized social identity keeps their partisanship and ideology distinctive and relatively stable.

The Myth of Political Homogeneity

Party and ideology have become closely aligned in the current era of polarized politics, especially among political activists, but partisan leanings and political ideology in the mass public can be different. There were conservative southern Democrats and liberal "Rockefeller" Republicans back in the 1950s, and there still are moderates in both parties today. Most political scientists regard partisanship and ideology as long-term political predispositions rather than as election-specific. Those predispositions can change, and there is some change in them even during election campaigns, but they generally stay steady across several election years.

There is some fluctuation in Jews' politics over time (as shown later in this chapter), but the 2013 Pew results are typical. After asking respondents whether they identified as Republican, Democrat, or Independent, Pew asked Independents which party they lean toward.[1] The Pew report combines leaners with partisans, and that decision is followed in this book. Pew found that 70% of Jews identified as Democrats or leaned toward that party, while national polls conducted by Pew around the same time period (2013, 96) found about half of the general public to be in the Democratic camp (fig. 7.1). Jews were second only to blacks in being Democratic: 85% of black Protestants were Democrats.[2]

Some sources emphasize that many Jews are politically independent. Indeed, when first asked if they are Democrats, Republicans, or Independents, 32% of the Pew sample answered that they were Independents, which is slightly lower than the 38% of the general public giving that answer in other Pew polls of the same year. Nearly all Jewish Independents

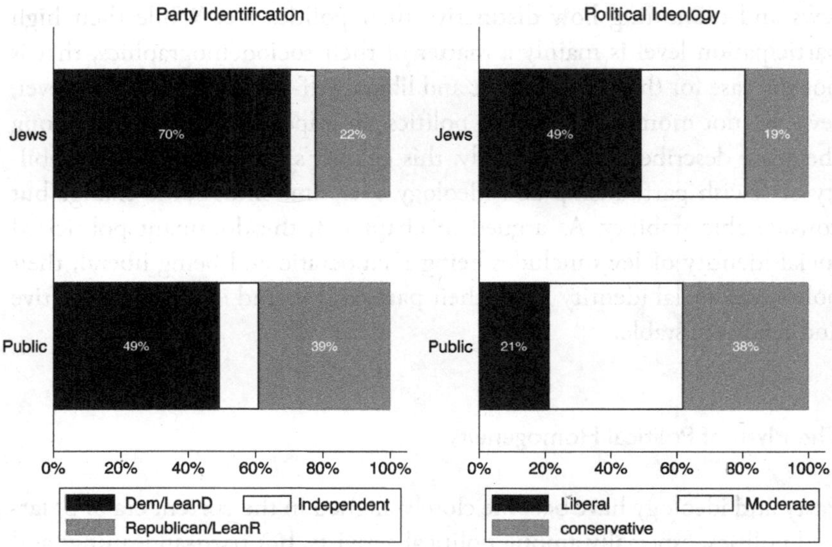

Fig. 7.1. Comparison of the politics of Jews and the politics of the public (*Note:* Data for Jews is based on analysis of the 2013 Pew Jewish survey; public data is from Pew Research Center 2013, 96. Percentages in the middle bars omitted to improve readability. Those responding "don't know" on political ideology have been combined with moderates.)

indicated that they were closer to one of the two major parties, with most being closer to the Democratic Party. Jewish surveys typically combine Independents who lean toward a party with those who identify with it, because surveys of the general electorate have found that leaners vote for that party's presidential candidate as much as partisans who weakly identify with their party (Keith et al. 1992). Not only are Jews predominantly Democratic, but Democratic Jews take a particularly negative view of the Republican Party.

Pew measured political ideology along a five-point scale, asking people, "In general, would you describe your political views as very conservative, conservative, moderate, liberal, or very liberal." Few people choose the "very" categories, so Pew combined the two categories at each end of this scale, and that practice is followed in this book.[3] As figure 7.1 shows, half of American Jews said they were liberal in their politics, versus just one-fifth of the general public. No other religious group was as liberal as Jews.

Comparing the two sides of figure 7.1 shows that there are more Jewish Democrats than Jewish liberals.[4] The figure also emphasizes that Jews are not fully monolithic in their politics. Three out of every 10 are not Democratic, and about half of Jews are not liberal. About one-fifth are Republicans, and about one-fifth are political conservatives.[5]

According to the 2013 Pew Jewish survey, only 46% of Jews are liberal Democrats, and that percentage again includes Independents who say they are closer to the Democratic Party. Table 7.1 displays the combined distribution of ideology and leaned partisanship. The largest category consists of liberal Democrats and includes just under half of Jews, which suggests that the other half are potentially susceptible to Republican campaign appeals. The second largest set of Jews consists of moderate Democrats, followed by conservative Republicans. Just under one-tenth are moderate Republicans, and slightly less than one-tenth are conservative Democrats. Only trace amounts of the other four possible combinations were found.

Incidentally, the Pew figures for Democrats and liberals among Jews are slightly larger than the values often given in the media, because of differing definitions of who is Jewish. In particular, Gallup and election exit polls ask only what one's current religion is, so Jews in those polls are Jews by religion (JBR). JBR are about 10 percentage points less Democratic and nearly 25 points less liberal than Jews of no religion (JNR).[6] Thus, media polls and exit polls likely understate the Democratic and liberal advantages among Jews as a whole.

TABLE 7.1. Jews' Ideology and Partisanship Combinations

Combination	Percentage
Liberal Democratic	46%
Moderate Democratic	19%
Politically conservative Republican	12%
Moderate Republican	8%
Politically conservative Democratic	6%
Moderate Independent	4%
Liberal Independent	2%
Politically conservative Independent	2%
Liberal Republican	1%
TOTAL	100%

Source: Analysis of the 2013 Pew Jewish survey.

Politically Distinctive

Jews' politics are distinctive and are not primarily due to their sociodemographics as was the case for their political participation. Distinctiveness is tested by whether the group's behavior differs from that of nongroup members who are similar to them in other sociodemographics. *The American Voter* (A. Campbell et al. 1960, 302–3) referred to this as comparing the group's behavior with that of people with similar "life situations" or "life circumstances." The extent of Jewish distinctiveness can be tested by using statistical controls, controlling for a wide range of sociodemographics at once as was done in some of the previous chapters.

Figure 7.2 shows the extent to which demographic controls reduce the apparent distinctiveness of Jews' partisanship and ideology. Recall from the previous chapter that the height of each line at the left side of each graph shows the difference between Jews and non-Jews before statistical controls. As one moves from left to right, sociodemographic controls are added first, then income is also controlled. The lines in these figures would fall to zero on the right-hand side if Jewish political distinctiveness were completely due to sociodemographics.[7]

The distinctiveness of Jews' Democratic identification remains under controls. As shown in the left half of figure 7.2, there was a 35-point difference between Jews and other nonblack Americans in the ANES data and a more than 25-point difference in the GSS data. Whereas chapter 6 showed that Jews' voting turnout is less distinctive when sociodemographic controls are instituted, their Democratic identification remains distinctive under controls. This result confirms studies for earlier years (Manza and Brooks 1997; Stanley and Niemi 2006; Wald 2015).

As shown in the right half of figure 7.2, in the liberal identification of American Jews compared to other nonblack Americans over the period, there was a 31-point difference according to the ANES data and a 25-point difference in the GSS data. Jews' liberal distinctiveness barely changes when sociodemographic controls are introduced.[8] Thus, their liberalism is not a reflection of their gender, age, education, income, or residence in the South. Jews are substantially more liberal in their self-identification than would be expected given their demographics.

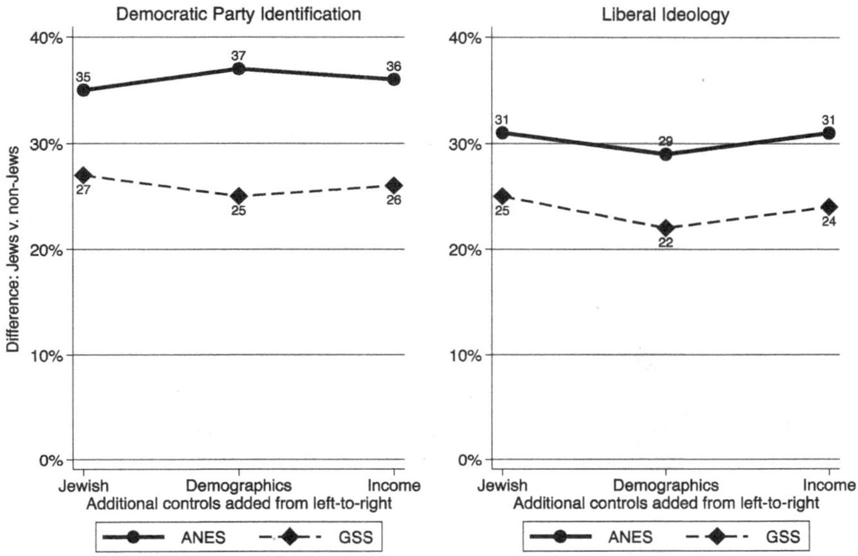

Fig. 7.2. Distinctiveness of Jews' politics
(*Source:* Analysis of American National Election Studies and General Social Survey.)

Political Differences among Jews

While their politics are distinctive, Jews are not as monolithic politically as they are often portrayed. Systematic denominational and sociodemographic differences exist. Such differences occur in the general electorate as well, with higher levels of Republican and conservative identification among evangelicals and people higher in class status. Similarly, the values underlying Jews' denominational differences lead to considerable political disparities between the Orthodox and non-Orthodox. By contrast, the self-interest differences across different socioeconomic categories do not lead to large political differences.

Denominational Differences. Some of the largest political differences among Jews are between adherents of the different branches of Judaism. As far back as the National Jewish Population Surveys for 1971 and 1990, Orthodox Jews were more politically conservative, while Reform Jews were

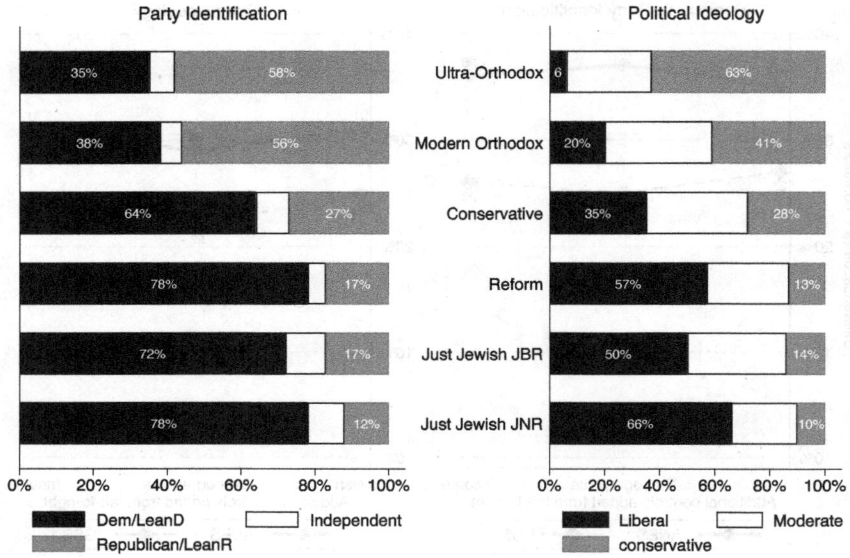

Fig. 7.3. Jews' politics by denomination
(*Source:* Analysis of 2013 Pew Jewish survey.)

more liberal (Lazerwitz et al. 1998). Lazerwitz and Harrison (1979) demonstrated that this difference was not just due to socioeconomic status.

Figure 7.3 presents the results on denominational differences for the 2013 Pew survey. As the left half shows, ultra-Orthodox Jews are the most Republican (58%) and the most politically conservative (63%). On the opposite end of the political spectrum, Reform Jews are the most Democratic (78%) and the most liberal (57%). To put their politics in context, the ultra-Orthodox are nearly as Republican and about as politically conservative as white evangelical Protestants. Reform Jews are a little less Democratic than black Protestants (85%) but are much more politically liberal.

These denominational differences permeate any analysis of the contemporary politics of American Jews. Orthodox Jews, especially the ultra-Orthodox, differ from most other Jews in their political orientations. As seen in chapter 2, only about one-tenth of Jews are Orthodox, which is why Jewish statistics overall show such a strong Democratic and liberal bent even when one of the three main streams of Judaism is neither Democratic nor liberal. The Orthodox are predominantly Republican, but they constitute such a small proportion of American Jewry that Pew found them to comprise only 28% of Republican Jews.

Adherents to Conservative Judaism are in between Orthodox and Reform Jews in their politics. Conservative Jews are less Republican and politically conservative than the Orthodox Jews and less Democratic and liberal than the Reform Jews. They are closer to Reform Jews on party identification but closer to the Modern Orthodox on political ideology.

There has been much attention in the media in recent years to the religious "nones," the growing proportion of the U.S. public without a religious affiliation. Jewish "nones" (the "just Jewish") are even more Democratic and liberal than religiously unaffiliated Americans. Interestingly, the "just Jewish" Jews by religion are less Democratic and less liberal than Reform Jews, possibly because they are a mixture of different types of people who consider themselves Jewish but do not identify with any of the three major branches.

Figure 7.4 provides an analysis of the relative impact of different factors on Jews' party identification and political ideology. Longer lines in the figure reflect greater impacts, with asterisks to signify statistical significance. Not only are the Orthodox more Republican and more politically conservative, but those who emphasize the importance of religion are significantly more Republican and more conservative. When controlling statistically on the other factors, Jews who are Conservative and Reform are not statistically different politically from the "just Jewish," and the importance people give to being Jewish is also not significant. Women and those with more education are more Democratic and liberal. Age and region do not have separate significant effects.

Though not looking specifically at Jews, Goren et al. (2016) analyzed how self-identified ideology is related to Schwartz's universal values described in chapter 4 in the present study. In the surveys they analyzed, people who favored conservation (tradition and security) were most likely to identify as conservatives, while those who favored self-transcendence (universalism and benevolence) were somewhat more likely to identify as liberals. That fits with the discussion of Jews' values in chapter 4, in that Orthodox Jews would most emphasize conservation values, whereas the non-Orthodox would be more likely to emphasize self-transcendence.

Sociodemographic Differences. Between Jews, there are also political differences along conventional sociodemographic categories, though those

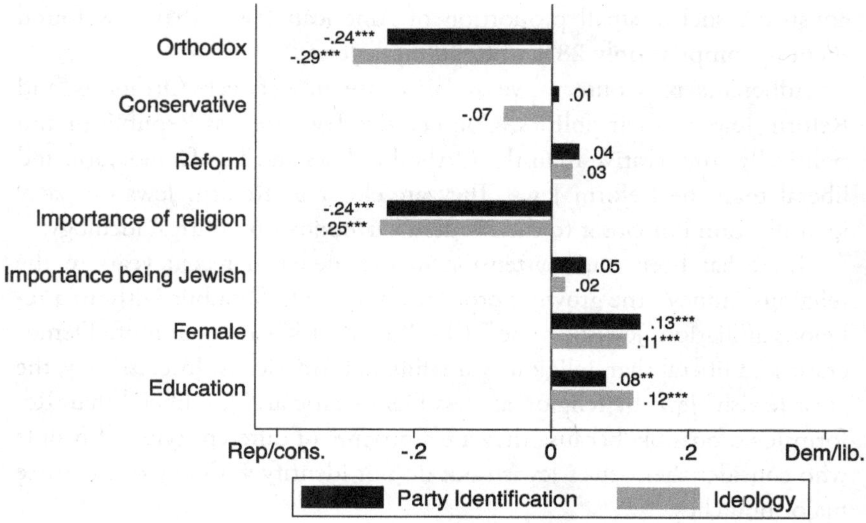

Fig. 7.4. Regression analysis of bases of Jews' politics
(*Source:* Analysis of 2013 Pew Jewish survey. "Just Jewish" is the baseline category; age and living in the South were not significant.)

differences are smaller than denominational differences. A Jewish gender gap echoes the gender gap that has existed in American politics since the 1980s, with Jewish women being more Democratic than Jewish men by 10 percentage points, as well as being more liberal. Age differences on party identification are minimal, except Jews under age 30 are more liberal than older Jews by about 7 points, even though more younger Jews are Orthodox.

As to education, those with advanced degrees are more Democratic and more liberal than those who did not get education past high school (fig. 7.5). Income differences exist but are smaller than educational differences, with middle-income Jews being more Republican and more politically conservative than those with high or low incomes.[9] Yet these income differences are weak, confirming the usual finding that politics are less affected by income for Jews than for the public as a whole.

While there are some political differences among Jews according to their sociodemographics, they are less than those between the adherents of the different branches of Judaism. Kotler-Berkowitz's (2017) analysis of the Pew data emphasizes that the denominational divisions are the most

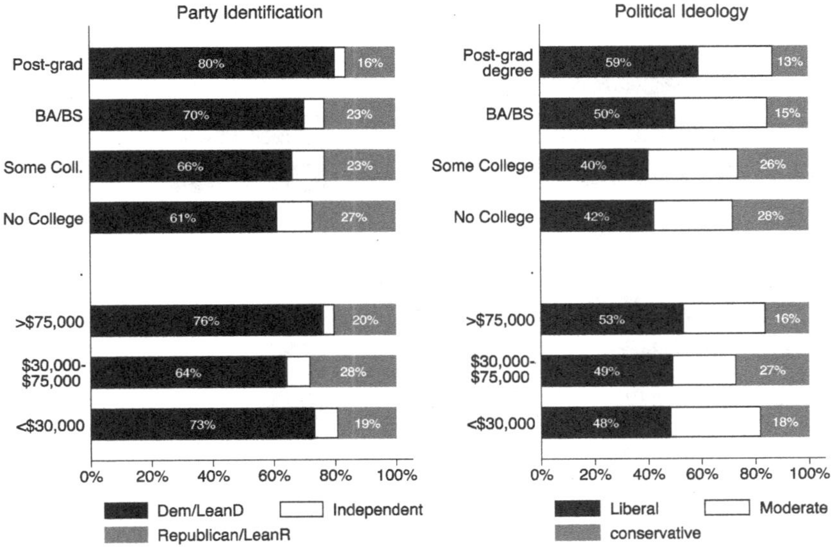

Fig. 7.5. Politics of Jews by sociodemographic characteristics
(*Source:* 2013 Pew Jewish survey.)

consistent political divisions among Jews, not only regarding partisanship and ideology but with respect to attitudes on issues regarding both U.S. domestic policy and Israel. That result raises the further question of the extent to which partisan differences for Jews on issues and voting are due to denominational differences, a question examined in subsequent chapters of the present study.

Political Fluctuation over the Years

Jews' partisan and ideological views have varied mildly over the years during which consistent measures have been taken. Figure 7.6 uses ANES surveys to trace Jews' party identification across three time periods: 1952–70, 1972–90, and 1992–2012. Ideology has been divided into only the two later periods because ANES did not ask the ideology question until 1972. The top set of bars shows results for Jews, with comparisons below for nonblack non-Jews.

The data on party identification show a small change back and forth for

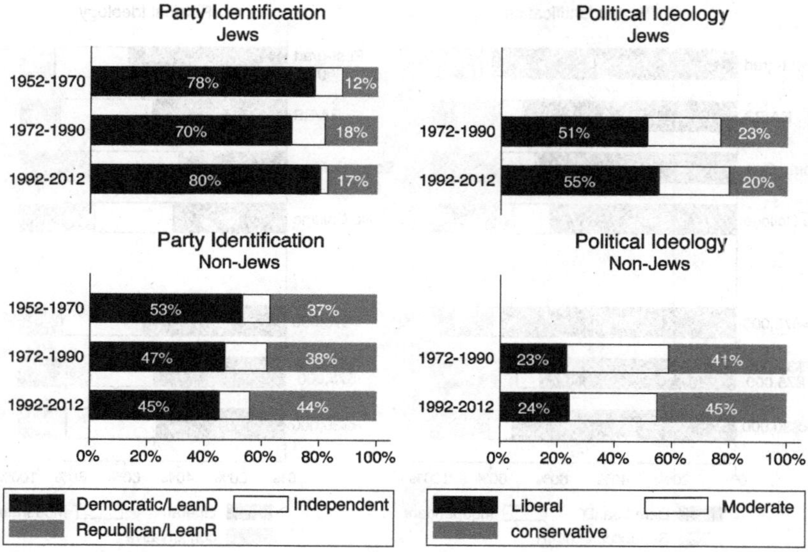

Fig. 7.6. Changes in politics of Jews and Non-Jews
(*Source:* Analysis of American National Election Studies surveys.)

Jews, with a majority always favoring the Democratic Party. Between the first two periods, the level of Democratic identification decreased among both Jews and non-Jews, but it went back up in 1992–2012 among Jews. Meanwhile, Republican identification among Jews increased in 1972–90,[10] but did not go up further in 1992–2012 as it did among non-Jews. The Republican Party became more associated with the Christian right and with social conservatism in the early 1990s, which may explain the different changes for Jews and non-Jews after that. Similarly, as shown in chapter 13 of the present study, Jews' presidential voting was less Democratic in the 1970s and 1980s than previously and became more Democratic again in the 1990s and early 2000s.

As to ideology, the right half of figure 7.6 shows that liberals have constituted the plurality among Jews throughout. Conservatives have been a plurality among non-Jews. There was an increase in conservatism among non-Jews as social issues such as abortion became prominent in the 1992–2012 period, whereas Jews became a few percentage points more liberal during those years.[11]

Pew's annual figures on party identification for registered voters show slight change in partisanship for Jews since 2001 (Pew Research Center 2018a). Democratic identification fell from a yearly average of 71% (compared to 23% Republican) in the Bush years to 67% (compared to 27% Republican) in the Obama years (see also Newport 2015; 2016), which was a somewhat larger shift among Jews than for the public as a whole. However, there was a shift away from the Republicans in the 2017 Pew figures for Jews (68% Democratic, 22% Republican), nearly back to their 2013 values in figure 7.1 (70% Democratic, 22% Republican).

Conclusions

While being Democratic and liberal are part of the dominant politicized social identity of American Jews, they are not totally monolithic in their politics. Most American Jews are Democratic and liberal in their political orientations, but not quite half are liberal Democrats. Importantly, more Jews are Democrats than are liberals. Jews are distinctively Democratic and liberal and are more distinctively Democratic than liberal.

As is the case among the general electorate, the most religious Jews are more Republican and more politically conservative. The main political division among Jews corresponds to the division between Orthodox and non-Orthodox, with the Orthodox more Republican and conservative. Reform Jews and the "just Jewish" are the most Democratic and liberal.

Party identification and, to a lesser extent, ideology have become part of Jews' social identity, making them resistant to change under normal circumstances and forming the basis for their politics of tradition. While there has been some fluctuation over the years, Jews' party identification and their ideological self-identification have been fairly stable. They did not join the public as a whole in becoming more Republican and more conservative in the 1992–2012 period.

This chapter has shown that fewer Jews claim to be liberals than one might have expected. The next question to arise is whether they are more liberal on political issues than their self-classified ideology suggests. Chapter 8 turns to Jewish attitudes on issues, examining how distinctively liberal Jews are on different issue types.

CHAPTER 8

Issue Replacement

The previous chapter showed that about half of Jews consider themselves liberals, with many fewer calling themselves political conservatives. Jews are usually thought to be very liberal on issues, especially on economics. After all, many voted for Socialist candidates in the early 1900s, when they helped elect two Jewish Socialists to Congress (Victor Berger, WI; Meyer Landon, NY), and senator Bernie Sanders has described himself as a democratic socialist. Jews may have been economic radicals back in the early 1900s, and they are still liberal on economics, but, Bernie Sanders notwithstanding, this chapter reveals that they are no longer very distinctively liberal on economic issues.

If Jews are not distinctively economic liberals, are they as liberal as they claim to be? The answer to this question is that they are distinctively liberal on social/cultural issues. Old economic issues have been replaced by post-materialist social/morality and science issues that have particular resonance to Jews, who are now more distinctively liberal on these new postmaterialist issues than on economic ones. As it happens, Jews are closer to the Democratic Party on these cultural issues, just as they used to be closer to the Democrats on economic issues.

Being liberal has been termed the "lay religion" of American Jews" (Yaffe 1968, 245). However, as sociologist Steven M. Cohen (1983, 151) recognized, the assimilation of the less-observant Jews has taken them into the more conservative general culture as opposed to the traditional liberal Jewish subculture, and that shift serves as a constraint on their liberalism. Liebman and Cohen (1990, 97) could still write in 1990 that Jews' liberalism is "a major component of their [Jews'] understanding of what it means to be a Jew," but it had become apparent by the mid-1990s that Jews were less liberal than usually claimed. As Raab (1996, 45) stated, "There will continue to be much truth to the notion that if you scratch an American Jew, you will find a Democratic voter. The complicating news today is that if you scratch somewhat deeper, you will not always find a liberal." Scratching deeper requires going beyond asking people if they are liberal or conservative, to examine how liberal their issue positions are.

The limitations of relying on ideological self-identification were shown by Ellis and Stimson's (2012) study *Ideology in America*. They found that a majority of the respondents who self-identified as conservatives in the General Social Survey from 1974 to 2006 instead had liberal positions on a measure of "operational ideology" based on federal spending in various areas (96). People's attitudes on specific issues do not necessarily correspond to their ideological self-identification, and this chapter finds similar results for Jews. After a preliminary discussion of Jews' liberalism on issues, this chapter shows that their attitudes on economic issues and government spending priorities are not particularly distinctive. The chapter then turns to social/cultural and science issues on which Jews' attitudes are more distinctive.

Jews' Liberalism

While Jews are sometimes described as having been wild-eyed radicals in the first half of the 20th century, there is no data as to how liberal they actually were. Jews were still on the liberal side of some economic/welfare issues in the 1956–68 period, with substantial majorities of them telling interviewers for the American National Election Studies (ANES) that the government should provide assistance for medical care (84%) and should provide people with guaranteed jobs and standard of living (71%). While Steven M. Cohen and Charles S. Liebman's (1997) analysis of 1972–94 data from the General Social Survey (GSS) found that Jews were "substantially" more liberal than non-Jews in nearly all issue areas, that measure was reduced considerably when controlling on sociodemographics. Showing, further, that Jews' attitudes were similar to those of other liberal religious groups, Cohen and Liebman concluded that Jews "think like Episcopalians" and that "in this respect, contrary to what others have argued, there is no anomaly of excessive Jewish liberalism" (426).

Later studies that have compared the policy views of Jews and non-Jews confirm that Jews' issue liberalism is limited. Tom Smith (2005, 56) determined that seeing liberalism "as the defining difference [between Jews and non-Jews] is wrong." Similarly, Abrams and Cohen (2016, 110) concluded, "The portrait of the Jewish population in America as a stalwart liberal group is called into question." More precisely, Liebman and Cohen (1996, 53) described Jews' liberalism as "selective." Abrams and Cohen (2016, 122) determined that even without demographic controls, "Jews' liberal tilt does not extend to all issue areas," with their liberalism "not so pronounced" on regulation of business and "restrained if at all present" in economic regulation. Still, they found "relatively strong liberal leanings" on social issues.

Economic Issues

The economic arena has been critical to defining the differences between liberals and conservatives in the United States since New Deal days. Jews were considered ultraliberal on economic issues in the early 1900s, and the Democratic Party became closer to them on these issues in the 1930s and 1940s. As more Jews have become well-off, the self-interest of many Jews pushes them in a more conservative economic direction. Jews are still liberal on some economic issues, but they are not much more liberal than would be expected given their sociodemographic characteristics. They are no longer distinctively liberal on the full range of economic issues.

While not looking specifically at Jews, Goren et al. (2016) determined that attitudes on economic welfare issues in the 2012 GSS were significantly related to Schwartz's "self-transcendence" values of universalism and benevolence (see fig. 4.1). People who are most universal and benevolent in their outlook are most favorable to such government policies as helping the poor, equalizing wealth, and government health care. Thus, policies that fit with Fuchs' (1956) Judaic value of *tzedakah* (charity) are most likely to be favored by many non-Orthodox Jews who stress self-transcendence values.

The approach taken in this chapter is to begin by comparing the levels of support of Jews and non-Jews on various issues, following the procedure used in table 5.1 as regards prayer in public schools. First, that table showed a difference of nearly 40 percentage points between Jews and non-Jews on the GSS question on disallowing Bible prayers in public schools. Next, that difference was recalculated after controlling on sociodemographic variables, specifically gender, age, education, income, and living in the South. The difference between Jews and non-Jews who were similar in those regards was somewhat lower, 32 points, but Jews were still significantly distinctive in their views. Finally, an additional control on political ideology was included, to see if Jews were more opposed to school prayer than non-Jews whose self-identified ideology was as liberal as that of Jews. The distinctiveness score for Jews again fell slightly, down to 27 points on school prayer. While that is lower than the original 40-point difference, it is still quite high, showing that Jews were unusually liberal on school prayer as compared to other liberals. Those results on school prayer provide a useful basis for comparisons with how distinctive Jews' attitudes are on other public issues.

The first numerical column in table 8.1 shows the percentage of Jews giving liberal answers on several economic issues in the ANES and GSS surveys since 1992. Jews' opinions on these economic matters are unex-

TABLE 8.1. Jews' Distinctiveness on Economic Issues

			Liberal answers		Distinctiveness scores[b]	
Survey	Variable[a]	Question	Jews	Non-Jews[c]	Control on demographics	Also control on Ideology
ANES	vcf0839	Government services and spending	52%	36%	23***	14***
ANES	vcf0809	Guaranteed jobs and income	36%	27%	17***	11*
GSS	helpnot	Government should solve more problems	31%	24%	10***	8**
GSS	eqwlth	Government should reduce income inequality	41%	43%	4	-1
ANES	vcf0806	Favor government health insurance	45%	42%	9	-2

Source: Analysis of the 1992–2012 ANES surveys (about 200 Jews) and the data for the 1992–2016 GSS (about 350 Jews).

[a]Variable names refer to the ANES and GSS codebooks.

[b]Positive values in this table show that Jews are more liberal even after controls.

[c]Comparison is with nonblack non-Jews.

***$p < .001$; **$p < .01$; *$p < .05$.

pectedly moderate, with the percentage of Jews giving the liberal answers to these questions never rising much above 50%. For comparison purposes, the second column in the table shows the percentages of non-Jews giving liberal answers.[1] Jews are somewhat more liberal on these issues than non-Jews, but the differences between the entries in those first two columns are fairly modest, never even half as large as on school prayer.

The third column in table 8.1 computes the distinctiveness score, controlling for gender, age, education, income, and living in the South.[2] This score has a maximum value of 100 for total distinctiveness, versus 0 if there were no difference between comparable Jews and non-Jews; it would be negative if Jews were less liberal than similar non-Jews. The rightmost column adds a control on ideology, to test if Jews take more liberal positions than non-Jews with a similar ideological self-identification profile as well as similar sociodemographics.[3] The distinctiveness scores in table 5.1 are generally less than half of the values found on school prayer, and Jews' attitudes are not at all distinctive on some of these economic issues.

Government Services. The choice between government services and small government is a classical economic trade-off, since providing more government services requires more government spending. Jews are generally seen as liberal on this topic, but they are less distinctive than might be expected. According to the ANES question (top row of table 8.1), Jews are significantly distinctive in favoring more government services, but the distinctiveness score is just 14 after adding the ideology control, showing that Jews are only somewhat more in favor of big government than are demographically comparable non-Jewish liberals. The 2013 Pew Jewish survey reveals denominational differences: only 35% of Orthodox Jews favor bigger government, versus around 60% in the other branches of Judaism. Jews of no religion are more in favor of larger government than are Jews by religion, 67% to 52%. The partisan divide among Jews is similar to that in the general population, with Democrats preferring a larger government by 72% to 20% and with Republicans preferring a smaller government by 78% to 16% (Pew Research Center 2013, 102).

The ANES also asks whether the government should guarantee jobs and a standard of living (second row of table 8.1). Jews have been distinctively in favor of such guarantees, but with a distinctiveness level of just 11. Indeed, when the Workmen's Circle, a Jewish organization that emphasizes social and economic justice, surveyed Jews in the spring of 2012,

37% opposed government job guarantees, and only 32% favored them, results emphasizing that Jews are not uniformly liberal on government economic guarantees.

Jews are somewhat more supportive of an expansive role for the government. The GSS asks whether the government in Washington tries to do too many things that should be left to individuals and private business or whether the government should do more to solve the country's problems (third row of table 8.1). Jews are significantly more favorable to the government doing more, but their 0.08 distinctiveness score on this issue is much smaller than would have been expected when Jewish liberalism was at its prime.

While the first three questions presented in table 8.1 lead to significant (albeit generally small) levels of distinctiveness, the remaining questions in the table yield negligible differences that are not significant. When the GSS asked whether the government ought to reduce the income differences between the rich and the poor, Jews were slightly less favorable to government action than were non-Jews, though the difference is not significant once demographics are controlled (fourth row of table 8.1). Jews might have been on the vanguard for economic reform two or three generations ago, but that focus weakened as many Jews became middle class. There is still an impetus toward social justice, particularly among Reform Jews, though that too may have weakened.

Another long-standing controversy related to the role of the federal government involves whether health insurance should be public or private. The 2008 National Annenberg Election Survey shows that more Jews were supportive of government health service than of the private system at that time (61%, versus 47% of non-Jews), though they only narrowly favored increased regulation in health care over increased competition (by 57%, versus 51% for non-Jews, a small, albeit significant, difference). However, surprisingly, Jews have not distinctively favored government health insurance over private plans, according to 1992–2012 ANES surveys (bottom row of table 8.1).

The 2008 Great Recession and the subsequent rediscovery of income inequality increased public concern with that inequality. In the 2012 survey of Jews by the Public Religion Research Institute (PRRI), 64% favored the government doing more to reduce the gap between rich and poor, and 73% agreed that the economic system unfairly favors the wealthy. Still, a slight majority (52% over 40%) indicated that they were not willing to pay more taxes for government programs to help the poor, and a similar small majority (54%) believed that poor people have become too dependent on government assistance programs.

Spending Priorities. Policy directions of modern governments are established by their budgets. While Jews are often stereotyped as big-government liberals who want the government to spend freely on a host of projects, surveys show considerable selectivity in their spending priorities. Djupe's (2007, 211) analysis showed Jews moving left on government spending in the 1972–2004 GSS data, but he still concluded that Jews "do not want to spend more money on every issue" (189). Analysis of more recent ANES and GSS surveys confirms that conclusion. Jews are distinctively liberal on spending in such areas as scientific research, the problems of the big cities, health, welfare, foreign aid, child care, education, and the environment, and most of these differences remain significant when ideology is also controlled, showing the impact of being Jewish. By contrast, Jews are not significantly willing to spend more on poor people, assistance to blacks, stopping crime, parks, space exploration, social security, or drug addiction. Neither the ANES nor the GSS finds Jews favorable to spending more money on defense. Indeed, the spring 2012 Workmen's Circle survey found that 38% of Jews wanted decreased defense spending, versus 23% favoring increased spending.

Affirmative Action and Immigration. Affirmative action and immigration policies raise issues regarding universal treatment of disadvantaged people, but they also have economic implications.[4] Jews might be expected to be distinctively liberal on these topics, given the history of discrimination against Jews and Jewish immigrants, as well as the universalism value of many non-Orthodox Jews. However, that is not the case. For example, on racial issues, GSS surveys show that only 23% of Jews feel that the government has a special obligation to help blacks improve their living standards, rather than opposing special treatment of blacks. That number is 10 percentage points higher than the percentage for non-Jews (top row of table 8.2), but the difference between them decreases when comparing Jews to non-Jews with similar ideological positions.[5] The spring 2012 Workmen's Circle survey similarly found that only 28% of Jews wanted the government to help blacks, while 45% favored blacks helping themselves.

Jews' support for affirmative action programs is limited. Because quotas were used in the early 20th century to restrict the access of Jews to colleges, Jews have favored meritocracy rather than the government pushing on behalf of particular groups of citizens, whether blacks or women. Greenberg and Wald (2001) found that Jews in their 2000 Jewish Public Opinion Study were not more liberal than non-Jews on affirmative action. According to the GSS questions in table 8.2, Jews' answers were only a few percentage points more favorable than non-Jews' answers on giving hiring priority to blacks, and Jews were not more favorable than non-Jews toward affirmative action for hiring and promoting women in the workplace.

Jews' opinions are also more mixed on immigration issues than might be expected given their experience with immigration controls. The ANES surveys find Jews distinctively less favorable to decreasing immigration than non-Jews with similar demographics, but the GSS surveys do not show a significant difference (see table 8.3).[6] A spring 2018 AJC poll found that only 17% of Jews favored decreasing the level of immigration.

The survey results in table 8.4 show that Jews do not view immigration as a burden but regard "illegal immigration" as a serious problem. For example, the 2012 PRRI survey reveals considerable acceptance of immigration, but the spring 2012 survey by the Workmen's Circle (WC) did not find majority support for a path for citizenship for "illegal immigrants."

TABLE 8.2. Jews' Distinctiveness on Affirmative Action according to the GSS

		Liberal answers		Distinctiveness scores[b]	
Variable[a]	Question	Jews	Non-Jews[c]	Control on demographics	Also control on ideology
helpblk	Government obligation to help blacks	23%	13%	9**	6*
affrmact	Hiring priority for blacks	22%	14%	10**	7*
fehire	Favor efforts to hire/ promote women	61%	61%	4	0
fejobaff	Favor priority for hiring women	24%	27%	3	0

Source: Analysis of the data for the 1992–2016 GSS (surveying 308–336 Jews on blacks, 108–155 on gender).

[a]Variable names refer to the ANES and GSS codebooks.

[b]Positive values in this table show that Jews are more liberal even after controls.

[c]Comparison is with nonblack non-Jews.

***$p < .001$; **$p < .01$; *$p < .05$.

TABLE 8.3. Jews' Distinctiveness on Decreasing Number of Immigrants

		Liberal answers		Distinctiveness scores[b]	
Survey	Variable[a]	Jews	Non-Jews[c]	Control on demographics	Also control on ideology
ANES	vcf0879	27%	52%	17***	14**
GSS	letin and letin1	46%	55%	6	8

Source: Analysis of the 1992–2012 ANES surveys (including 191 Jews) and the data for the 1996–2014 GSS (including 132 Jews).

[a]Variable names refer to the ANES and GSS codebooks.

[b]Positive values in this table show that Jews are more liberal even after controls.

[c]Comparison is with nonblack non-Jews.

***$p < .001$; **$p < .01$; *$p < .05$.

The 2008 National Annenberg Election Survey (NAES) found little difference between Jews' and non-Jews' views of a path to citizenship for those in the United States illegally, though Jews were less favorable to building a fence along the Mexican border. These surveys show somewhat greater tolerance of undocumented immigrants by Jews than among the American public at large, but not complete Jewish support for the immigrants' cause. All in all, Jews do not react very differently from other Americans on affirmative action and immigration topics.

Economic Issues Conclusions. Contemporary Jewish liberalism is less focused on economic issues today than it was previously. The change is likely due to a combination of several factors. First, Jews' socioeconomic status has improved, making economic well-being less of a self-interest concern. Second, there has been generational change, with the baby boom and later generations of Jews growing up with less materialist focus than the World War II and earlier generations. Third, the political polarization of America in the early 2000s has focused less on economic matters than on other issues.

Bernie Sanders's emphasis on economic justice may have led to an impression that Jews are still extremely liberal on economic matters, but that impression is mistaken. Jews are not now predominantly conservatives, but they are not much more liberal on most economic issues than comparable non-Jews. Even when they are distinctively liberal, the differences are generally small, no more than 14 points and usually below 10. Neither their self-interest nor their values move Jews to be exceptionally liberal on these issues today. That raises the question of why so many Jews still self-identify as liberal, which is examined in the following sections of this chapter.

TABLE 8.4. Jews' Attitudes on Immigration Policy

Year	Survey	Question	Jews	Non-Jews[a]
2014	RLS	A growing population of immigrants is a change for the better v. worse	44%–21%	25%–41%
2012	PRRI	Growing number of newcomers strengthens American society v. threatens traditional American customs and values	57%–32%	
2012	Autumn WC	Today's immigrants are a burden because they take jobs, housing, and health care	17%	
2012	Autumn WC	Support DREAM Act to allow legal residence for illegal immigrants brought to U.S. as children if they join military or go to college	70%	
2012	Spring WC	Support making it possible for illegal immigrants to become citizens v. oppose	34%–38%	
2010	AJC	Support Arizona law for police to ask people they have stopped to verify their residency status	52%	
2007	AJC	Consider illegal immigration a serious problem for the U.S.	79%	
2007	AJC	Deport illegal immigrants v. let them work in U.S. and become citizens if they meet certain requirements	15%–67%	
2008	NAES	Support path to citizenship for those in U.S. illegally	54%	56%
2008	NAES	Favor driver licenses for illegal immigrants	32%	17%
2008	NAES	Build fence along Mexican border	48%	59%

Source: Analysis of surveys in the Religious Landscape Study and by the Public Religion Research Institute, Workmen's Circle, and American Jewish Committee and of the 2008 National Annenberg Election Survey.

[a]Comparison is with nonblack non-Jews.

Social/Morality Issues

Several studies have emphasized Jews' liberalism on cultural issues. Greenberg and Wald (2001) found that Jews in their 2000 Jewish Public Opinion Study were more liberal than non-Jews on most social issues. Tom Smith (2005, 29) concluded that the greatest issue differences between Jews and non-Jews in the GSS were on abortion rights and sexual morality. However, Djupe's (2007, 211) analysis of 1972–2004 GSS data showed Jews moving left on civil liberties but not on moral issues.

Table 8.5 examines the distinctiveness of Jews' attitudes on a variety of cultural issues for the 1992–2014 period. Their distinctiveness on many of these issues is close to that found on school prayer and much greater than for economic issues. Jews are particularly more supportive than the general

TABLE 8.5. Jews' Distinctiveness on Social Issues

			Liberal answers		Distinctiveness scores[b]	
Survey	Variable[a]	Question	Jews	Non-Jews[c]	Control on demographics	Also control on ideology
ANES	vcf0838	By law, should abortion be allowed	81%	41%	36***	26***
GSS	homosex	Same-sex sexual relations not wrong	70%	36%	29***	22***
GSS	abany	Allow abortion for any reason	79%	42%	29***	22***
GSS	evolved	Humans developed from animals	80%	54%	23***	15***
GSS	grass	Should marijuana be legalized	56%	37%	18***	13***
ANES	vcf0876a	Protect gays from discrimination	88%	66%	17***	10**
GSS	gunlaw	Favor gun permits	92%	77%	12***	9***
GSS	letdie1	Allow incurable patients to die	84%	72%	10**	5
GSS	cappun	Oppose death penalty for murder	33%	26%	7**	3

Source: Analysis of 1992–2012 ANES surveys (164 to 226 Jews) and the data for the 1996–2014 GSS (324 to 501 Jews, except 123 for the variable "evolved").
[a]Variable names refer to the ANES and GSS codebooks.
[b]Positive values in this table show that Jews are more liberal even after controls.
[c]Comparison is with nonblack non-Jews.
***$p < .001$; **$p < .01$; *$p < .05$.

public on having abortion be unconditionally legal and on society accepting, rather than discouraging, homosexuality. They are also more acceptant than the public as a whole on marijuana legalization and protecting gays from discrimination. Those issues are not the issues that brought Jews into the Democratic Party in New Deal days. They are new, postmaterialist issues that invoke universal and self-direction values, opposing government interference with individual choices on moral matters. Not only do a sizable majority of Jews give liberal answers to nearly all the questions presented in table 8.5, but Jews are more distinctively liberal on most of these issues than on most of the economic issues in table 8.1.

Jews' attitudes on social issues are distinctive because the partisan and ideological divides among Jews on those issues are smaller than the same divides among non-Jews. As shown in later chapters of this book, most Republican Jews and most politically conservative Jews take the liberal position on those issues, whereas their non-Jewish counterparts are conservative. Cohen and Liebman (1997) suggest three important explanations of Jews' distinctive liberalism on these issues: that Jews are not bound by conservative Christian tradition on sexuality, that "they associate conservative morality in the public square with obstacles to their full inclusion in American society" (410), and their religious modernism (425).

When Goren et al. (2016) examined the 2012 GSS and an early 2011 online survey to see how Americans' attitudes on several issue domains were related to their values, morality issues in both surveys were significantly related to Schwartz's "conservation" values of tradition, conformity, and security. People who most emphasize tradition and conformity values, as Orthodox Jews would, tend to be most against abortion and homosexuality. Indeed, there are sizable differences between Orthodox and non-Orthodox Jews on these issues. Traditional values are invoked for the Orthodox, while the impact of universalism, egalitarianism, self-expression, and secular-rational values is particularly evident among the views of the non-Orthodox. This division is similar to the difference between evangelicals and mainline Protestants, except that the Orthodox constitute a much smaller proportion of Jews than the evangelical proportion of non-Jews. The Modern Orthodox, in particular, are more liberal than Christian evangelicals on these social issues, and the non-Orthodox have more liberal attitudes than mainline Protestants.

Homosexuality. Orthodox Jewry literally accepts the biblical prohibitions on homosexual activities, as seen when the Orthodox Union's Rabbinical Council of America (which is associated with the Modern Orthodox movement) expressed its regret at the Supreme Court's 2015 decision on gay marriage. By contrast, the Conservative and Reform movements recognize same-sex marriage ceremonies, though officiating at them is at the discretion of each rabbi. In 2012, when support for allowing gay marriage was reaching the 50% level among the public at large for the first time, Jewish surveys found about 80% support (Cohen and Abrams 2013, 16; Jones and Cox 2012, 24). The denominational difference is echoed in public opinion data, such as the 2012 PRRI survey finding that 85% of the non-Orthodox and 49% of the Orthodox were favorable to allowing gay couples to marry legally. Still, finding that about half of Orthodox Jews favor allowing gay couples to marry legally reemphasizes how liberal Jews are on social issues.

Abortion. Judaism considers a mother's life to take precedence, so a fetus must be aborted to save the mother's life. Orthodox Judaism prohibits abortion generally but views it as mandatory if it is necessary for saving a woman's life. Conservative Judaism accepts abortion as justifiable when continuation of the pregnancy could cause harm to the mother, and Reform Judaism views women as "moral agents" with the right to act on their own behalf. Tom Smith's (2005, 10–11) summary of GSS results found that of all ethnic, racial, and religious groups, Jews are the most supportive of abortion rights. The 2012 PRRI survey found that 55% of Jews felt that abortion should be legal in all cases, an additional 39% felt it should be legal in most cases, and only 6% wanted it illegal in most or all cases. Even 62% of Orthodox Jews in that survey felt that abortion should be legal in most or all cases (Jones and Cox 2012, 24).

Not only are Jews significantly more favorable to a complete pro-choice position, as shown in the top row of table 8.5, but that is true in the ANES data even when also comparing Jews with non-Jews who are comparable in church attendance and on whether they view religion as important, with the distinctiveness score still 20 when those factors are also controlled. Jews' attitudes on abortion are so distinctive that more detailed analysis is appropriate. Table 8.6 presents the results of analysis of the PRRI question. As to be expected, liberals are more pro-choice, though party identification does not have an additional significant effect. Jews who identify with the Conservative and Reform movement are significantly more pro-choice than are the "just Jewish." There were not enough Orthodox Jews in the sample for their lower support for abortion to be significant, but those who consider religion important are significantly less pro-choice. It is notable that sociodemographics are not significant, particularly that gender does not have an additional effect on Jews' attitudes on abortion.

Moral Issues. In a Gallup summary of American's views on the acceptability of various moral issues (Jones 2016), based on combining samples from 2000 to 2016, Jews stood out as more liberal than Catholics and Protestants on nearly every issue, including abortion, doctor-assisted suicide, cloning animals, gay-lesbian relations, having a baby outside of marriage, divorce, gambling, premarital sex, and stem cell research. Jews were also less supportive of the death penalty. Still, table 8.5 shows Jews are not very distinctive on a few social issues. They are more favorable to legalizing marijuana than non-Jews by 53% to 35%, a difference that is significant under controls but falls to just 13 points when controlling on demographics and ideology. Jews are more supportive than non-Jews of requiring permits to own guns, by 92% to 77%, a difference that is significant under controls but falls to just 9 points. They are more supportive of allowing incurable patients to die and are more opposed to the death penalty for murder, but those differences are not statistically significant under controls for demographics and ideology.

TABLE 8.6. Regression Analysis of Jews' Acceptance of Abortion

Variable	Coefficient
Party identification (Democrat = 1; Republican = 0)	.04
Ideology (liberal = 1; moderate = .5; conservative = 0)	.14***
Orthodox	–.13
Conservative	.08**
Reform	.04*
Importance of religion	–.08**
Female	.00
constant	.70***

Source: Analysis of the 2012 Jewish Values Survey by the Public Religion Research Institute.

Note: Baseline is "just Jewish." Positive values are more pro-choice. Age, education, living in the South, income, and marital status were also controlled but were not significant.

***$p < .001$; **$p < .01$; *$p < .05$.

Gender Roles. Like most other ancient religions, traditional Judaism was male-dominated. That dominance was exemplified by just counting men for the minyan of ten adults needed to hold public services. Moreover, in services, only men were allowed to read from the Torah, and men were separated from women by a wall (*mechitza*). Orthodox Judaism still follows those strictures, most Conservative synagogues practice egalitarianism, and the Reform movement is gender-neutral.

This large change in Conservative and Reform practices occurred because most Jews are supportive of equality for women. Indeed, Jews were early supporters of equality, with more than 75% of Jews versus fewer than 60% of non-Jews favoring equal roles for women when asked about the issue by the ANES in the 1970s. While still more favorable to gender equality, Jews appear less distinctive on this issue today because non-Jews have become increasingly liberal about it (Smith 2005, 37). For example, in the first decade of the 2000s, 90% of Jews and 80% of non-Jews favored equal roles. The significant distinctiveness on this question is not eliminated by controls on standard demographic variables, but it disappears when Jews are compared to non-Jews with similar ideological positions. Yet differences remain, as when the 2014 Pew Religious Landscape Study found that 80% of Jews and just 68% of non-Jews considered more women in the workplace to be a change for the better.

Science Issues

Jews have been open to rational thought and science since the writings of the Jewish philosopher Maimonides in the 12th century. That openness is still evident in terms of their distinctively liberal attitudes on science, education, and medicine. As Tom Smith (2005, 31) points out, Jews "have notably more confidence in science than non-Jews do."

This modernity in science matters is exemplified by most Jews' acceptance of the theory of evolution, which is less controversial among Jews than among Christians. The ultra-Orthodox are least likely to accept evolution. Yet even the Modern Orthodox Rabbinical Council of America issued a statement in 2005 noting that Jewish authorities have considered evolutionary theory, "properly understood," as "not incompatible with belief in a Divine Creator" (though it also recognized that some respected Jewish voices follow a literalist view of the biblical account of creation).

Conservative Judaism views God as having created the universe and life within it but does not make claims as to how that occurred that reject evolutionary theory. Reform Judaism does not view evolutionary theory as dealing with theological questions, including how the universe was formed. Jews' distinctiveness in acceptance of science is evident on the evolution question in table 8.5. Similarly, the 2014 Pew Religious Landscape Study found that 84% of Jews, compared to only 65% of the public as a whole, agree that "humans and other living things have evolved over time." Even 46% of Orthodox Jews accepted the evolution explanation, as did upwards of 85% of the other branches of Judaism.

The different branches of Judaism have similar perspectives on the environment. The Orthodox Union's Rabbinical Council of America adopted a statement in 2006 encouraging its members "to teach that the preservation of the environment is of importance in the eyes of the Torah and the Rabbis" and calling for both ecological awareness and protecting the environment. Consequently, Jews have taken liberal positions on the environment. For example, the 2012 Workmen's Circle survey showed that 72% of Jews agree that climate change has been occurring and that some action needs to be taken, versus 28% who feel either that it is not occurring or that we do not know enough about it yet to take action. Jews have favored protection of the environment even when that involves economic tradeoffs, as when 69% of the respondents in the 2012 PRRI survey supported tougher environmental protection laws even if they cost jobs or raise prices. However, ideological differences still affect Jewish views, with liberals stressing environmentalism more than conservatives.

Conclusions

While Jews are usually described as liberal across the board, surveys reveal far greater complexity. Steven M. Cohen (1983, 151) argued that assimilation of the least-observant Jews would serve as a limitation on their liberalism, and it has indeed diminished their distinctiveness on economic issues. They are more liberal than non-Jews on some economic questions, though not as liberal as they might have been in New Deal days. Jewish views are distinctively liberal on a few questions of economics and government size, but the level of distinctiveness is muted, and Jews are not distinctive in their views on other economic issues. Differences between Republican and

Democratic Jews on these issues mirror partisan differences among the population at large. Denominational differences are minor because values differences between the Orthodox and non-Orthodox are not invoked. Jews favor more government spending in some areas but are selective about which ones.

As described earlier, studies by Liebman and Cohen (1996), Greenberg and Wald (2001), Smith (2005), Djupe (2007), and Abrams and Cohen (2016) have previously pointed out that Jews are particularly liberal on social issues, though not all of those studies examined whether Jews were more liberal than comparable non-Jews. This chapter extends those studies by arguing that issue replacement has kept Jews liberal. After moderating their positions on economic issues, they have remained liberals because of being liberal on a new set of cultural issues. They have stayed Democratic because the Republican Party moved away from them on morality issues, becoming identified with the conservative side when most American Jews became very liberal on abortion, gay rights, and climate change.

The key to understanding this development is an additional factor, the very high rate of college and postgraduate education for Jews. In college, Jews have been expected to recognize the preeminence of scientific findings and have been exposed to cultural diversity that fosters a universalistic outlook on many social issues. Jews' distinctiveness on both social and science issues is based on willingness to reject traditional views. Whether the topic is abortion, homosexuality, evolution, or climate change, liberal positions challenge established modes of thinking. This tendency recalls Cohen and Liebman's (1997) "argumentative individualism" explanation of Jewish liberalism, mentioned in chapter 4 of the present study. Contemporary Jews are willing to question conventional authorities and to adopt a position of modernity in social life and in scientific realms.

Goren and Chapp's (2017) analysis of several panel surveys of the general public underlines the potency of morality issues. They demonstrate that "culture war" issues (abortion and homosexuality) affect partisan predispositions and even religious orientations. The social issues on which Jews are most distinctive involve their values, primarily universalistic ones, more than their self-interest. The non-Orthodox tend to be postmaterialists, emphasizing secular rationality, self-expression, self-direction, universalism, and egalitarianism values. The influence of those values is very evident in views on social issues. Orthodox Jews who emphasize Schwartz's values of tradition and conformity are only a small minority of American

Jews. While less surveyed, the other set of issues on which Jews' attitudes are distinctive are the church-state separation issues discussed in chapter 5. Indeed, the distinctiveness scores on school prayer in table 5.1 are greater than all the values reported in the present chapter.

To the extent to which Jews' values predominate in their voting, their views on social issues make it difficult for Jews to vote for socially conservative Republicans, even if their economic self-interest goes in the Republican direction. Given how distinctively liberal Jews are on social issues, it may be puzzling that even more Jews do not describe themselves as liberals, though that likely occurs because their positions on economic issues are more mainstream. Before this study examines that possibility further, the next chapter turns to another potentially important set of attitudes that could have a substantial effect on Jews' politics: their attitudes regarding Israel and, especially, Israeli policies.

CHAPTER 9

Politicized Attitudes on Israel

One of the largest misconceptions about American Jews' politics is that their political views are based on their unconditional support of Israel. Evangelical Protestants are the group that gives Israel the most unconditional support. An overwhelming majority of Jews say they "care" about Israel, but there are large disagreements among them about specifics of U.S. policy regarding Israel and threats to its security. Views on Israel have become one of the most visible splits among U.S. Jews, threatening increased separation from Israeli Jewry. Furthermore, partisan differences have developed and endanger the traditional bipartisan American consensus on Israel.

Israel's security inherently evokes Jews' self-interest in terms of concern and responsibility for fellow Jews. However, many Jews also value universalism, which makes them concerned about recent Israeli government actions regarding the Palestinians. There is honest disagreement among U.S. Jews about what is in Israel's self-interest, especially about whether its West Bank settlements are justified and whether a two-state solution would strengthen Israel's security. Adherents of both sets of views are sincere in their values and in their evaluations of Israel's best interest, but they are led to opposite policy conclusions.

This chapter begins by discussing American Jews' sense of connection to Israel. It then summarizes the Israeli-Palestinian dispute, with discussion of American public opinion and of the attitudes of American Jews toward that conflict. Next is consideration of the Iranian dispute, with a focus on U.S. Jews' attitudes. The fracturing of the long-standing consensus on Israel is a recurring theme of this chapter.

American Jews and Israel

Just as being Democratic has become part of the politicized social identity of many American Jews (see chap. 3), Wald and Williams (2006) have shown that Israel has become part of many Jews' "politicized ethnic identity." As Lederhendler (2017, chap. 4) argues, American Jews have always been distinctive in being transnational in their focus, with an emphasis first on Spain and then on Germany and Russia. Their transnational emphasis has shifted to Israel, though there was considerable disagreement among Jews in the early 1900s about the wisdom of creating a Jewish state in Palestine. Some Orthodox Jews did not believe that a Jewish state should exist there before the Messiah arrives, while the Reform movement did not want Judaism to be nation-based. The Holocaust tragedy caused most Jews to accept that having their own state was important for their self-protection; only a few ultra-Orthodox sects remained opposed by the time that Israel proclaimed its statehood. In the words of Hartman and Hartman (2000, 395), there followed a gradual "evolution of Israel into the symbolic center of Jewish ethnicity." The 1967 Six-Day War increased the focus of American Jews on Israel (Barnett 2016, 159–64), with widespread pride in how the little nation fought off its larger Arab neighbors in a battle for survival. The organized Jewish community took up Israel as the "centerpiece of Jewish public life" (Liebman and Cohen 1990, 84).

Connection to Israel. Surveys consistently show that most American Jews feel a connection to Israel. The 2013 Pew study is typical in finding that 88% consider caring about Israel to be an important part of their being Jewish and that 69% are emotionally attached to Israel. However, there are differences between Jews in their level of connection. Only 43% consider caring about Israel to be an essential part of their being Jewish, and just 30% consider themselves very attached to Israel. Thus, Israel does not predominate over all other potential factors for most Jews. Not surprisingly, the 2013 Pew survey found that only one-third as many of Jews of no religion as compared to Jews by religion feel very attached to Israel (12% versus 36%).

Social networks are important in reinforcing connections with Israel. Analysis of the 2000–01 National Jewish Population Survey (NJPS) found that, with other factors controlled, Jews who had more Jewish organization memberships and whose personal networks included more

Jews were more supportive of Israel (Kadushin and Kotler-Berkowitz 2006). Many Jews who are strongly connected to Israel are among the American Jews who have a family member or close friend who lives there (45% in the 2000–01 NJPS). The 2017 AJC Annual Survey of American Jewish Opinion found that 50% of Jews had been to Israel, which helps reinforce those connections.

As shown in table 2.4 earlier in the present study, there are differences in feelings of connection to Israel between the main branches of Judaism. The Modern Orthodox are most likely to consider Israel essential and to feel very attached to it. Lower support by the ultra-Orthodox is due to ultra-Orthodox groups, including the large Satmar Hasidim and the extreme Neturei Karta, that still consider Israel's establishment a violation of biblical injunctions against returning to Israel before God redeems Jews.

There are also partisan differences among Jews in feelings of connection to Israel, though these partisan differences could simply reflect the denominational differences between the Orthodox and the non-Orthodox. To test this possibility, Jews' feelings of connection to Israel were analyzed while controlling statistically for denomination, ideology, and demographics.[1] The results are presented in figure 9.1, where line lengths show the magnitude of the relationships after these controls. The top pair of lines shows that party identification matters to caring about and feeling attached to Israel, with Democrats feeling less connected to Israel. However, partisanship matters much less than denomination, as shown by the lines for the different denominations. Orthodox, Conservative, and Reform Jews all care more about Israel and are more attached than the "just Jewish," with denomination mattering more on feeling attached to Israel than on caring about it. Ideology also has a larger effect than party on caring about Israel, with liberals tending to care less; party has a larger effect than ideology on feeling attached to Israel. The largest demographic difference is that older people feel more connected to Israel. This analysis confirms that political views have become relevant to how American Jews feel toward Israel, and it shows that these differences are not wholly a matter of denomination or demographics.

Jews can have different meanings when they say they "care" about or are "emotionally attached" to Israel. Feeling connected to Israel does not necessarily imply agreement with its political decisions. Many people are attached to it because they have a family member there, while others view it as an important cultural center. Some may regard Israel as a homeland,

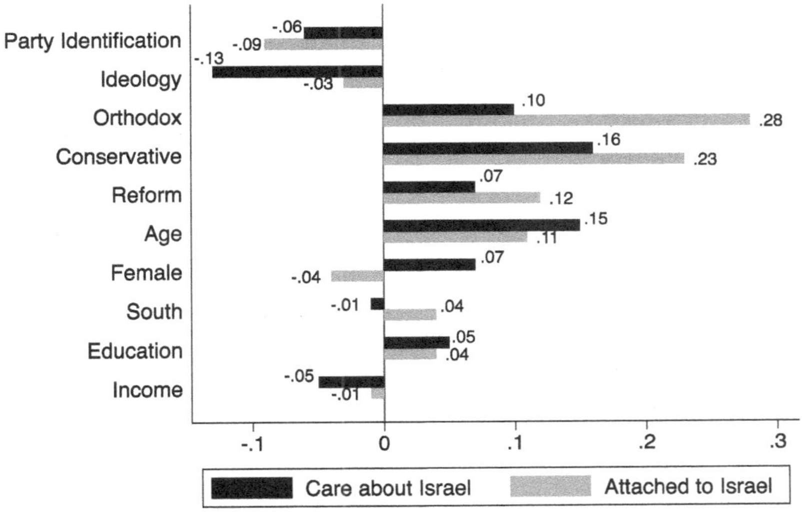

Fig. 9.1. Regression analysis of Jews' feelings of connection to Israel
(*Note:* Analysis of 2013 Pew Jewish survey. Bars show regression coefficients, with Just Jewish as baseline.)

while others value it as a Jewish refuge. As discussed below, many Jews are concerned about maintaining Israel's security, even if they do not feel strongly connected to Israel.

The Israeli-Palestinian Dispute

Britain administered Palestine with a League of Nations mandate after the defeat of the Ottoman Empire in World War I. The British government's 1917 Balfour Declaration "view[ed] with favour the establishment in Palestine of a national home for the Jewish people," though Britain also promised independence to the Arabs in exchange for their support in World War I. The Nazis' murder of six million Jews amplified the pressure on Britain to permit an independent Jewish state after World War II ended. The United Nations General Assembly voted in November 1947 to partition Palestine into separate Jewish and Arab states. Accordingly, the State of Israel declared its independence when the British Mandate ended in May 1948. Israel successfully defeated invading armies from its Arab neighbors in its subsequent War of Independence, which displaced many original Palestinian inhabitants (Morris 2004; Shavit 2013). However, tensions remained between Israel and both Egypt and Syria.

When neighboring armies were mobilized on its borders in 1967, Israel made a preemptive strike; the Six-Day War ended with Israel capturing the West Bank, East Jerusalem, the Gaza Strip, the Golan Heights, and the Sinai Peninsula. In 1973, Arab armies sought to regain these territories with a surprise attack on Yom Kippur, the most holy day of the Jewish calendar, but Israel eventually repulsed the attack. A major-power conflict then threatened, with the U.S. helping Israel while the Soviet Union backed Egypt and Syria. The two superpowers worked to establish a cease-fire instead.

Israel still controls area on the West Bank of the Jordan River that it captured during the 1967 Six-Day War, but many nations consider its settlements there to be an illegal occupation. While Israel unilaterally withdrew from Gaza in 2005, there has been persistent conflict with Gaza's elected Hamas government, which is committed to "liberating Palestine." The summer 2014 Gaza War stopped rocket fire into Israel and destroyed Sinai Desert tunnels that Hamas used to supply Gaza with weapons, but that war was controversial because of the large number of civilian Palestinian casualties.

Negotiations up through the Obama administration focused on a two-state solution with an independent Palestinian state, but the parties have not been able to agree (Ross 2015). President Donald Trump indicated that he "could live" with either a one-state or a two-state solution, whichever the sides choose. Given Israeli Arabs' higher birthrate, continuation of the current situation without moving to a two-state solution could make it impossible for Israel to continue as a Jewish state if it remained a democracy with full voting rights for its non-Jewish citizens.

American Public Opinion. American support for Israel has traditionally been bipartisan, although relations between the two countries' governments have not always been easy. Nearly every U.S. president has had differences with the Israeli government. As former defense secretary Robert Gates remarked, "Every President I worked for [Carter through the first Bush], at some time in his presidency, would get so pissed at the Israelis that he couldn't speak" (quoted in Ross 2015, 221). There is little reason to think that later presidents were very different in that regard. Such differences, though, have not led to unraveling of the American public's strong support for Israel. As Alba (2006, 355) wrote, "Much of Gentile America has accepted support for Israel as its own cause." This support was evident when the February 2018 Gallup survey found the public sympathizing significantly more with Israel than with the Palestinians, by a 64% to 19% margin (Saad 2018).

Yet there have been important shifts in the profile of group support. Evangelicals have become some of the strongest supporters of Israel, seeing the country as a fulfillment of biblical prophecies related to the Second Coming of Jesus. Studies by Mayer (2004) and Baumgartner, Francia, and Morris (2008) confirm that evangelicals are significantly more sympathetic toward Israel even with demographic characteristics controlled (also see Phillips, Lengyel, and Saxe 2002). There are, however, expectations that younger evangelicals, who are less committed to biblical inerrancy, will become less supportive of Israel.

In 1995, Lipset and Raab (1995, 145) could still write that "support for Israel . . . has not been a partisan political issue between the major parties." However, partisan divisions developed as evangelicals moved to the Republican camp, and the divisions grew as partisan polarization intensified in the early 2000s (Cavari 2013). Israel maintains strong support among Republicans, while support has begun sliding among Democrats. By early 2018, Gallup found that 87% of Republicans sympathized more with the Israelis than with the Palestinians, versus 49% of Democrats, with most of the remaining members of both parties being neutral rather than sympathizing more with the Palestinians (Saad 2018).

There are also generational differences. For example, a January 2018 Pew poll (Pew Research Center 2018b) found those under age 30 split by just 32% to 23% on sympathy for Israel over the Palestinians, compared to a split of 56% to 13% among those over 50. This weaker support for Israel among the younger generation may just reflect less media coverage of the dispute during their lifetimes, but it could still have serious implications going forward.

American Jewish Opinion. Few surveys of the U.S. public that ask questions about Israel include enough Jews to compare their opinions with those of the public at large, but a comparison is possible using the 2015 survey on Iran by the *Jewish Journal of Greater Los Angeles* (*JJLA*), which interviewed separate Jewish and national samples. Reflecting the greater attention that

Jews pay to Israel, two-thirds (65%) of the Jews interviewed sympathized a lot with Israel in its dispute with the Palestinians, versus only 26% of the general public, with less than one-tenth in each sample sympathizing a lot with the Palestinians. Political conservatives in both the Jewish and general samples had the most sympathy with Israel: 91% of politically conservative Jews sympathized a lot with Israel, as did 58% of Jewish liberals, 53% of conservatives nationally, and 15% of liberals nationally.

While nearly all U.S. Jews are generally supportive of Israel, specific policy matters regarding the disputes between Israel and the Palestinians are controversial. The 2012–15 *JJLA*, Pew, and Workmen's Circle (WC) polling results in table 9.1 show that many American Jews were skeptical of the peace efforts of the Israeli government, which was led by Benjamin Netanyahu. They were even more skeptical about the Palestinian Authority, which was led by Mahmoud Abbas. A small majority thought that the Israeli government truly wanted peace, but nearly half believed that it wanted to prevent the emergence of a Palestinian state. Few American Jews blamed Israel alone for lack of success in peace negotiations, but many blamed both sides equally. Little more than one-third of U.S. Jews thought that the Israeli government was making a sincere effort to bring about a peace settlement, and a 2014–15 survey of Israeli Jews found that 40% of them did not consider their government's effort toward peace to be sincere (Pew Research Center 2016a). There were denominational differences among American Jews: 61% of the Orthodox and 52% of the Conservative regarded Israeli efforts as sincere, versus only 36% of Reform and 27% of the "just Jewish."

TABLE 9.1. American Jews' Attitudes on the Goals of Palestinians and Israel

Year	Survey	Question	Palestinian leadership	Israeli government
2015	*JJLA*	Making a sincere effort to bring about a peaceful settlement	10%	37%
2013	Pew	Making a sincere effort to bring about a peaceful settlement	12%	38%
2012	WC	Truly wants peace	5%	58%
2012	WC	Palestinians seek Israel's destruction	78%	
2012	WC	Israeli government wants to prevent the emergence of a Palestinian state		45%

Source: Analysis of surveys by the *Jewish Journal of Greater Los Angeles*, Pew Research Center, and the Workmen's Circle.

Most Jews support a firm Israeli response to terrorism but, at the same time, favor resolving the dispute with Palestinians peacefully, a combination that Waxman (2016, 126) aptly terms "hawkish dovishness." The 2013 Pew study found that 44% of U.S. Jews viewed continued building of Jewish settlements as hurting Israel's security. According to that survey, 61% of Jews felt that Israel and an independent Palestinian state could coexist peacefully, but that number fell to 49% in the 2016 AJC poll.

Surveys of American Jews find widely varying results about whether they favor a two-state solution, partly because surveyors often word their questions to get respondents to agree with survey sponsor's policy positions. The 2012 PRRI Jewish Values Survey asked a neutrally worded question: "Generally speaking, would you support or oppose the establishment of a Palestinian state?" It found 53% of Jews supportive and 42% opposed (Jones and Cox 2012, 38). A similar question in the 2017 AJC poll obtained virtually identical results: 55% support and 40% opposition. In the June 2016 Joint Palestinian-Israeli Pulse Poll, Israeli Jews supported a two-state solution by a margin of 53% to 37%, versus a nearly even split of 51% to 47% among West Bank Palestinians.

A 2010 Brandeis University survey (Sasson et al. 2010) found U.S. Jews less favorable toward a two-state solution when asked about possible compromises "as part of a permanent settlement with the Palestinians." Respondents expressed less than majority support for dismantling settlements (46%) and even less support for compromising on Israeli control of Jerusalem (29%). Of course, surveys are a poor guide to the compromises required in negotiations, as it would be poor strategy to agree in advance to concede more than is necessary. Still, these results show that American Jews' attitudes are more complex than shown in surveys that claim exceedingly high levels of support for a two-state solution.

Partisan differences permeate Jews' attitudes on specific policy matters. Back in 1998, partisan differences on the peace process were not significant in a national survey of Jews by the *Los Angeles Times*, though liberals were more positive toward the process, while the more religious (Orthodox) were more negative (Wald and Martinez 2001). By 2012–13, partisan differences were present (table 9.2). Jewish Democrats were more likely than Jewish Republicans to believe that Israel and a Palestinian state could coexist, to doubt the sincerity of the Netanyahu government in peace negotiations, to support the establishment of a Palestinian state, and to favor having the United States serve as an impartial broker in negotiations.

Jews in the United States and Israel also see these matters differently, as shown in a Pew comparison of polls in the two countries (Pew Research Center 2016a, 1–2). More American Jews than Israeli Jews (66% to 38%) saw security threats including violence and terrorism as the most important long-term threat facing Israel. Many Israeli Jews (39%) viewed economic problems as their most important threat, while just 1% of U.S. Jews recognized that concern. U.S. Jews were more likely to feel that Israel and an independent Palestinian state can coexist peacefully (61% v. 43% of Israeli Jews), but they were less likely to think that West Bank settlements help Israel's security (17% v. 42% of Israeli Jews).

Opinions among Young Jews. Surveys find that young American Jews are less supportive of Israel than are older people. The older generation remembers Israel as a young country that had to fight neighboring Arab countries to survive. As Cohen and Kelman (2007, 3) wrote, the younger generation instead knows only the Lebanon wars and the intifadas (Palestinian uprisings), which are "perceived as far more morally and politically complex than the wars Israel fought between 1948 and 1974, casting Israel in a more troubling light." The younger generation also sees Israel in perpetual conflict with Palestinians over West Bank settlements and in Gaza.

The young do not consider Israel to be as central to their Judaism as

TABLE 9.2. Jews' Attitudes on Israel-Palestinian Negotiations by Party

Year	Survey	Question	Democrats	Republicans
2013	Pew	There is a way for Israel and an independent Palestinian state to coexist peacefully	69%	38%
2013	Pew	Palestinian leadership is making a sincere effort to bring about a peace settlement	15%	6%
2013	Pew	Israeli government is making a sincere effort to bring about a peace settlement	32%	62%
2012	PRRI	Support the establishment of a Palestinian state	60%	23%
2012	J Street	U.S. should serve as an impartial broker v. side with Israel during peace negotiations	53%–32%	33%–55%

Source: Analysis of surveys by the Pew Research Center, the Public Religion Research Institute, and J Street.

earlier generations did. Table 9.3 displays the generational differences. Younger Jews are less likely either to view caring about Israel as essential to their Judaism or to feel attached to Israel. Answers on whether continued building of West Bank settlements hurts Israel's security show less of a generational divide. The younger generations are more cynical about the Israeli government's sincerity in peace efforts and are more likely to believe that a way can be found for peaceful coexistence between Israel and a Palestinian state.

There has been a vigorous debate over how to interpret this age difference. According to the "distancing hypothesis," young people have become more alienated from Israel (e.g., Cohen and Eisen 2000). Steven M. Cohen's analysis of the 2013 Pew data found that one-fifth of young non-Orthodox Jews were "Israel-alienated," feeling unattached to Israel and thinking that the U.S. is too supportive of it (Guttman 2014). On the other side of the debate, a comparison of annual AJC surveys over time by Sasson, Kadushin, and Saxe (2010; also Sasson et al. 2010) found that young adults have long been less supportive of Israel. Their support of Israel has not declined over the years; instead, young Jews become more supportive as they become older. Kotler-Berkowitz and Ament (2010) pointed out, however, that those AJC surveys were not based on probabilistic samples and did not include Jews of no religion. Furthermore, Cohen and Kelman (2007) argue that the current generation of young adults is unlikely to become stronger supporters of Israel as they age, even if earlier generations did (see also Waxman 2016, 137–38). The different research teams agree that the Taglit-Birthright Israel program, which has given free

TABLE 9.3. Jews' Attitudes on Israel by Generation

Generation	Age in 2013	Year born	Caring about Israel is essential	Very or somewhat attached to Israel	Settlements hurt Israel's security	Israeli government making sincere effort for peace	Peaceful coexistence is possible
Millennial	18–32	1981–	33%	62%	48%	32%	71%
Gen X	33–48	1965–80	36%	58%	39%	46%	61%
Boomer	49–67	1946–64	46%	74%	46%	46%	63%
"Silent" and "Greatest"	68+	–1945	56%	81%	42%	55%	56%

Source: Analysis of the 2013 Pew Jewish survey.

trips to Israel to 400,000 North American Jewish young adults, is a useful approach for increasing feelings of connection to Israel. However, surveys attempting to demonstrate the effectiveness of such programs (e.g., Cohen and Kopelowitz 2015; Shain et al. 2015) cannot control for the likelihood that Jews who apply for a Birthright trip are already more sympathetic to Israel than those who do not apply.

The Intermarriage Effect. Another important correlate of attitudes on Israel is intermarriage. Indeed, Cohen and Kelman (2007, 9–16; 2008, 16–17) called it "the key factor." Stephen M. Cohen's analysis of the Pew data pointed to Israel alienation being higher among those who were raised in intermarried households (Guttman 2014). Two mechanisms that could underlie this finding are less engagement with Israel for people who were raised by intermarried parents and less engagement for adults who intermarry.

Table 9.4 separates the effect by whether respondents are intermarried and/or whether their parents were.[2] A substantial difference between the table's top and bottom rows is associated with intermarriage. According to the top two rows, which compare intermarried people, children of intermarried parents are less attached to Israel. This result shows a lower attachment associated with growing up in an intermarried household. According to the bottom two rows, which compare children of inmarried parents, those children who are intermarried feel much less connected to Israel. But their intermarriage may not be a cause of this lower attachment, since it is at least equally possible that Jews who are less involved in Jewish topics (including Israel) are the ones who intermarry. The differences are smaller on the specific policy questions in the table's two right-hand columns, about

TABLE 9.4. Non-Orthodox Jews' Attitudes on Israel by Intermarriage

Respondent	Parents	Caring about Israel is essential	Very or somewhat attached to Israel	Israeli government making sincere effort for peace	Settlements hurt Israel's security	Peaceful coexistence is possible
Intermarried	Intermarried	28%	38%	22%	55%	67%
Intermarried	Inmarried	34%	60%	32%	55%	68%
Inmarried	Inmarried	53%	82%	52%	48%	59%

Source: Analysis of the 2013 Pew Jewish survey.
Note: The category of intermarried parents and respondent inmarried was too small to include.

the West Bank settlements and the possibility of peaceful coexistence between Israel and a Palestinian state: there are modest differences between people who are inmarried and intermarried, with no differences related to whether parents were intermarried.

The Iranian Dispute

Iranian leaders make Holocaust-denial statements and speak of annihilating the Zionist regime, so the possibility of a nuclear-armed Iran is considered a direct threat to Israel. Iran was found to be conducting nuclear enrichment activities in noncompliance with the Nuclear Proliferation Treaty, resulting in the UN Security Council imposing sanctions against that country in 2006. President George W. Bush had the United States join multinational nuclear talks with Iran. The Obama administration controversially started negotiations to remove sanctions in exchange for verified stopping of their nuclear program.

The situation was politicized in March 2015, when the Republican Speaker of the House, John Boehner, did not inform Obama in advance before inviting the Israeli prime minister, Benjamin (Bibi) Netanyahu, to speak to Congress. Netanyahu used the talk to criticize Obama's Iran policy. An agreement between Iran and the United States, Russia, China, Britain, France, and Germany was announced in the summer of 2015, over the vigorous opposition of Republican politicians and the Israeli government. Supporters emphasized that the accord required the removal of 98% of Iran's uranium stockpile and imposed restrictions on its nuclear program for at least 15 years. Opponents saw the agreement as conceding to Iran the right to eventually develop a nuclear capability that could be used against Israel. In any case, the agreement did not stop Iran's military aid to the Hamas movement in Gaza and to Hezbollah forces in Lebanon that threaten Israel. In May 2018, President Trump withdrew the United States from the multilateral accord and reinstituted American sanctions on Iran.

There has been disagreement in the American Jewish community on U.S. policy about preventing Iran from getting nuclear weapons. Table 9.5 shows survey results from around the 2012 presidential election that concern taking military action against Iran. American Jews had considerable willingness to have military confrontation with Iranians over their development of nuclear weapons, if economic sanctions were not successful, especially if Israel, rather than the United States, took that military action. There were slight differences between the different denominations, but none favored having the United States set a red line on Iran's nuclear progress that, if crossed, would trigger an American military attack on its nuclear facilities.

Still, the 2012 surveys emphasize how much American policy toward Iran had become a partisan topic even among Jews. In the J Street survey, Republicans supported setting a red line with Iran (57%), while that approach received only half as much support (29%) among Democrats. When PRRI asked about American military action if economic sanctions are unable to stop Iran's nuclear weapons program, 78% of Republicans supported military action, compared to only 52% of Democrats.

Surveys of Jews in 2015 disagreed about reactions to the nuclear agreement that John Kerry negotiated with Iran. A high-quality survey taken by SSRS in mid-July found that 49% of Jews supported the accord, with 31% disapproving (S. Cohen 2015; Guttman 2015). However, that survey was taken before opposition to the agreement could ramp up, which may be why 20% of the sample did not take a position. An AJC survey taken with an online panel in mid-August found 51% approval and 47% disapproval, suggesting that many Jews who did not know enough about the treaty in July turned against it after more negative information about it was publicized. The split was partisan: 66% of Democrats approved the accords, and 87% of Republicans disapproved. Approval was greatest among the "just Jewish" (69%) and Reform Jews (54%), while 67% of Orthodox and Conservative Jews disapproved.[3]

Ominously, the Iran controversy has further fractured the American Jewish community, with the legitimacy of dissent being questioned. Sev-

TABLE 9.5. Jews' Attitudes on Responses to Iran Nuclear Program

			U.S. action		Israeli action	
Year	Survey	Question	Favor	Oppose	Favor	Oppose
2012	J Street	Set a red line	35%	47%	—	
2012	PRRI	Military action	59%	37%	—	
2012	AJC	Military action	64%	35%	72%	26%
2013	AJC	Military action	52%	45%	67%	30%

Source: Analysis of surveys by the American Jewish Committee, J Street, and the Public Religion Research Institute.

eral decades ago, Hertzberg (1979, 223) pointed out that opposition to Zionism had become grounds for ostracism from organized American Jewish life.[4] Similarly, during the 2015 controversy about whether Congress should block the Iran accord, those Jews who questioned Israeli policies were often charged with disloyalty.[5] This raises the broader question of the nature of the relationship American Jews have with Israel.

The Relationship between American Jews and Israel

When Israel was formed, there was an understanding that American Jewish organizations would support or at least not criticize Israeli policies, particularly on security matters. Since U.S. Jews were not putting their lives at stake in defending Israel militarily, the view was that they should not criticize the decisions that Israeli Jews made to defend themselves (Ginsberg 2001, 22–23). As longtime Anti-Defamation League director Abraham Foxman said, "Israeli democracy should decide; American Jews should support" (Beinart 2012b, 50). That unquestioning view was epitomized by the American Israel Public Affairs Committee, the major pro-Israel lobbying group, which became known for supporting Israeli government decisions, though Waxman (2016, 160–61) documents how its support for the Oslo peace process was "half-hearted at best." Disunity became public in 2008, when J Street was formed as a lobby organization favoring a two-state solution to the Israeli-Palestinian conflict and willing to oppose Israeli policies that the organization views as obstacles to such a solution.

Conflict has developed between Jews who believe it is essential to give Israel unconditional support and those who consider it appropriate to express their disagreements with Israeli policies. Politically conservative American Jews tend to be totally supportive of Israeli policies: regarding Palestinian opposition to Israel as unlikely to abate, they think that concessions, including giving up territory taken during the 1967 Six-Day War, would just weaken Israel without corresponding gains. By contrast, many liberal American Jews view the Israeli government's hard line in negotiating as inhibiting a solution to the conflict and regard Israeli government policies as harmful to its long-term security. As Waxman (2016, 94–108) delineates, the extreme right among American Jews wants Israel to include all the West Bank and views the Palestinians as having no legitimate claims to Judea and Samaria, while the extreme left is anti-Zionist and supports the Boycott, Divestment, Sanctions movement as part of its opposition to occupation of the West Bank. However, most U.S. Jews take more centrist positions: a large center-right blames Palestinians for the conflict and opposes any action that could weaken Israel's security, and a large center-left is committed to Israel as a Jewish state but favors recognizing Palestinian rights.

The nature of Israeli governments has been another factor affecting how American Jews feel about Israel's policies. Its early governments were formed by the socialist Labor (originally Mapai) Party, whose base consisted of European settlers. The infusions of eastern (*Mizrahi*) Jews from Muslim countries and of Jews from several Asian and African nations after Israel gained statehood changed Israel's political balance of power. These new immigrants largely supported the right-wing Likud Party, which displaced Labor as the governing party in 1977. The governing coalitions since then have gone back and forth between the two, and liberal American Jews have been less comfortable with Likud governments than with Labor governments.

A related factor is the inclusion of ultra-Orthodox political parties in Israeli governments. Israel's proportional representation system has given small religious parties considerable power when none of the major parties receives an electoral majority. For example, after the 2015 election, Likud leader Benjamin Netanyahu pulled together a bare majority of 61 in the 120-seat Knesset (Israel's parliament) only by making concessions to bring two ultra-Orthodox parties into his governing coalition.

The inclusion of religious parties in coalition governments has led to the Orthodox being given wide latitude in religious matters, even though most Israeli Jews are secular. For example, Israel does not provide for secular marriages but instead requires that Jewish marriages be Orthodox. The Israeli Orthodox rabbinate does not recognize Reform and Conservative rabbis or accept marriages or conversions they conduct. In the extreme, that means that American Jews who move to Israel cannot have a Jewish marriage there if their mother had converted under the supervision of an American non-Orthodox rabbi. Other controversies involve Orthodox restrictions on the religious role of women in Israel, requiring women to sit in the back of public buses in Orthodox areas, and not permitting women to pray along with men at the Western Wall in Jerusalem. Most of the American Jewish community opposes this treatment of Reform and Conservative Jews and of women. For example, the 2018 AJC poll of Jewish opinion found that 80% of U.S. Jews favored non-Orthodox rabbis being permitted to officiate at Jewish weddings, divorces, and conversions in Israel; 81% supported changing Israeli law to allow for civil marriages and divorces; and 73% supported a mixed-gender prayer area adjacent to the Western Wall.

In July 2018, Israel's Knesset enacted a new "basic law" (which has the legal effect of a constitutional rule) entitled "Israel as the Nation State of the Jewish People." It declares that "the right to exercise national self-determination in the State of Israel is unique to the Jewish people," without mentioning either democracy or the principle of equality. While many people view the Jewishness of Israel as self-evident, many American Jews have struggled with the question of whether Israel can be both Jewish and democratic. The 2015 AJC survey of American Jews found that 62% favored separation of religion and state in Israel or, at least, a lesser role there for religion.

Conclusions

American Jews retain a large sense of connection to Israel. However, "caring" about Israel does not necessarily translate into agreeing with its government's policies. Most American Jews still favor Israel in its disputes with the Palestinians, but many are skeptical of the Israeli government's sincerity in peace negotiations.

Polls have traditionally found strong support for Israel in both American political parties, but by 2015, survey responses reflected the tensions between Obama and Netanyahu. Many young adults and Democrats, including many young Jews and Jewish Democrats, are distressed by Israel's continued creation and expansion of settlements in the West Bank. Republicans are more supportive of Israel on these matters, and Jewish Republicans are more likely to accept the old stricture that American Jews should not be second-guessing the decisions that Israeli Jews make for their own security. Dealing with the possibility of a nuclear Iran threatening Israel's existence also became a partisan issue. Jewish views might change if there was an existential threat to Israel from Iran, but there is much greater skepticism of claims about nuclear capabilities of Middle East nations since weapons of mass destruction, which were the justification for the 2003 invasion of Iraq, were found not to exist there. The

Republican Party's emphasis on Israel as an issue may be mainly intended to maintain its strong evangelical vote, with any gains it obtains by using this as a wedge issue among American Jews being icing on the cake. Still, a breakdown of the bipartisan consensus on U.S. policy toward Israel could have serious implications for U.S. support, though history suggests that any administration would try to maintain a policy that is acceptable to most American Jews.

The politicization of support for Israel became evident when Israeli prime minister Benjamin Netanyahu was seen as supporting his friend Mitt Romney in the 2012 election and then working with congressional Republicans to try to forestall the Iran nuclear accord. Yet the overwhelming proportion of American Jews still voted for Obama's reelection, and a majority of them did not oppose the nuclear accord even though there were many public statements from Jewish groups against the agreement. Nevertheless, it is paradoxical when most American Jews express feelings of connections to Israel but, at the same time, support the political party that is less supportive of Israel's policies. As discussed in chapter 14 of this study, support for Israel was still highly politicized during the early years of the Trump administration, regardless of several changes in American policies regarding the Middle East.

The discussion of domestic issues in the previous chapter and of attitudes on Israel in this chapter demonstrate that relying on conventional self-identification of liberal/conservative ideology limits our understanding of Jews' partisan choices. Chapters 10 and 11 explore this matter in considerable detail. They also uncover related anomalies in the relationship between partisanship and ideology among Jewish Americans.

CHAPTER 10

The Missing Jewish Republicans

One rarely thinks of Jews being Republican and/or conservative, but many Jews are. What is unexpected is that many Jewish political conservatives are not Republicans. There are fewer Jewish Republicans than there should be given Jews' political attitudes more generally.

Who are these "missing Jewish Republicans," and why are they missing? Answering these questions requires a closer look at Jews' partisanship and ideology. This chapter begins by examining the relationship between their party ties and ideology. Next, it details the politics of Jewish political conservatives and considers the politics of nonconservatives. This analysis finds that social issues are critical to understanding why there are not as many Jewish Republicans as might be expected given Jews' attitudes on other issues.

A Mismatch between Partisanship and Ideology among Jews

Jews' Ideology Does Not Conflict with Their Partisanship. As American politics have become polarized at the beginning of the 21st century, we have become accustomed to party identification and ideology matching one another: being politically conservative and Republican or being liberal and Democratic go together. Indeed, the ideology of most Jews does not conflict with their partisanship. Both the Pew and the ANES surveys find that less than one-tenth of Jewish Republicans are liberals and that equally few Jewish Democrats are conservatives. There may have been less congruence back in the 1950s, when the Republican Party had a liberal wing and the Democratic Party had a conservative wing, but Jewish partisans today do not think of themselves as an ideological grouping opposing their party's mainstream. Most Jewish Republicans have realized that their team does not contain liberals, and most Jewish Democrats recognize that theirs does not include conservatives.

Jews' Partisanship Is Not in Accord with Their Ideology. Remarkably, the opposite is not true: Jews' partisanship is not well aligned with their ideology, in that many Jewish political conservatives are not Republicans. The only previous discovery of this result was by Lipstadt, Pruitt, and Woocher (1984; Medoff 2002, 202). Writing in the Jewish magazine *Moment* before the 1984 election, they pointed out, "Only half or less of the Jews who call themselves conservatives identify as Republicans." They continued, "It's as if conservatism has gained a measure of respectability within the Jewish community that Republicanism has not." The discrepancy is not quite as large now, but it is still the case that many Jewish conservatives do not choose to be Republicans.

This point is best illustrated with some data. Jewish liberals are overwhelmingly Democratic, 93% in the 2013 Pew Jewish survey. If conservatives were similarly Republican, one would expect about 93% of conservatives to be Republicans. Instead, only 61% of Pew's Jewish political conservatives were Republicans. That is a 32% difference in the proportions of liberals who were Democrats and of conservatives who were Republicans, showing that many conservative Jews were not identifying as Republicans.[1]

Figure 10.1 displays this asymmetric relationship; the top bar represents liberals, and the bottom bar represents conservatives. Comparing these two bars shows the considerable discrepancy between how ideology translates into partisanship for Jewish liberals and conservatives. The left half of the figure shows Republicans at a disadvantage according to the 2013 Pew Jewish survey, because Jewish conservatives are not as Republican as Jewish liberals are Democratic; the right half of the figure replicates this finding through the 1992–2012 ANES surveys. This is a general result for Jews across many surveys,[2] but it is specific to Jews: among non-Jews in the ANES, the percentage of conservatives who are Republicans is only five percentage points below the percentage of liberals who are Democrats, and even less (three points) in the 2014 Pew Religious Landscape Study. While it is possible that the Jewish conservatives were voting Republican even if they do not identify that way, that was not the case in the ANES data: just 50% of politically conservative Jews voted Republican. Similarly,

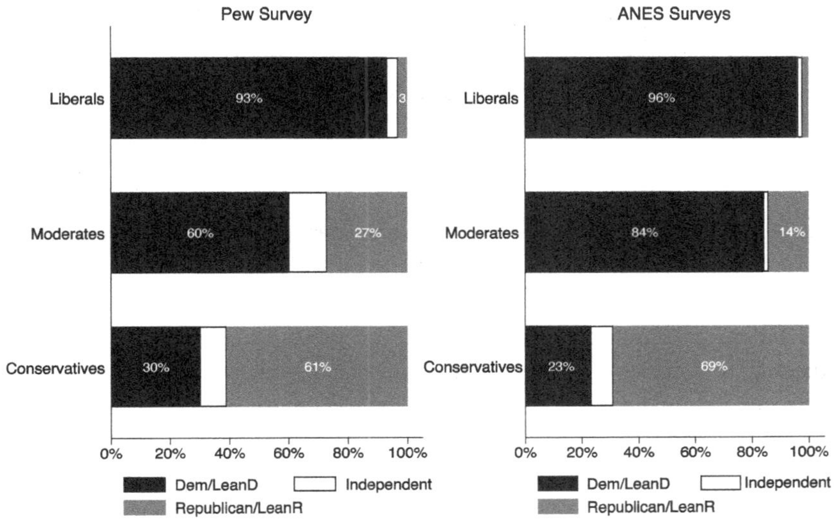

Fig. 10.1. Jews' partisanship by their ideology
(*Source:* Analysis of Pew and ANES surveys.)

election-day polls by J Street found that only 62% of Jewish conservatives in 2012 and 53% in 2016 voted for the Republican presidential candidate.

Thus, Jewish political conservatives have been considerably less likely to accept Republican partisanship than Jewish liberals are to embrace Democratic partisanship. This misalignment means that the Republican Party does not get the level of support from conservative Jews that a conservative party usually obtains from political conservatives, costing the GOP support that it should reasonably expect to receive. The GOP loses about 6% of the Jewish vote because political conservatives are not as Republican as liberals are Democratic.[3] Understanding why these Republicans are missing requires examining the views of conservative Jews.

The Politics of Jewish Conservatives

Who are the Jewish conservatives, and why are they not more Republican? Jewish conservatives might be expected to be mainly Orthodox Jews, but the bottom row of table 10.1 shows that they are spread out quite evenly across the Orthodox, Conservative, Reform, and "just Jewish" (bottom row of table 10.1). The table's top row reveals that Republicans are missing in each denomination, with at most two-thirds of political conservatives in any denomination being Republican. The greatest concentration of missing Republicans is among conservative Jews in the Conservative movement, with barely more being Republican than Democratic.[4]

Israel. An important possibility is that attitudes on Israel could explain the missing Republicans. Table 10.2 shows the attitudes of Jewish conservatives and liberals on some of the questions relating to Israel in surveys by the Pew Research Center and the Public Religion Research Institute. As to be expected, a majority of conservatives express hard-line positions on most of these topics, while only a minority of liberals do so on most of them.

TABLE 10.1. Partisanship by Denomination for Jewish Political Conservatives

	Denomination				
Party identification	Orthodox	Conservative	Reform	Just Jewish	Total
Republican	68%	49%	64%	65%	
Independent	4%	9%	7%	16%	
Democrat	28%	42%	29%	19%	
Total	100%	100%	100%	100%	
Republican minus Democrat	40%	7%	35%	46%	
% of conservatives	28%	27%	25%	21%	101%

Source: Analysis of the 2013 Pew Jewish survey.

TABLE 10.2. Partisanship of Jewish Conservatives and Liberals by Their Attitudes on Israel

		Politically conservative Jews			Liberal Jews		
		% with this position	Party identification		% with this position	Party identification	
Year	Survey		% Rep.	% Dem.		% Rep.	% Dem.
2012	PRRI	79%	79%	21%	50%	1%	99%
POSITION: *U.S. should take military action to prevent Iran's development of nuclear weapons if economic sanctions are unable to stop their nuclear weapons program*							
2012	PRRI	71%	83%	17%	28%	6%	94%
POSITION: *Oppose establishment of Palestinian state*							
2013	Pew	52%	68%	22%	25%	6%	87%
POSITION: *Israel and Palestine cannot coexist*							
2013	Pew	82%	62%	29%	40%	6%	83%
POSITION: *Settlements do not hurt peace process*							

Source: Analysis of surveys by the Pew Research Center and the Public Religion Research Institute.

If Israeli attitudes were crucial to Jews' partisanship, those with hard-line positions would be expected to be Republican. However, Jewish political conservatives are not all hard-liners on Israel, and issues concerning Israel do not move them into the Republican camp. Averaging across the four issue positions in table 10.2 shows that 22% of conservative hard-liners are Democrats. That result is in contrast with how united liberals are in their loyalty to the Democratic Party regardless of their position on Israel issues.

Domestic Issues. Turning to domestic issues, table 10.3 presents analysis of an index of four domestic issue questions in the 2008 National Annenberg Election Survey (NAES): abortion, gay marriage, taxes, and health insurance. As to be expected, Jewish conservatives who take a greater number of liberal stands on these issues are less likely to consider themselves Republican: only 30% of those who are liberal on three to four issues are Republican, versus 86% of those who are liberal on one issue at most. Striking is that Jewish conservatives tend to take more liberal stands on these issues than do non-Jewish conservatives. While 30% of Jewish conservatives take predominantly liberal stands, only 10% of non-Jewish conservatives do so. Instead, 52% of non-Jewish conservatives take predominantly conservative stands on these issues, compared to only 21% of Jewish conservatives. Many Jews who think of themselves as politically conservative do not adhere fully to Republican positions on domestic issues, and, correspondingly, many do not identify with the more conservative party.

The right-hand side of table 10.3 shows that Jewish liberals are more likely to give liberal answers to at least three of these issues than are non-Jewish liberals, by a 90% to 68% margin. Jewish liberals are not conflicted

TABLE 10.3. Comparison of Jews and Non-Jews on a Domestic Issues Index by Ideology

	Jewish conservatives		Non-Jewish conservatives		Jewish liberals		Non-Jewish liberals	
Number of liberal answers	% Rep.	% with score	% Rep.	% with score	% Dem.	% with score	% Dem.	% with score
0–1	86%	21%	83%	52%	—	0%	55%	9%
2	73%	49%	70%	38%	88%	10%	69%	24%
3–4	30%	30%	43%	10%	96%	90%	88%	68%
Total		100%		100%		100%		101%

Source: Analysis of the 2008 National Annenberg Election Survey.

on these issues, and they overwhelmingly identify with the more liberal party. Thus, self-proclaimed ideology lines up better with domestic issue positions for liberal Jews than for conservative Jews.

Comparison with Non-Jewish Conservatives. The puzzle of low Republican identification by Jewish political conservatives can be explored further by examining differences between Jewish and non-Jewish conservatives on specific issues. Enough Jews were interviewed in the 2008 NAES and the 2014 Pew Religious Landscape Study (RLS) to permit comparisons with non-Jews in those surveys. The results presented in table 10.4 show that Jewish conservatives were more liberal than non-Jewish conservatives on social issues—by 45 percentage points on abortion, 21 on legalizing gay marriage, and 10 on accepting homosexuality)—as well as by 15 points on accepting the theory of evolution.

By contrast, the attitudes of Jewish conservatives were generally similar to those of non-Jewish conservatives on economic issues such as taxes and government services. Conservative Jews and non-Jews have virtually identical views on cutting taxes on a question in the 2008 NAES, while the RLS found very little difference between Jews and non-Jews of the same ideological position on attitudes toward the size of government. Thus, Jewish conservatives are distinctive from non-Jewish conservatives on social issues but not on economic ones, so their choice of party may depend on which set of issues they care about the most.

TABLE 10.4. Comparison of Jewish and Non-Jewish Conservatives on Domestic Policy Issues

Year	Survey	Question	Jewish conservatives	Non-Jewish conservatives
2008	NAES	Abortion should be available	76%	31%
2014	RLS	Evolution is best explanation for origins of human life	63%	48%
2014	RLS	Homosexuality should be accepted by society	51%	41%
2008	NAES	Legalize gay marriage	31%	10%
2008	NAES	Want taxes cut	49%	50%
2008	NAES	Favor one government system for health insurance	48%	32%
2014	RLS	Larger government with more services	23%	19%

Source: Analysis of the National Annenberg Election Survey and the Pew Religious Landscape Study.

Conflicted Conservatives. Many politically conservative Jews are conflicted on domestic issues, and those conflicted conservatives are less likely to consider themselves Republican in their partisanship. For example, in the 2013 Pew Jewish survey, the self-identified political conservatives who are not conservative on domestic issues are the ones who are not Republicans: only 26% of conservatives who gave the liberal answers on questions about both gay acceptability and size of government were Republicans.[5]

This analysis of Jewish political conservatives is reminiscent of the Ellis and Stimson (2012, 96) analysis of ideology referred to in chapter 8 of the present study. They found that a majority of self-identified conservatives in the General Social Survey took liberal positions on a measure of operational ideology based on federal spending on various topics. Only 15% of the public were consistent conservatives. About 30% were conflicted conservatives who identified as conservatives while taking liberal positions on operational ideology, and only 54% of those conflicted conservatives were Republican. By contrast, nearly 30% were consistent liberals, with only 4% being conflicted liberals who took conservative issue positions. The results presented in this section of the present analysis are similar, while emphasizing policy issues rather than spending areas. Many Jewish self-identified political conservatives are not conservative on issues and do not identify as Republicans, and there are many more conflicted conservatives than conflicted liberals among Jews.

The Politics of Nonconservative Jews

Surprisingly, there may also be missing Republicans among Jewish moderates and liberals. The analysis in this section is similar to that above, finding that many actually favor small government while still disagreeing with Republican positions on social issues. Indeed, because they are more numerous than Jewish political conservatives, this is a large loss for the GOP.

Moderates. Ideological moderates might be expected to split fairly evenly between the two parties. Figure 10.1 shows that they instead split two-to-one Democratic over Republican (60%–27%) in the Pew data and even more Democratic (84%–14%) in the 1992–2012 ANES surveys. Thus, the Republicans lose many Jews among moderates.

The denominational choices of moderates are similar to those of Jews as a whole, with most being Reform and the fewest being Orthodox, as shown in the last row of table 10.5. While half of the Orthodox among the moderates are Republicans, only one-third of Conservatives, one-quarter of Reform Jews, and one-sixth of the "just Jewish" moderates identify with that party.

To examine further why more Jewish moderates are not Republicans, table 10.6 revisits the index of four domestic issue questions from the 2008 NAES: abortion, gay marriage, taxes, and health insurance. Moderates who are Jewish tend to take more liberal stands on these issues than do non-Jewish moderates, with 59% of Jewish moderates taking liberal stands on at least three of the four issues, versus just 35% of non-Jewish moderates. Half of the non-Jewish moderates who take one liberal stand at most on these issues are Republican, but only 4% of Jewish moderates are that conservative on these issues. Thus, Jewish moderates have enough liberal positions on domestic issues that they are less likely to identify as Republicans.

TABLE 10.5. Partisanship of Jewish Political Moderates by Denomination

	Denomination				
Party identification	Orthodox	Conservative	Reform	Just Jewish	Total
Republican	51%	33%	24%	18%	
Independent	12%	12%	12%	18%	
Democrat	37%	55%	64%	65%	
	100%	100%	100%	101%	
Republican minus Democrat	14%	–22%	–40%	–47%	
% of moderates	11%	22%	36%	31%	100%

Source: Analysis of the 2013 Pew Jewish survey.

TABLE 10.6. Comparison of Jewish and Non-Jewish Moderates on a Domestic Issues Index

Number of	Jewish moderates		Non-Jewish moderates	
liberal answers	% Rep.	% with score	% Rep.	% with score
0–1	—	4%	51%	19%
2	53%	37%	40%	46%
3–4	18%	59%	24%	35%
Total		100%		100%

Source: Analysis of the 2008 National Annenberg Election Survey.

Additional results on moderates in the Pew study are given in table 10.7. Most Jewish moderates want a smaller federal government, but they still lean slightly Democratic. Tellingly, the vast majority of moderates are acceptant of homosexuality, and they are Democrats rather than Republicans by a three-to-one margin. Their positions are more hard-line on the settlements than on the possibility of Israel coexisting with a Palestinian state, but most are Democrats even if they have hard-line positions on these issues.

Liberals. As to Jewish liberals, 95% of liberals in the Pew study who want more government services are Democrats, which is not surprising. However, it is surprising that 85% of self-identified liberals who want fewer government services are also Democrats. Those small-government liberals could be Republicans if economic issues mattered more to them than other issues.

Conclusions

Jewish Democrats who are political conservatives are about as rare as Jewish Republicans who are liberals. This suggests that party identification has become primary for most Jews: they become Democrats or Republicans and then generally accept the ideological position that goes with that partisanship or, at least, do not adopt the opposite ideological position. As Achen and Bartels (2016, 234) state, studies "suggest that ideology is more often an *effect* of partisanship than its *cause*" (emphasis in original). Kinder and Kalmoe (2017) similarly conclude that ideology is a "mere summary" of policy views, rather than a causal factor.

TABLE 10.7. Partisanship of Jewish Political Moderates by their Issue Positions

Position	% of moderates with this position	Party identification	
		% Rep.	% Dem.
Smaller federal government	55%	38%	46%
Favor accepting homosexuality	83%	21%	65%
Israel and Palestinian state cannot coexist	37%	38%	51%
Settlements do not hurt peace process	65%	34%	54%

Source: Analysis of the 2013 Pew Jewish survey.

However, many Jewish political conservatives are not Republicans. A possible explanation for this fact would be that conservative Jews are conservative because of their hard-line positions on Israel. The data shows that is not the case: they are not united on hard-line positions, and many of the conservatives who voice hard-line positions are still not Republicans. Thus, positions on Israel do not explain the missing Jewish Republicans.

Instead, the puzzle of the missing Republicans involves social issues that seemingly prevent many conservatives from being Republicans. Many conservative Jews are conflicted ideologues who are fairly liberal on social issues even though they favor a small government and lower taxes. Of course, any gains that the Republican Party might make among Jews by changing its position on social issues could be overwhelmed by losses from non-Jewish social conservatives—though the latter are unlikely to find the Democratic Party any more to their liking. Even without changing their positions on social issues, Republican candidates wanting to increase their vote among Jews could emphasize their small-government positions, while Democratic candidates wanting to maintain their vote advantage among Jews should emphasize social issues.

While this chapter has emphasized the role of social issues in decreasing Republican support among Jews, it may well be that feelings about the Christian right and/or attitudes on church-state separation are the basic underlying factors. This analysis has emphasized the Pew survey, which lacked questions on those two topics, but the very negative attitudes of most Jews toward the Christian right, discussed in chapter 5, are a reminder of the important role that social groups play. Attitudes on the Christian right and on church-state issues are likely correlated with Jews' positions on social issues, so a survey that measured those attitudes might find that the association of the Christian right with the Republican Party is what keeps many Jews from becoming Republican (see fig. 5.4).

The interplay between Jews' attitudes on economic and social issues has been fundamental to this examination of the missing Jewish Republicans. The results show that Jews' attitudes in the two domains are not identical, which calls into question the usual measure of self-identified ideology. The next chapter shows that a broader classification of Jews' ideology would be more useful.

CHAPTER 11

Jewish Libertarians

Many Jewish business owners and professionals who vehemently complain that government regulation of businesses has become excessive simultaneously view government prohibitions of homosexuality and abortion as unwarranted. That pattern does not fit into the usual classification of political ideology as either liberal or conservative, and we usually assume that it is a rare combination of attitudes. However, these "Libertarians" are fairly common, with about one-quarter of contemporary Jews being small-government social liberals.

The discussion of missing Republicans in the previous chapter implied that the conventional liberal/conservative distinction does not fully capture ideological differences among Jews. The usual liberal/conservative classification commingles economic and social ideology rather than recognizing that they can be distinct. This chapter separates out these two liberal/conservative dimensions and constructs a four-category ideological classification. Understanding Jews' politics requires recognizing this enlarged classification, particularly the prevalence of Libertarians. That prevalence accounts for why the "missing Republicans" are missing. Additionally, views on Israel affect the politics of these Libertarians more than is the case for the other ideological types.

Expanding the Ideology Classification

Two basic domains for government regulation in the domestic policy arena should be distinguished when considering ideology. The first domain involves the market and the extent to which the government should interfere with the economy in the pursuit of equality. Government spending on antipoverty efforts is one example of such an initiative, and affirmative action programs are another. The question is whether individuals and employers should make their own choices without the government intruding. In the early 20th century, Jewish immigrants who worked in sweatshop conditions favored limitations on market mechanisms through the enactment of laws regulating workplace hours and safety. The movement of subsequent generations into owning and managing businesses has led some Jews to prefer market mechanisms rather than government regulations on commerce, though many still use the Judaic value of charity as a basis for supporting government aid to the needy.

The second domain involves social order and the extent to which the government should impose order at the expense of restricting individual liberties. Requiring that marriage involve people of opposite genders is an example, as is prohibiting the use of marijuana. The government can impose laws and penalties in the social domain, rather than let individuals make their own choices. Jews are sensitive to such restrictions on individual liberty, because they have historically suffered from limitations on their religious practice. That sensitivity has led many Jews to favor minimal government constraints on individual rights, rather than government enforcement of traditional moral codes. A prime exception is that Orthodox Jews' strong support of traditional morality leads some to favor government restrictions on gay marriage.

While it is customary to talk about Americans' political ideologies as either liberal or conservative, that categorization blurs the differences between economic and morality issues. Peoples' positions on the proper role of government on economic and social-welfare issues need not coincide with their views on the government's role regarding moral and social issues. People who want the government to provide welfare programs may or may not favor government enforcement of morality. Recognizing the distinction between these two separate types of issues leads to four possible ideological categories, shown in figure 11.1.[1]

Corresponding to the usual distinction between the political left and right, the people represented on the left of the figure favor considerable economic regulation, and those on the right want minimal regulation of the economy by the government. The figure's vertical dimension separates both the political left and the political right into two categories. At the top

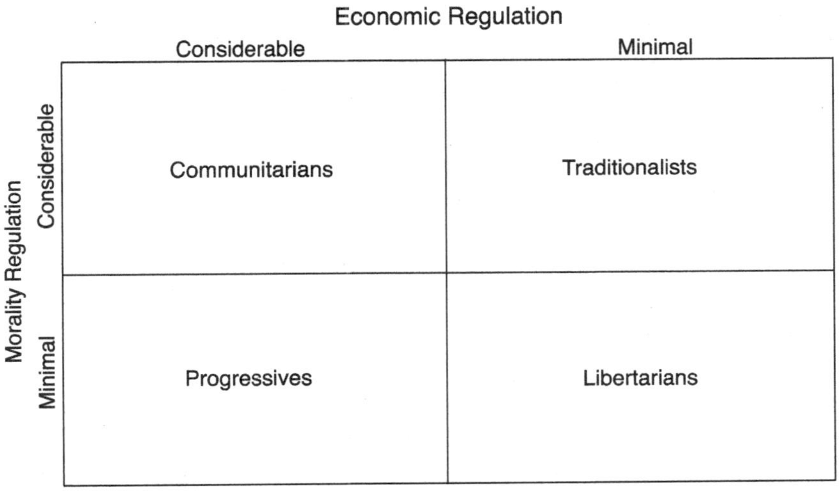

Fig. 11.1. An expanded ideological classification

left are "Communitarians," who are consistent in wanting the government to play a large role, both in the economy and the moral sphere. At the bottom left are those who favor government intervention in the economy but want individuals to be allowed to make their own decisions on morality. The present discussion refers to these "left liberals" as "Progressives." At the top right are those who expect government intervention in the moral/social arena but oppose government intervention in the economy. This discussion refers to these "right conservatives" as "Traditionalists," to avoid further confusion with self-identified conservatives and the Conservative movement in Judaism.[2] At the bottom right are "Libertarians," who are consistent in wanting minimal government intervention, whether in the economy or in the moral sphere.

Classifying Jews' Domestic Ideology

Both the 2013 Survey of U.S. Jews by the Pew Research Center and the 2012 Jewish Values Survey by the Public Religion Research Institute (PRRI) included questions that can be used to apply this typology. The Pew survey addressed only two issues of domestic public policy (response percentages are shown in parentheses):

- Social issue: respondents were asked whether they thought that "homosexuality should be accepted by society" (82%) or that "homosexuality should be discouraged by society" (13%).
- Economic issue: respondents were asked whether they would prefer "a smaller government providing fewer services?" (38%) or "a bigger government providing more services" (54%).

The PRRI study addressed more issues of domestic public policy. Chosen for this analysis are the two that are most comparable to the issues addressed by the Pew survey:

- Social issue: respondents were surveyed about "allowing gay and lesbian couples to marry" (81% favor; 18% oppose).
- Economic issue: respondents were asked whether they thought that "the government should do more to reduce the gap between the rich and the poor" (64% agree; 35% disagree).

The Pew and PRRI questions are not identical, but they are analyzed together in this section to see how much difference occurs because of question wording and other sources of variation between the surveys.[3]

Table 11.1 gives the distribution of Jews on these pairs of questions.[4] Progressives are the largest response category, with Libertarians being second. That those two categories are the largest fits the permissiveness of most Jews on social issues. By contrast, no more than 10% are Traditionalists, and under 10% are Communitarians.[5] The small size of those two cat-

TABLE 11.1. Size of Ideology Types

	2013 Pew	2012 PRRI	2014 RLS	
Ideology type	Jews	Jews	Jews	Non-Jews
Progressive	47%	55%	49%	28%
Libertarian	28%	25%	32%	34%
Communitarian	5%	8%	6%	8%
Traditionalist	7%	10%	9%	24%
Ambiguous[a]	13%	2%	4%	6%
Total	100%	100%	100%	100%

Source: Analysis of surveys by the Pew Research Center, by the Public Religion Research Institute, and in the Religious Landscape Study.

[a]The "ambiguous" category includes those who did not answer at least one of the questions.

egories is consistent with the finding in the 2007 Pew Religious Landscape Study (RLS) that only 22% of Jews favored the government doing more "to protect morality in society," while 71% were worried that the government "is getting too involved in the issue of morality."

The 2014 RLS surveyed the general public on the same pair of questions used in the 2013 Pew Jewish survey, so the RLS results are also included in the table to permit a comparison of Jews with non-Jews. The Libertarian category is not unique to Jews; many people in the general population are small-government social liberals. Libertarians are as common among non-Jews in the 2014 RLS as among Jews. However, the RLS reveals important differences in the ideology of Jews and non-Jews: Jews are ideologically distinctive in that they have a much higher proportion of Progressives and correspondingly fewer Traditionalists.

Characteristics of the Ideological Categories

This section examines the difference characteristics of the types of people who fall into the new ideological categories introduced in this chapter. Demographic differences are examined, along with denominational and political differences. These differences are helpful in explaining the puzzle of the "missing Republicans" among Jews.

Demographic Differences. There are minor demographic differences between these groups, some of which are shown in table 11.2. Men are overrepresented among Libertarians and Traditionalists because they are more likely to oppose government regulation in economic matters, while

TABLE 11.2. Demographic Characteristics of Ideology Types

	Male		Income above $100,000		College graduates	
Ideology type	Pew	PRRI	Pew	PRRI	Pew	PRRI
Progressive	41%	46%	41%	30%	65%	66%
Libertarian	56%	55%	52%	44%	59%	65%
Communitarian	58%	44%	12%	9%	23%	31%
Traditionalist	63%	61%	29%	32%	39%	55%

Source: Analysis of the 2013 Pew Jewish survey and the 2012 Jewish Values Survey by the Public Religion Research Institute.

women are disproportionately Progressives. Libertarians have the highest incomes. The groups with the fewest people having high incomes are the Communitarians and Traditionalists, and they are least likely to be college graduates.

Not shown in the table is that Progressives are overrepresented proportionately in the West and underrepresented in the East. Young people are disproportionately Progressives, even though a greater percentage of young Jews than older Jews are Orthodox. Older people are more likely not to answer one of the Pew questions, with 11% saying that society should be acceptant of homosexuality but not answering the question on government size.

The demographic profile of Libertarians is of particular interest. They fit the characteristics that would be associated with businesspeople, professionals, and managers, in that they are more male than the Progressives and earn a higher income than the Progressives without being more educated than them.

Liberal/Conservative Differences. The next step is to compare this typology with people's self-identification as liberals or conservatives. As seen in table 11.3, liberals are overwhelmingly Progressives. Most of the remaining liberals are Libertarians, which calls attention to the importance of recognizing that some Jews are small-government liberals. Most ideological moderates were also either Progressive or Libertarian. Political conservatives were expected to fall in the Traditionalist category, but

TABLE 11.3. Ideological Classification of Jews by Their Self-Identified Ideology

	Pew			PRRI		
Ideology type	Liberal	Moderate	Political conservative	Liberal	Moderate	Political conservative
Progressive	72%	29%	15%	80%	47%	13%
Libertarian	14%	44%	37%	17%	30%	36%
Communitarian	2%	7%	10%	1%	14%	14%
Traditionalist	2%	5%	23%	1%	8%	36%
Ambiguous[a]	10%	15%	15%	2%	1%	0%
Total	100%	100%	100%	101%	100%	99%

Source: Analysis of 2013 Pew Jewish survey and the 2012 Jewish Values Survey by the Public Religion Research Institute.

[a]The "ambiguous" category includes those who did not answer at least one of the questions.

they split between that category and Libertarians, because many Jews who are economic conservatives do not want the government regulating moral matters.[6]

Denominational Differences. Denominational differences are also to be expected. Table 11.4 shows that most non-Orthodox Jews are Progressives or Libertarians. By contrast, the Orthodox have higher proportions of Traditionalists and Communitarians, due to their less-permissive stances on morality issues such as homosexuality.

Political Views. Table 11.5 summarizes the political views of Jews in the different categories. The values shown are averages for each category based on zero-to-one scoring; higher scores represent being more Democratic

TABLE 11.4. Ideological Classification of Jews by Their Denomination

	Pew				PRRI			
Ideology type	Orthodox	Conservative	Reform	Just Jewish	Orthodox	Conservative	Reform	Just Jewish
Progressive	10%	38%	55%	54%	34%	55%	59%	56%
Libertarian	19%	31%	31%	26%	12%	25%	26%	28%
Communitarian	20%	9%	1%	3%	24%	8%	8%	3%
Traditionalist	32%	5%	3%	5%	25%	11%	5%	10%
Ambiguous[a]	18%	16%	10%	12%	4%	1%	1%	2%
Total	99%	99%	100%	100%	99%	100%	99%	99%

Source: Analysis of the 2013 Pew Jewish survey and the 2012 Jewish Values Survey by the Public Religion Research Institute.

[a]The "ambiguous" category includes those who did not answer at least one of the questions.

TABLE 11.5. Jews' Political Views by Their Ideology Type

	Pew		PRRI	
Ideology type	Party	Ideology	Party	Ideology
Progressive	.94	.84	.87	.80
Libertarian	.59	.50	.55	.52
Communitarian	.56	.37	.67	.37
Traditionalist	.21	.24	.21	.19

Source: Analysis of the 2013 Pew Jewish survey and the 2012 Jewish Values Survey by the Public Religion Research Institute.

Note: Higher average values represent being Democratic and liberal. Party is coded with 1.0 as Democratic, 0.5 Independent, and 0.0 Republican; ideology as 1.0 liberal, 0.5 moderate and 0.0 conservative.

and liberal.[7] Progressives are the most Democratic and liberal, while Traditionalists are the most Republican and politically conservative. Libertarians and Communitarians are in the middle on both measures. The basic patterns in table 11.5 hold in a separate analysis (not shown) of only the non-Orthodox, confirming that denomination does not determine these results.

Bartels's (2018, 1489) analysis of a 2017 YouGov survey found that Democratic identifiers are more concerned with opposition to limited government than with opposition to cultural conservatism, while the Republican base is more concerned with cultural conservatism than with limited government. That suggests that Libertarians would be put off by the emphasis in each party, forcing them to decide which they consider the least objectionable.

The 2014 RLS survey shows an important difference in the partisanship of Jewish versus non-Jewish Libertarians. While Jewish Libertarians in that study are split fairly equally between the two parties, there is a 3-to-2 ratio of Republicans to Democrats among non-Jewish Libertarians. The economic question seems to be more important for the partisanship of non-Jewish Libertarians, while the social issue is at least of equal importance with the economic one for Jewish Libertarians.

This classification helps resolve the mismatch discussed in the previous chapter between the large percentage of liberal Jews who consider themselves Democratic versus the smaller percentage of politically conservative Jews who are Republican. Many politically conservative Jews are Libertarian, and according to the Pew data, only 64% of them are Republican, which puts Republicans at a considerable disadvantage. Thus, the partisan mismatch between liberal and conservative Jews occurs because social and economic issues do not divide Jews in the same way.

The Effect of Attitudes about Israel

Attitudes on the Middle East also affect the politics of these groups, as is shown by constructing a two-question index on that topic for both the Pew and PRRI surveys. Pew asked whether peaceful coexistence would be possible between Israel and a Palestinian state and whether Israel's West Bank settlements hurt the peace process, while PRRI asked about military action against Iran if sanctions were ineffective and about support for the creation of a Palestinian state. Those with a hard-line stance would have opposed the creation of a Palestinian state, believed that such a state could not coexist peacefully with Israel, felt that the settlements did not hurt the peace process, and viewed military action against Iran as appropriate; those who support coexistence would have given the opposite pattern of responses. More respondents were on the coexistence side in the Pew survey while more took the hard-line positions in the PRRI data, with 45% of respondents in both surveys falling between those two positions.

As is to be expected, Jews who took "coexistence" positions on both questions were more Democratic and liberal, while hard-liners were more Republican and conservative (see the average values in table 11.6). Progressives are very Democratic and liberal regardless of their positions on Israel. The politics of Libertarians varies with their positions on Israel, with those favoring coexistence being predominantly Democratic and liberal, while those with hard-line positions are mostly Republican and politically conservative. Only hard-line Traditionalists are overwhelmingly Republican, while Traditionalists who are not hard-liners are somewhat more moderate politically.

Another interesting Pew survey question asked whether the Obama ad-

TABLE 11.6. Jews' Political Views by Ideology Type and Attitudes toward Middle East

		Pew		PRRI	
Ideology type	Middle East	Party	Ideology	Party	Ideology
Progressive	Coexistence	.99	.91	.94	.86
Progressive	Mixed	.92	.76	.80	.78
Progressive	Hard-line	.83	.73	.83	.72
Libertarian	Coexistence	.73	.65	.95	.83
Libertarian	Mixed	.66	.46	.53	.48
Libertarian	Hard-line	.38	.40	.33	.37
Communitarian	Coexistence	—	—	—	—
Communitarian	Mixed	.50	.30	.70	.49
Communitarian	Hard-line	—	—	.62	.30
Traditionalist	Coexistence	—	—	—	—
Traditionalist	Mixed	.36	.38	.39	.26
Traditionalist	Hard-line	.09	.16	.06	.12

Source: Analysis of the 2013 Pew Jewish survey and the 2012 Jewish Values Survey by the Public Religion Research Institute.

Note: Higher average values represent more Democratic and more liberal. Results are shown only for categories that include at least 2% of U.S. Jews. Party is coded with 1.0 as Democratic, 0.5 Independent, and 0.0 Republican; ideology as 1.0 liberal, 0.5 moderate, and 0.0 conservative.

ministration was too tough on Israel. The survey was taken at a time when the media was emphasizing the outcry from people who felt that it was. Overall, 12% of Jews instead answered that they considered the administration too supportive of Israel; similarly, about a tenth of Jews gave that opinion in the 2010 Brandeis survey of American Jewish attitudes about Israel (Sasson et al. 2010, 20). Of course, there are many possible ways in which respondents could interpret being "too supportive," but Jews giving that response in the early 2010s were probably indicating substantial estrangement from Israeli policies.

Ideological Context

Jewish Libertarians are not necessarily Libertarian in the full sense of Cato Institute Libertarians, since many Jewish Libertarians would favor a more pro-Israel stance. A natural question is how Jewish Libertarians relate to other ideological groupings. Are they the neoconservatives of the late 1900s and early 2000s? Are they the Rockefeller Republicans of the 1950s and 1960s, or are they the Goldwater Republicans of that era? They have some similarities to each, but there are differences too.

Jewish neoconservatives came from a big government background, though they felt that the Democratic Party left them. Their main focus became an interventionist foreign policy with strong support for Israel, while Jewish Libertarians are not as solidly pro-Israel as the neoconservatives. As to domestic policy, the early neoconservatives favored welfare reform, supporting a more conservative welfare program. They rejected the counterculture of the 1960s and most emphasized traditional morals. Thus, they would differ from Jewish Libertarians in being opposed to abortion and probably to same-sex marriage.

Rockefeller Republicans were liberal on the moral matters of the mid-1900s, so they might be expected to take Libertarian positions on respecting people's own decisions on abortion and same-sex marriage. However, they supported some welfare programs and some New Deal programs, rather than advocating small government. Rockefeller Republicans are better described as moderates than as Libertarians.

In a sense, Jewish Libertarians are closer to Barry Goldwater's Republicanism, because Goldwater favored small government rather than welfare programs. He emphasized individual liberties, so he would be expected to take Libertarian positions on today's issues concerning moral values. However, he was strongly in favor of states' rights, as when he voted against the 1964 Civil Rights Act because he opposed a federal role in antidiscrimination legislation. That stance suggests that he would have opposed federal decisions on abortion and gay marriage, wanting those issues to be decided by the states.

Conclusions

The usual classification of ideology as liberal or conservative does not fit cleanly for Jews. As shown in chapter 8, Jews are distinctively liberal on most social issues, but they are no longer distinctively liberal on most economic issues. That disparity draws attention to the need to expand the usual view of ideology to reflect the differences between Jews' ideology in the morality and economic realms. The expanded ideological classification presented in this chapter consists of four categories: Libertarians, who are consistent in opposing government regulation in both spheres; Traditionalists, who support government regulation of social issues but oppose government economic regulation; Progressives, who favor government regulation of the economy but oppose government restrictions in the social arena; and Communitarians, who support government regulation across the board.

Most Jews are either Progressives or Libertarians. However, Jewish political conservatives are split mainly between the ranks of Traditionalists and Libertarians. As to politics, Progressives are the most Democratic, and Traditionalists are the most Republican. The reason that many Jewish political conservatives are not Republicans is that many are Libertarians who are split in their partisan choices. Attitudes toward the Middle East particularly make a difference in the politics of Libertarians, with those having different positions on the Middle East having opposite politics. Thus, the finding that a large number of Jews are Libertarians is important because it means that many Jews are between the parties and could vote for either party, depending on the circumstances. The chapters in this part of this book have examined these and several other factors that affect the political views of American Jews. The chapters in the next part put the different factors together in an examination of Jews' voting.

PART IV

Presidential Voting

While Democratic presidential voting has become part of most Jews' politics of tradition, traditions are not immutable. There are always exceptions to traditions, limits to them, and possibilities of changing them. Understanding the possibilities of change requires recognizing the factors that affect Jews' voting, what subgroups are most susceptible to change, what evidence of change there has been in and since the latest election, and how changes in Judaism may affect changes in their politics.

This final part of this book begins with analysis in chapter 12 of how different factors affect Jews' voting. Attitudes toward Israel are shown to be one factor in their voting, albeit not the most important factor. The chapter theorizes an attitude triad in which economic issues, social issues, and attitudes on Israel are crucial. Chapter 13 evaluates the possibilities for the long-awaited political realignment of the Jewish vote, along with a consideration of the politics of Jewish millennials and of Orthodox versus non-Orthodox Jews. Chapter 14 examines the 2016 presidential election campaign, Jews' voting in that election, and how the beginning of the Trump presidency has affected Jews' political attitudes. Finally, chapter 15 summarizes the earlier chapters and presents an overall account of Jews' politics of tradition, along with the prospects for Jews breaking out of that tradition.

CHAPTER 12

What Makes Jews' Voting Distinctive?

It has been said that Jews are like everyone else, just more so. The same has been said about their voting: that they respond to the same trends as the rest of the public but more so. Quips aside, Jewish voting is distinctive, but it has been unclear what factors account for that distinctiveness. Does it have to do with their religion? Most authors agree that it is not religion per se that causes Jews to be liberal, but what, then, makes their voting distinctive? Is it all a matter of their party identification? How do issues factor in? How important are attitudes on Israel? Peter Beinart (2012a) has claimed that Jews "don't really vote as Jews at all. . . . They vote as secularists." Does that mean that Jews' positions on Israel do not affect their political views?

This chapter begins by demonstrating that Jewish voting has been distinctive. It then analyzes the impact of Jews' views on Israel policy on their voting. This is a controversial matter because of its political implications. Some analysts interpreted decreases in the Jewish vote for Jimmy Carter in 1980 and for Barack Obama in 2012 as being due to dissatisfaction with those incumbents' sterner policies toward Israel, with the implicit message being that presidents must treat Israel better to get Jews' votes. Other analysts point out that the lessened support for Carter and Obama in their reelection attempts just followed national voting trends, implying that Jewish voters pay little mind to American policies regarding Israel. The analysis of several surveys in this chapter yields an in-between conclusion: attitudes on Israeli policy are among the important factors affecting Jews' voting but are not the most important factor.

This chapter then proposes an "attitude triad" theory of Jews' voting based on the previous chapters' analyses of economic issues, social issues, and the Israel issue. Economic issues set a baseline vote, from which Jews shift as they weigh two potential threats: a foreign threat to Israel's security and a domestic threat to their liberties. Different sets of Jews respond to those two dueling threats, with some focusing more on the potential threat to Israel and others being more concerned with threats to their own liberties. The analysis in this chapter goes through 2012, with the unusual 2016 election discussed separately in chapter 14.

Politically Distinctive

Jews have been distinctively Democratic in their party identification (see chap. 7), so it comes as no surprise that they have been voting distinctively Democratic for president. Combining surveys covering the 1992–2012 elections, data from the American National Election Studies (ANES) shows that Jews voted 34 percentage points more Democratic than non-Jews, and the General Social Survey (GSS) estimates a 29-point greater Democratic vote.[1] Finding about a 30-point voting difference in two well-regarded surveys corroborates a substantial voting gap.

The distinctiveness of Jews' voting barely changes as sociodemographic controls are instituted, as illustrated in figure 12.1.[2] The height of the lines in the figure does not diminish from left to right as more controls are added. Sociodemographic characteristics do not render the distinctiveness of Jewish voting spurious. These data establish that Jews have been voting more Democratic for president than would be expected given their sociodemographics.

Even when the analysis includes controls for ideology (not shown in fig. 12.1), Jews are significantly more Democratic in their vote, though the difference drops to 14 points in the ANES data. However, once party identification is also controlled, Jewish voting no longer appears distinctive: the difference is a nonsignificant 6 points. Thus, their combined partisanship and ideology largely account for Jews voting more Democratic than the rest of the electorate.[3] Not surprisingly, the factors that cause Jews to vote so Democratic are, to a considerable extent, incorporated in their party loyalty and ideology. However, Jewish surveys that include questions about Israel permit a more nuanced investigation.

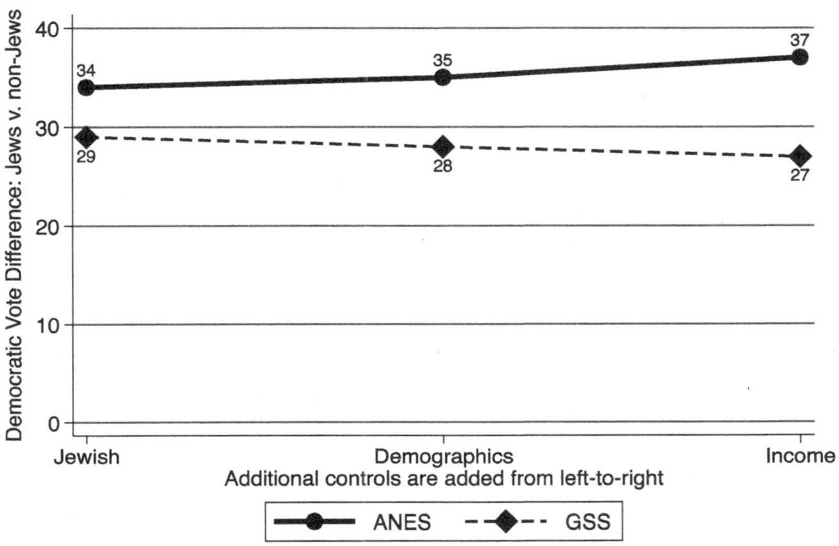

Fig. 12.1. Distinctiveness of Jews' Democratic presidential voting, 1992–2012 (*Source:* Analysis of ANES and GSS surveys.)

Israel as a Voting Issue

Is Israel a voting issue for American Jews? As already mentioned, this question is controversial. For example, Jimmy Carter's win of less than half of the Jewish vote in the three-candidate 1980 election has been ascribed to his poor relations with Israel (e.g., Lazarowitz 2010), although he also obtained a lower vote from the public at large, due to dissatisfaction with the hyperinflation and prolonged Iranian hostage crisis during his presidency.

Differences in Question Wording. Jewish voting surveys reach different conclusions on the importance of Israel to Jews' voting, depending on the questions that are asked. According to an election-day survey sponsored by the Republican Jewish Coalition, Israel mattered substantially to Jews' voting decisions in 2012. That survey directly asked respondents how important issues concerning Israel were in their vote decisions, and 30% of the respondents considered Israel very important, 46% said somewhat important, and only 22% stated that it was not important.

Israel looked much less important in a J Street survey conducted that same day, which presented respondents with a list of 13 issues and asked them to choose the 2 issues that they considered most important in deciding how to vote for president. Although respondents could give two answers, only 10% of respondents chose Israel, putting it in a tie for sixth place; Iran was the least chosen issue, at just 2%. J Street obtained a similar result in its 2016 election-day poll: Israel came in ninth, at 9%, and Iran was last, at 2%. Likewise, when the AJC 2015 Annual Survey of American Jewish Opinion gave people a list of 10 issues and asked which would most affect their 2016 vote, the most popular answer was the economy (42%); U.S.-Israel relations came in fifth, at 7%, and only 4% chose Iran's nuclear program. According to these results, Israel appears to be a crucial voting issue for relatively few Jews.

Correlational Results. Social psychologists would consider neither of the tests discussed in the preceding subsection to be definitive. Skeptical about the ability of people to give the reasons for their behavior (Nisbett and Wilson 1977), those researchers prefer to analyze the correlations of people's attitudes with actual behavior. Table 12.1 shows that several ques-

TABLE 12.1. Correlations of Attitudes on Israel Issues with Presidential Approval and Vote

Survey	Timing	Question		Correlation	Control on party
PRRI	Early 2012	Support establishment of Palestinian state	Approve Obama	$.32^{***}$	$.20^{***}$
J Street	Nov. 2012	U.S. should not set a red line with Iran	Democratic vote	$.27^{***}$	$.13^{***}$
J Street	Nov. 2012	U.S. should vote in UN to recognize Palestinian state	Democratic vote	$.16^{***}$	$.13^{***}$
Pew	Spring 2013	There is a way for Israel and Palestinian state to coexist peacefully	Approve Obama	$.22^{***}$	$.07^{***}$
Pew	Spring 2013	Settlements hurt Israel's security	Approve Obama	$.29^{***}$	$.10^{***}$
AJC	Aug. 2016	Israel can coexist peacefully with Palestinian state	Democratic vote intention	$.37^{***}$	$.24^{***}$
AJC	Aug. 2017	Support establishment of Palestinian state	Democratic vote recall	$.38^{***}$	$.27^{***}$

Source: Analysis of surveys by the American Jewish Committee, J Street, the Pew Research Center, and the Public Religion Research Institute.

$^{***}p < .001$; $^{**}p < .01$; $^{*}p < .05$.

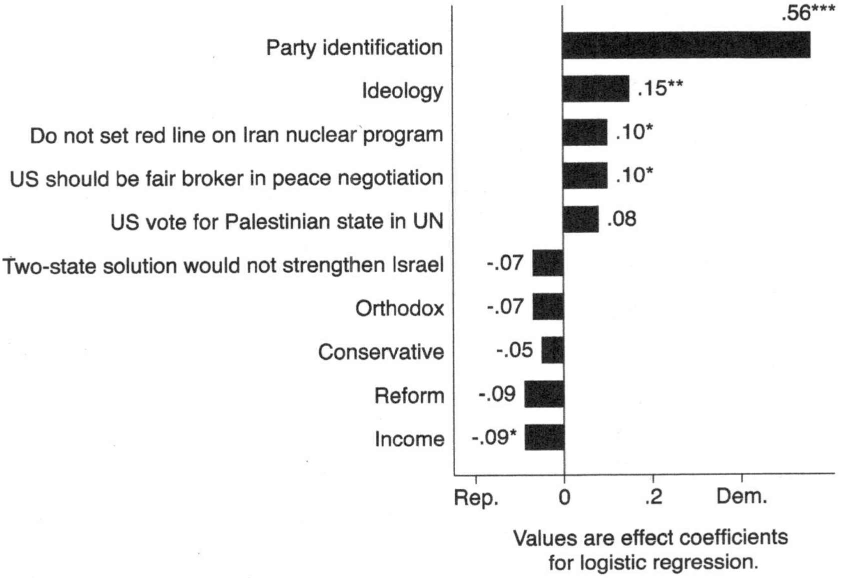

Fig. 12.2. Regression analysis of Jews' 2012 presidential vote
(*Note:* Analysis of 2012 J Street survey. Values are coefficients for logistic regression.)

tions about issues related to Israel have moderate-sized correlations with presidential approval or vote.[4] The rightmost column shows that most of the correlations are only partially reduced when party identification is statistically controlled,[5] so the relationship between attitudes on Israeli policies and presidential approval and vote is more than just a partisan effect. Comparing different surveys can be problematic, but the correlations are highest for the 2016 and 2017 AJC surveys, which implies that Israel may be becoming more important to Jews' political decisions. Those two AJC surveys are analyzed in more detail in chapter 14.

The 2012 J Street election-day survey included questions on Israel-related policies, permitting further tests of their importance in Jews' voting. The analysis shown in figure 12.2 finds that party identification and ideology are both significant predictors of vote, as is income, with higher-income Jews being less likely to support Obama's reelection. (Longer lines in the figure indicate greater effects of the variables, with asterisks denoting statistical significance.) Two questions about American policy in the Middle East are also significant: whether the United States should be a fair broker in peace negotiations between Israelis and Palestinians, rather than support Israel's positions, and whether the United States should set down a red line on Iran's nuclear progress. This survey did not include direct questions about domestic social or economic issues, but its results emphasize the extent to which the Israeli issues were related to Jews' voting in 2012.[6]

Table 12.2 summarizes several studies of Jewish voting, briefly describing each survey and indicating the five most important predictors in each analysis.[7] Questions about Israel are among the five top predictors in all of these studies. As to be expected, party identification was the most important predictor of vote in every study. While the questions asked and included in the analysis differ across surveys, most found important either social issues (e.g., gay marriage) or thermometer ratings of evangelicals or the Tea Party. Table 12.2 demonstrates that Israel is not the main factor or even one of the two top predictors of Jews' voting but that it still plays a significant role in their vote decisions.

Conditional Effects. The Israel issue is likely to affect some types of Jews more than others. The ideological classification developed in the previous chapter is useful for exploring such differences. Table 12.3 employs that typology in showing the level of presidential approval for Barack Obama in the 2012 PRRI Jewish Values Survey and the 2013 Pew Jewish survey. An average of 1 would indicate that everyone approved his performance, while 0 would show that everyone disapproved.[8] As to be expected, Progressives, at the top of the table, most approved of Obama's presidential performance, while Traditionalists, at the bottom of the table, most disapproved. Libertarians and Communitarians are in the middle. Presidential approval would be strongly related to voting on reelection, so the order of Democratic voting in 2012 would likely approximate the pattern in the table.

Table 12.3 also classifies respondents on the basis of an index of attitudes on the Middle East, developed in the previous chapter. Those who expressed coexistence positions on both questions approved Obama's performance more than those with hard-line positions on both. Among Progressives, the largest of these ideological groups, there was strong approval of Obama's performance, though there was some slippage among Progressive hard-liners. By contrast, there was a considerable difference among Libertarians according to their stance on the Middle East, which is important since they constitute about a quarter of the Jews. Thus, issues concerning Israel had an impact on approval of Obama's performance, but the impact was conditioned on Jews' positions on domestic issues.

TABLE 12.2. Five Most Important Predictors in Studies of Jewish Voting

SURVEY:	NJDC	AJC	WC	J Street	J Street reanalysis
DATE:	Summer 2004	Autumn 2004	Spring 2012	Election day 2012	Election day 2012
MODE:	Internet panel	Telephone panel	Internet panel	Internet panel	Internet panel
MEASURE:	Vote intention	Vote intention	Vote intention	Reported vote	Reported vote
Largest	Party identification	Party identification	Party identification	Party identification	Party identification
Second	Evangelicals rating	Ideology	Social issues	Tea Party rating	Ideology
Third	Direction of country	Orthodox	Economic justice	Direction of country	U.S. role in peace talks
Fourth	Importance of Israel	Gay marriage	Economic issues	Income	Iran red line
Fifth	Health care	Gaza withdrawal	Israel attachment	Israel questions	Income
SOURCE:	Uslaner and Lichbach 2009	This chapter	Cohen and Abrams 2012	Uslaner 2015	This chapter

Summary. The evidence presented so far indicates that issues regarding Israel have an intermediate impact on Jews' voting. While most Jews will say that such issues are important in their voting decisions, few who are asked to select from a list of issues choose Middle East concerns as their most important issue. Attitudes on Israel and Palestine were significantly correlated with presidential approval and vote and are significant in the analysis of vote in the 2012 J Street survey. That impact varies across different types of Jews. The next step is to compare the importance of Israel with that of domestic issues, as a test of whether attitudes on Israel have an independent impact on Jewish voting.

The Role of Issues in Jewish Voting

While economic issues, social issues, and attitudes on Israel could all affect Jews' voting, few Jewish surveys include questions on all those topics. The 2012 PRRI and 2013 Pew surveys are the most complete in this regard.

TABLE 12.3. Approval of Obama by Domestic Issue Typology and Attitudes toward Middle East

	Pew		PRRI	
Progressive	.88		.80	
Coexistence		.91		.89
Mixed		.88		.77
Hard-line		.74		.66
Libertarian	.49		.46	
Coexistence		.63		.65
Mixed		.54		.50
Hard-line		.33		.26
Communitarian	.59		.44	
Coexistence		—		—
Mixed		.67		.53
Hard-line		—		.32
Traditionalist	.25		.17	
Coexistence		—		—
Mixed		.37		.26
Hard-line		.18		.10

Source: Analysis of the 2013 Pew Jewish survey and the 2012 Jewish Values Survey by the Public Religion Research Institute.

Note: Higher average values represent higher proportion approving of Obama's handling of his job. Results are shown only for categories that include at least 2% of U.S. Jews.

Neither asked about vote, but both asked whether respondents approved or disapproved of Barack Obama's performance as president. The PRRI survey was conducted a few months before the presidential election, and the Pew survey occurred a few months after the election, so those surveys' measure of presidential approval should closely correlate with how respondents voted on Obama's reelection. To put the 2012 election issues in context, Obama's position had "evolved" to support gay marriage that spring, the economy was recovering slowly from the Great Recession that Obama had inherited, and Republicans charged that the Obama administration was not sufficiently supportive of Israel.

Table 12.4 presents a parallel analysis of these two surveys, with the goal of checking the relative importance of the Middle East index versus the domestic questions. The first three columns for each study show the impact of each predictor on Obama approval, party identification, and liberal/conservative ideology, without using partisanship or ideology as

TABLE 12.4. Regression Analysis of Jews' Political Views

	Pew				PRRI			
Variable	Obama	Party identification	Ideology	Obama	Obama	Party identification	Ideology	Obama
Sizegovt/ reducegap	.34***	.36***	.34***	.10*	.33***	.37***	.33***	.10
Acceptgays/ gaymarriage	.16**	.21***	.17**	.02	.17**	.20**	.34***	.02
Middle East index	.15***	.21***	.16***	.03	.19***	.17***	.17***	.09*
Female	−.02	.10**	.07	−.08**	.03	.14**	.06	−.04
Education	.01	.01	.04	.00	.05	.00	.07	.04
Age	−.02	.03	.01	−.04	−.03	.11*	−.05	−.08*
Income	.02	.02	.03	.01	.08	.02	.05	.06
Orthodox	−.06	−.07	−.15**	.00	−.06	−.08	−.09	−.01
Conservative	−.04	−.02	−.11**	−.01	−.02	.01	−.13**	.00
Reform	−.03	.01	.00	−.03	.00	.00	−.10*	.01
Party identification				.52***				.47***
Ideology (3-category)				.12*				.16*

Source: Analysis of the 2013 Pew Jewish survey and the 2012 Jewish Values Survey by the Public Religion Research Institute.

Note: Values shown are beta coefficients. The baseline category is "just Jewish." Party identification in PRRI is 5-category.

***$p < .001$; **$p < .01$; *$p < .05$.

predictors. The last column in each block adds party identification and ideology as additional predictors of Obama approval.

Looking at the first column in each block, approval ratings for Obama depend, primarily, on the economic issue and, secondarily, on the social issue and the Middle East index, when party identification and ideology are not included in the equation. Similarly, the middle two columns in each block emphasize the economic issue's effect on Jews' party and ideological identifications but also show the significant effects of the social and Middle East issues. The economic question has the largest effect, serving as the main basis for Jews' political attitudes. Social/morality issues and the Middle East index generally have about half the impact of the economic issue, though the economic and social issues are equally important in the PRRI ideology column.

The rightmost column in each block in table 12.4 shows that ratings of Obama are significantly affected by partisanship and, to a lesser extent, by ideology. Attitudes on the Middle East have a significant (though small) direct effect on Obama approval in the PRRI survey, as does the Pew survey's question about size of government. While these issues do not have consistent significant effects in the rightmost column for each survey, they have substantial indirect effects through their impact on party and ideology. Jews who favor small government, oppose gay rights, and have hard-line positions on the Middle East are significantly more Republican and politically conservative, which, in turn, leads to lower approval of Obama and presumably to less likelihood of voting for his reelection.[9]

These two surveys allow direct comparisons of social issues versus matters related to Israel. Those who gave coexistence answers to both Middle East questions experienced little conflict in their politics, as only 5% gave the conservative answer as regards homosexuality. However, more than two-thirds of those who took hard-line stands on both Middle East issues were acceptant of homosexuality or same-sex marriage, and more of them are Democrats than Republicans. Thus, attitudes on domestic social issues seem to mitigate the political effects of hard-line views on policies concerning Israel.[10]

An "Attitude Triad" Theory. This analysis provides strong evidence that attitudes relating to Israel do affect the politics of Jews, above and beyond their attitudes on economic and social issues. Strictly speaking, these results apply only to the 2012–13 period, but the results suggest an "attitude triad" theory, which begins with two main points:

1. Economic attitudes are primary in influencing Jews' political positions. Jews' attitudes on these issues are not distinctive as compared to comparable non-Jews, but economic matters still provide a baseline for their party and ideological identifications.
2. Domestic social issues and Israel are secondary in influencing Jews' party identification and ideology and thus indirectly affecting their voting. Jews' attitudes on these topics are distinctive, so social issues and attitudes on Israel are the major factors leading to the distinctiveness of Jews' voting. While social issues and attitudes on Israel were equally important in the 2012 election, their relative importance could vary between elections, depending on current campaign issues.

A "Dueling Threats" Postulate. Social issues and attitudes on Israel can be seen as countervailing factors in Jews' voting, moving different group of Jew in opposite directions. These results suggest a "dueling threats" postulate: Jews who are most concerned with restrictive policies on social issues, threats to church-state separation, and the political power of the Christian right are moved in the Democratic and liberal direction, while Jews who are most concerned by threats to Israel's security from insufficient American support are moved in the Republican and conservative direction.

This postulate is based on an insightful article on Jews' voting intentions in the 2004 election in which Eric Uslaner and Mark Lichbach (2009) described the battle for Jewish votes as a "two-front war." George W. Bush was seeking another four years in office, against John Kerry, in a year in which prohibiting gay marriage was a ballot issue in several states. Analyzing a summer survey of Jews that was sponsored by the National Jewish Democratic Council, Uslaner and Lichbach found that attitudes on Israel and attitudes toward evangelicals were countervailing factors affecting vote intention, with the latter attitudes mattering more. The Israel issue pushed vote intentions toward the Republicans, but it impacted only a few Jewish voters. Uslaner and Lichbach emphasized that "for a much greater share of Jewish voters, the 'zero-sum' identity issue of evangelicals loomed much larger" (408), with negative feelings toward evangelicals pushing the Jewish vote in the Democratic direction.[11]

The analysis by Uslaner and Lichbach nicely captures the "dueling threats" postulate, according to which there are forces that push the voting of different groups of Jews in opposite directions. Some Jews' concern with Israel's security leads them to vote Republican, while Jews who are most concerned about evangelicals are more supportive of Democrats. Uslaner and Lichbach (2009, 401) consider Jews' concern with evangelicals to be largely due to their positions on church-state separation. Attitudes toward evangelicals would also be highly correlated with stands on social issues, though Uslaner and Lichbach found that attitudes on civil unions for gay couples did not have a significant effect on 2004 vote intentions.

The AJC survey that was conducted in late August 2004 confirms aspects of the "dueling threats" postulate. Gay marriage and attitudes on withdrawal of Israel from Gaza were both significant predictors of vote intentions, behind only partisanship, ideology, and being Orthodox (fig. 12.3). Orthodox Jews, those who opposed gay marriage, and those who opposed withdrawal from Gaza were more likely to vote Republican. Notably, viewing evangelicals as anti-Semitic was not significant in the AJC analysis, even though that study examined the same election as Uslaner and Lichbach. Still, the AJC results support the "dueling threats" postulate. involving attitudes on Israel versus a social issue.

Conclusions

Jews do not vote like everyone else. They have been voting distinctively Democratic for president. Additionally, their differences on Israel are related to their partisanship and their voting, as are their views on social and economic issues. When asked to choose from a list of issues, only about one-tenth of Jews choose Israel as their most important issue in voting, presumably those who are most supportive of Israel. Recall from the previous chapter that about one-tenth of Jews indicate that the Obama administration was too supportive of Israel, which suggests that the two opposite extremes on Israel among American Jews are fairly equally balanced. Even though few choose Israel as their most important issue in voting, most Jews tell pollsters that Israel is important in their voting. Issues related to

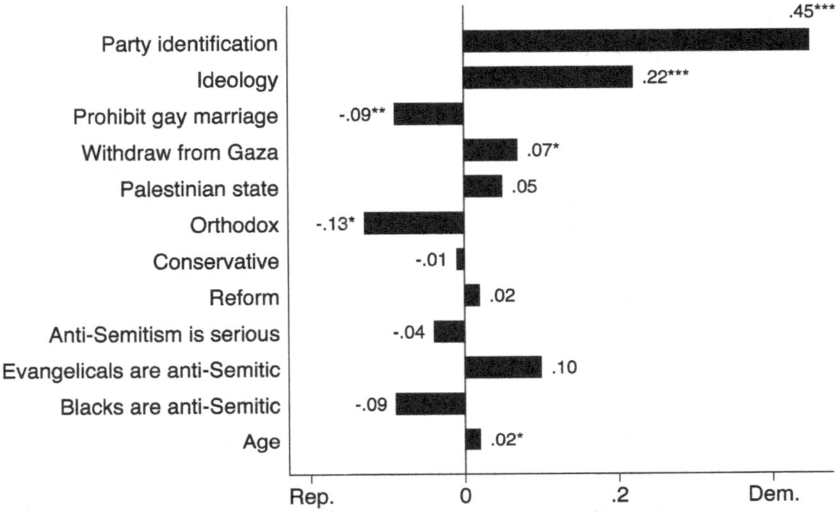

Fig. 12.3. Regression analysis of Jews' 2004 vote intention
(*Note:* Analysis of 2004 American Jewish Committee survey. Values are effect coefficients for logistic regression.)

Israel are correlated with their votes, and Israel-related issues are consistently among the five most important issues in different studies of Jews' voting. Equally critical, issues about Israel have also become incorporated into their party identification.

Three factors are crucial to understanding Jews' voting. First, attitudes on size of government and on reducing the gap between rich and poor serve as a baseline determinant of Jews' political positions. Jews' attitudes are not very distinctive on economic matters, but these economic views underpin their political positions, with economic liberals voting more Democratic and with economic conservatives tending more Republican. The other two crucial factors, attitudes on Israel and attitudes on social issues, operate as opposite potential forces that move Jews' votes off the economics baseline. Jews who focus particularly on the security threat to Israel vote more Republican, while those most concerned with a domestic threat—from a combination of the Christian right, decreased church-state separation, and cultural/morality regulations—vote more Democratic. Later studies may alter the conclusions reached in this chapter as to the relative importance for Jews of economic issues, social issues, and attitudes about Israel, but at least these results counter claims that Israel is not a relevant factor in Jews' voting.

Finding that attitudes about Israel affect some Jews' voting does not mean that American Jews vote the way that Israelis want. Quite to the contrary, for example, most Israeli Jews questioned why American Jews were not voting for Mitt Romney in 2012 and for Donald Trump in 2016. Attitudes on Israel have effects in both directions: hard-liners are more Republican, while those who believe that coexistence between Israel and an independent Palestinian state is possible are more Democratic. The latter are more numerous than the former.

In any case, the survey results analyzed in this chapter challenge the usual view that Israel is not a voting issue among Jews. It is a voting issue, just not *the* voting issue. It is among the factors that affect Jews' votes, although it is definitely not the main basis for how most Jews vote. The next chapter considers the possibilities for political realignment of Jewish voters, along with how attitudes about Israel affect those possibilities.

CHAPTER 13

Still Waiting for Realignment

Every presidential election campaign during the last several decades has provoked speculation about whether the Jewish vote would finally realign toward the Republicans (e.g., Himmelfarb 1981; Friedman 2003). Jews voted Republican in some state and local elections in the mid-20th century (Fisher 1979, 116), but the growing political polarization in recent years has made defection from Democratic partisanship less common even at those levels. Meanwhile, Jews' presidential voting has changed little. Whenever it has looked like the long-awaited realignment was beginning to occur, circumstances have intervened to bring Jews back solidly into the Democratic camp. As Shapiro (2000) suggested, waiting for American Jews to change politically has become reminiscent of playwright Samuel Beckett having Vladimir and Estragon wait endlessly for the arrival of Godot.

While Jews have not realigned, the previous chapters have highlighted several fissures that have opened up in Jews' voting patterns. Orthodox Jews are more politically conservative and Republican, as are Jews from the former Soviet Union. People occupied professionally and in business management also are somewhat more politically conservative. There are indications of higher-income people voting somewhat more Republican than other Jews, as evidenced by the significance of income in the preceding chapter's analysis of data from the 2012 J Street survey (see fig. 12.2). The old liberal/conservative split has become multifaceted, with Libertarian Jews split in their politics. Furthermore, there is a serious fracture among American Jews on supporting the Israeli government's policies. These several splits create an opening for realignment.

This chapter begins with a brief recapitulation of Jewish voting history, followed by discussion of the nature of realignments and that nature's implications for Jewish voting. The chapter argues that expectations for Jews' realigning are based on an oversimplification about how their voting changed in New Deal days, along with insufficient appreciation of the forces that lead to partisan realignment. The second half of this chapter focuses directly on groups of Jews that could realign, especially millennials, Orthodox and Conservative Jews, and Libertarians. It considers the factors that could lead them to realign and the factors that hamper their changing parties.

Jewish Presidential Voting History

In 1944, after upward of 90% of Jews had voted Democratic in the two preceding presidential elections, Judge Jonah J. Goldstein famously stated, in a Yiddish play on words, "The Jews have three *velten* [worlds]: *di velt* [this world], *yene velt* [the next world], and Roosevelt." By the 1948 election, however, pollster Sam Lubell (1951) described his Jewish respondents as feeling lost at Roosevelt's death and as moving away from the Democratic Party. According to a recent reconstruction, only 54% voted for Truman that year (Weisberg 2012). Though not at the level of the Roosevelt years, the Jewish vote remained Democratic through the Eisenhower-Stevenson contests of the 1950s. With many Jews moving to the suburbs, there was some speculation that they would shift to voting Republican, but their vote for Democratic presidential candidates bounced back up in the 1960s elections.

There was renewed attention to the Jewish vote in the 1970s, as other parts of the New Deal coalition were pulling away from the Democratic Party. Jews' vote for Democratic candidates fell that decade and then went below 50%, for the first time in nearly half a century, when Jimmy Carter ran for reelection in 1980. Though Republicans thought the fall meant that Jews were ready to realign, Jewish support for Reagan instead decreased a few percentage points in 1984 according to the regular exit poll. Republicans commissioned a special exit poll of Jews in 1984, emphasizing strongly Jewish precincts. Their poll showed an increase in the Republican vote by Jews, but a response memo written by Reagan's pollsters discredited that poll as a nonprobability sample, since Jews who live in mainly Jewish areas are different from those who do not (Weisberg 2012).

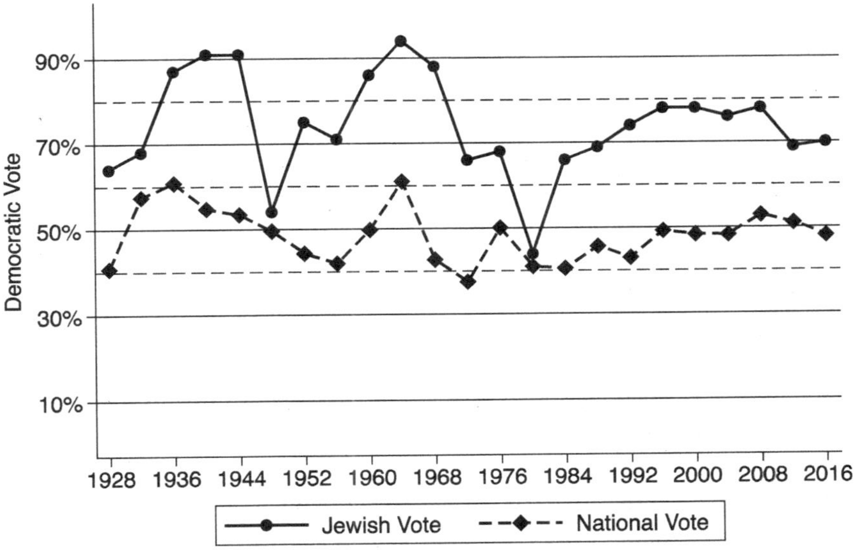

Fig. 13.1. Democratic presidential vote, 1928–2016
(*Source:* Updated from Weisberg 2012.)

Instead of realigning, the Jewish vote for Democratic candidates went back up in 1992–2008 (fig. 13.1).[1] This timing coincided with the Christian right becoming more associated with the Republican Party (see chaps. 5 and 7). The Moral Majority movement in the 1980s, Pat Buchanan's "Culture War" speech at the 1992 Republican convention, and the selection of Sarah Palin as the GOP candidate for vice president in 2008 all linked the Republican Party with conservative positions on cultural issues in the minds of many Jews. The religion-infused campaigns for the Republican presidential nomination by Pat Robertson in 1988, Pat Buchanan in 1992, Mike Huckabee in 2008, and Ben Carson in 2016 served to reinforce most Jews' identification with the Democratic Party at a time when the New Deal origin of that identification had lost its motivating power. As Cohen and Blitzer (2008, 4) insightfully wrote, "To many Jews, a more overtly Christian America or a more moralistic America translates into an America that may be less accepting of difference in general and of Jews in particular."

For Obama's reelection in 2012, the Democratic vote went down slightly among Jews, as it did among the public as a whole. It looked like Jews' affinity toward the Democrats might be declining back to the level of the 1970s and 1980s. But in 2016, as is discussed in chapter 14, the Democratic vote stayed steady, while declining a few percentage points among the general public.

The Basis of Realignments

The usual story is that Jews had been voting Republican up through the mid-1920s and then switched over to the Democratic Party to support Franklin Roosevelt's attempts to tame the Great Depression. However, that story is incomplete, because it does not take account of the mechanisms underlying party realignments. The usual mechanisms include conversion, mobilization, and generational and group influences.

Conversion versus Mobilization. Analyses by Kristi Andersen (1979) and John Petrocik (1981) find that the New Deal realignment was not based on conversion of Republicans into Democrats. Party identification is usually resistant to change, so most people who had been voting Republican through the 1910s and 1920s would not have changed parties, regardless of the Great Depression. Instead, Andersen and Petrocik show that the New Deal realignment involved mobilizing previous nonvoters into the Democratic Party.

There was massive immigration to America from the 1880s through 1924. Several studies have demonstrated that many of the new immigrants had not become citizens and therefore could not have started voting.[2] Similarly, many newly enfranchised women did not start voting immediately in 1920, so they were potential targets for mobilization. Most establishment German Jews who had been voting Republican would likely have continued doing so, while new Russian Jewish immigrants and Jewish women who had not been voting were being mobilized into the Democratic Party. Gerald Gamm (1989) documented, for example, that voting turnout in Boston's Jewish areas was low through the early 1930s and did not jump up until 1936, after Roosevelt began battling the Depression aggressively. Gamm found that some conversion to the Democratic side occurred in Boston, especially among Jewish men in the early part of the realignment, but that mobilization of new voters could explain most of the increased Democratic vote for Jewish women.

Conversion of people from one party to another is always difficult, and the high degree of partisan polarization today makes it even harder to accomplish. Even a mobilization-based realignment of Jews would be unlikely today, because most Jews already vote. Increased mobilization of young Jews might be possible, since the voting rate of young people is generally low. But on the whole, political realignment of Jews would have to depend on other factors.

Generational Theory of Realignment. There have been claims that American politics realign in cycles of about 28 to 36 years (Sellers 1965). This cyclical theory implied that realignment was due in the late 1960s or early 1970s. While that was a time of considerable political turmoil, national politics did not realign. Instead, a weakening of party ties occurred. Paul Allen Beck's (1979) generational theory of partisan change helps explain this development.

Beck's theory suggests that the children who grow up during a political realignment period will follow their parents politically but that the subsequent (third) generation will not care about the issues that caused the realignment. In the instance under consideration here, the Great Depression was too far in the past to matter to the generation that came of political age during the 1960s and 1970s. They were instead "ripe for realignment," ready to change their party loyalties if a new issue arose. If no such issue emerged, many in that third generation would become Independents, creating what is termed a "political dealignment." Thus, the Vietnam War and the Watergate cover-up did not cause party realignment but increased public cynicism about politics and fueled political independence among young people. Issue change also occurred around that time, with New Deal economics becoming less important and with social issues like abortion receiving more attention. This shift fits with the findings in chapter 8 that Jews are no longer distinctively liberal on economic issues but are distinctively liberal on morality issues.

Polls of Jews' partisan leanings after 1968 found some movement away from the Democrats. But a funny thing happened on their way to the GOP party: the Republican Party changed—the party of the business establishment became a religiously conservative party. That change attracted many Orthodox Jews, but it did not attract young non-Orthodox Jews. Most Jews remained Democratic because the Democratic Party became the liberal party on cultural issues, as it had been on 1930s economic issues. Some young Jews became Independents who usually voted Democratic for president. Still, the generational theory may imply that it is time for another realignment in the 2010s, with economic inequality and resentment being potential realigning issues.

Social Group Realignments. Realignment of a social group is difficult if the group's members have come to see their party identification as part of their group's social identity. A politics of tradition then develops, in which members of the social group reinforce each other's partisan ties. Under those circumstances, conversion to the other party becomes very unlikely, unless the group's own party pushes the group's members out by acting against their subjective self-interest.

The realignments of blacks and southern whites starting in the mid-1960s illustrate how social groups can convert politically. To the extent to which blacks could vote before the 1965 Voting Rights Act, they split between the two parties. However, blacks who had been voting Republican felt that they were pushed out of their party when the GOP nominated Senator Barry Goldwater for president, after he had voted against the Civil Rights Act of 1964 that outlawed discrimination in public accommodations and employment. At the same time, the Democratic Party's role in passing civil rights legislation caused southern whites to see the Democratic Party as not representing their interests as much as it had in the past, and they were attracted by the Republican Party's "southern strategy." For both blacks and southern whites, the policy changes that motivated their party switch involved their party deserting them on an issue that was central to their subjective self-interest.

Blacks quickly moved over to the Democratic side, but the realignment of white southerners took several decades. Many white southerners did not change parties until their states' prominent white politicians switched parties, which made clear to their constituents that it was acceptable to be Republicans. That gradual realignment of white southerners is known as a "secular realignment," in contrast to the more dramatic, "critical realignment" of blacks that occurred when a sudden event precipitated a sharp change.

The realignments of blacks and southern whites show three aspects of party change by a social group: (1) it is based on the group's feeling that it has been pushed out of its party, along with the pull of the other party, (2) it may take several elections to reach full fruition, and (3) it is accelerated when major politicians belonging to that group switch parties. Those elements have not been evident for American Jews. Some Jews began to feel pushed out of the Democratic Party in the 1980s, when Jesse Jackson was running for the Democratic presidential nomination, but Pat Robertson's campaign for the Republican presidential nomination neutralized the pull that Jews might have felt from the GOP side. By the 2012 election, there were claims that the Obama administration was not sufficiently protecting Israel against the potential existential threat of Iran building nuclear weapons. However, that threat was not direct enough for most Jews to view the Democrats as having deserted them concerning Israel, particularly when Obama had given Israel access to the Iron Dome technology to protect itself against incoming missiles. The debate in 2015 as to whether Congress should block the implementation of the multinational nuclear accord with Iran split the Jewish community, with conflicting polls on the sentiment of rank-and-file Jews. Some Jewish Democrats in Congress opposed the accord, but none switched parties.

The lack of prominent Jewish Republicans also serves as a restraint on Jews thinking of switching parties. The most successful Jewish Republican in modern times was Eric Cantor, the first Jew to be House majority leader. He could have been a role model for Jews in the Republican Party if he had moved up to become the first Jewish Speaker of the House. However, that possibility disappeared when he lost his party's 2014 congressional primary to a Tea Party Republican who emphasized his own religion during the campaign. Other leading Jewish Republicans do not have the cachet that Cantor would have had to attract Jews to the GOP.[3]

By contrast, Jews' Democratic partisanship is reinforced by Jews in high elective office being primarily Democrats, including all 9 Jewish senators and all but 2 of the two dozen Jewish members of the House of Representatives after the 2018 election. Moreover, Jews have attained high roles in the Democratic Party. Senator Joseph Lieberman (CT) became the most successful Jewish politician when the Democratic Party nominated him for vice president in 2000.[4] Not only did Bernie Sanders make a strong run for the 2016 Democratic presidential nomination, but 2017 opened with Democrat Charles (Chuck) Schumer becoming the first Jew to serve as Senate minority leader.

Converting Jews to Republicanism

Conversion to the Republican Party has long been discussed in terms of socioeconomic convergence of Jews with the rest of the electorate, with higher-income Jews becoming more Republican than lower-income Jews, as is the case among non-Jews. Sigelman (1991a, 991) was speaking of economic voting by Jews when he wrote, "Jews are simply not that politically distinctive, and as they become more and more integrated into the American mainstream . . . their erstwhile distinctiveness fades into sameness." While the fading Sigelman wrote about has been very slow, there is some evidence of higher-income Jews voting more Republican than lower-income Jews (see chaps. 4 and 12).

Conversion also depends on Jews' values and self-interest, as well as the interplay between the two. For example, many younger Jews since the 1960s have been postmaterialist, but that could change if new generations have difficulty getting jobs that are as good as those of their parents. Another possibility is that American Jews' view that their self-interest requires a high wall of separation between church and state may change as more Jews want government aid for their religious day schools. Additionally, how best to achieve the goal of a secure State of Israel could motivate realignment, particularly if the Democratic Party becomes more positive toward the Palestinian movement, though there is still considerable disagreement among American Jews about which policies would make Israel most secure.

John Zaller (1992) has proposed a theory of public opinion that is relevant to why Jews have not converted to become Republicans. He sees public opinion as being affected by exposure to elite discussion. People who are interested in politics are more likely to receive elite messages, though they are unlikely to accept messages that are inconsistent with their preexisting attitudes. What particularly matters in Zaller's theory is whether the messages that people receive come from just one side of political debates or from both sides. There is little reason to reassess one's political positions when political messages in a homogenous community are primarily one-sided; political conversion is unlikely until one also hears credible messages from the other side. Ryan and Milazzo (2015) used this point in explaining partisan change among Catholics, attributing their decreased Democratic identification to Catholics moving from homogeneously Democratic northern cities to Republican suburbs and to the South, where they heard pro-Republican messages.

In accord with Zaller's theory, the large majority of Jews whose family and friends are predominantly Democratic have had little reason to reconsider their political positions. The 2015 debate over the Iran nuclear agreement was a significant exception. While there was Jewish support for the accord, there were vigorous arguments against the pact by important Jewish voices, including the American Israel Public Affairs Committee and the Anti-Defamation League. Some prominent Jewish members of Congress came out against the accord. Jewish members who ultimately supported the agreement conceded that it had problems needing remedies, though they argued that defeating it would have worse consequences. Thus, even Democratic Jews heard a clear message of weaknesses in the Iran accord, creating the possibility that those Jews might reconsider their support for the Democrats. Indeed, one line of thinking is that Bibi Netanyahu's real aim was to create a realignment of Jews so that the American Jewish community would end up in a Republican camp that is more unconditionally acceptant of Israel's policies.

The controversy over the Iran nuclear agreement was not enough to dislodge most American Jews from their ties to the Democratic Party. The consensus among the polls with the most transparent sampling (see chap. 9) was that Jews were either supportive of the accord or evenly split. In any case, as is discussed in the next chapter of the present study, the unusual nature of Donald Trump's candidacy stole attention away from Republican attempts to use the Iran agreement as a wedge issue in the 2016 election.

Potential Realignment Targets

The groups of Jews with the greatest potential to change their partisanship are millennials, Orthodox and Conservative Jews, and Libertarians. Here again, generational and group influences are active realignment mechanisms.

Millennials. Young people are particular important to group realignment, because they may be motivated by different national problems than concerned earlier generations. Older Jews have voted strongly Democratic, but their generation is being replaced by the millennial generation, which is more universalistic on social and economic issues but also less viscerally attached to Israel. Many young people are politically independent when they join the electorate, so mobilizing them into a party could shift the partisan balance of Jews. A complicating factor is that the higher fertility rate of Orthodox Jews means that young Jews are disproportionately Orthodox, which may counterbalance the Democratic and liberal direction of non-Orthodox millennials. The continued growth of the Orthodox branch of Judaism could give the Republicans a considerable boost, though demographic-based realignment is so gradual that it can easily be overridden by unforeseen future events.

How sizable are generational differences on politics among Jews? The 2013 Pew Jewish survey and the 2012 PRRI Jewish Values Survey were large enough to permit comparing Jews across generations.[5] Jews' political attitudes are remarkably similar across generations in both the Pew and PRRI surveys (tables 13.1 and 13.2, respectively). All generations are predominantly Democratic; none are politically conservative. The younger generations are not particularly distinctive ideologically, even though 10% of the Pew sample of millennial and Gen X Jews are ultra-Orthodox, compared to just 3% of older Jews.[6]

The two surveys agree that all generations of Jews are very liberal on social issues and are liberal on economic issues (see also Abrams and Cohen 2016, 116–17). The overriding conclusion is that millennials and Gen Xers have replicated the liberal attitudes of their parents and grandparents.

TABLE 13.1. Political Attitudes by Generation, Pew Survey

Generation	Year born	Age in 2013	Republican v. Democrat	Political conservative v. liberal	Accept homosexuality	More government services
Millennial	1981–	19–32	21%–73%	18%–52%	88%	64%
Gen X	1965–80	33–48	24%–66%	18%–46%	82%	51%
Boomer	1946–64	49–67	23%–72%	21%–50%	83%	54%
"Silent" and "Greatest"	–1945	68+	21%–71%	20%–46%	84%	56%

Source: Analysis of the 2013 Pew Jewish survey.

TABLE 13.2. Political Attitudes by Generation, PRRI Survey

Generation	Year born	Age in 2012	Republican v. Democrat	Political conservative v. liberal	Legalize gay marriage	Legalize abortion mostly	Reduce income gap
Millennial	1981–	19–31	34%–66%	19%–55%	85%	90%	66%
Gen X	1965–80	32–47	32%–68%	16%–45%	85%	92%	63%
Boomer	1946–64	49–66	28%–72%	19%–42%	82%	95%	63%
"Silent" and "Greatest"	–1945	67+	22%–78%	19%–41%	75%	96%	66%

Source: Analysis of the 2012 Jewish Values Survey by the Public Religion Research Institute.

Generation replacement has not materially modified Jews' politics. Jews may be less liberal on economic issues than in the 1930s and 1940s, but issue replacement has kept them on the very liberal side of politics, with even the older generations accepting liberal positions on new social issues.

The spring 2013 Pew survey did not find generational differences in evaluations of Barack Obama's job performance, with approval near 70% in every generation, including millennials. The 2012 Cooperative Congressional Election Study (CCES) found that 70% of Jews under 30 years of age voted for Obama's reelection, so even with their larger concentration of Orthodox, young Jews did not pull the Jewish vote toward the Republican side.

Are young Jews likely to realign? The non-Orthodox might be drawn to the Republicans by an economic program that would increase their chances to obtain good jobs as they enter the job market. However, surveys suggest that they would not be attracted by the Republicans' conservative morality stands and hard-line positions on Israel's disputes with the Palestinians and Iran.

The larger question is whether the young generation will become engaged in Jewish topics. The causes that mobilized young Jews in earlier decades are no longer as relevant to the current generation of young Jews. Even support for Israel is weaker among young Jews, though the Birthright program of free trips to Israel may help increase that support. Most Jewish organizations have been "defensive," as in the Anti-Defamation League's work against anti-Semitism, but the younger generation has shown less interest in defensive organizations. To the extent that they are interested in "organized Judaism," Waxman (2016, chap. 6) finds that their interest is in "positive organizations" focused on social justice, the environment, and similar causes, such as the efforts of Mazon to end hunger in the United States and Israel (see also Barnett 2016, 234–42, on international humanitarianism). How this focus of young people on positive organizations will translate into politics remains to be seen.

Orthodox Jews. The Orthodox would be a likely source for further party conversion and increased political mobilization, because they are the most politically distinctive segment of the American Jewish community. The 2013 Pew survey found 41% of Orthodox saying that they are Republican when first asked, going up to 58% when Independents are asked to which party they are closer.[7] These figures are much higher than for the other branches of Judaism, but there is still room for considerable movement into the Republican Party. However, evidence about Orthodox politics is somewhat mixed, partly because the ultra-Orthodox are a difficult group to survey. Those who separate themselves from secular society would have been underrepresented in the early AJC surveys that relied on consumer panels, and they are also unlikely to agree to participate in election-day surveys. The Pew survey's repeated phone attempts increased the likelihood of obtaining Orthodox respondents, though the ultra-Orthodox might still not have been completely surveyed.[8]

Most of the data on Orthodox voting is based on election results in predominantly Orthodox precincts, though those precincts generally also contain some non-Orthodox Jews and some non-Jews (Fingerhut 2008). In early references to the politics of the Orthodox as distinctive, Liebman (1973) pointed out that they were more conservative on matters such as abortion and homosexuality, and Maller (1977) mentioned that they were voting more Republican in 1969 municipal elections in New York City and Los Angeles. Change was noticed when Hasidic areas in New York City voted strongly Republican for president in the 1970s and 1980s (Hertzberg 1985; Himmelfarb 1989; Balinska 1988, cited in Sigelman 1991b, 200–201), though there are accounts that Modern Orthodox areas voted Democratic in some of those elections. A 1984 poll by the National Jewish Coalition for Reagan-Bush found that 59% of Orthodox Jews and 94% of Hasidic Jews voted for Reagan (Weisberg 2012). A poll by Market Opinion Research found that George H. W. Bush received 75% of the 1988 Orthodox vote (Carroll 1988). Since the Orthodox were the only Jewish denomination that followed the nation in voting Republican in those years, Shapiro (1992, 219) wrily observed, "Paradoxically, the Orthodox appeared politically 'more American' and 'less Jewish' than the non-Orthodox."

Ultra-Orthodox precincts voted Democratic in 2000 when Senator Joseph Lieberman, an Orthodox Jew, was the Democratic nominee for vice president (Fingerhut 2008). Most of those precincts voted Republican in 2004, though their 2008 vote was more mixed (Fingerhut 2008). In one of the most complete analyses of Orthodox precincts, Rocklin (2017) compared ultra-Orthodox and Modern Orthodox voting starting in the 2000 presidential election. There were large shifts in several ultra-Orthodox neighborhoods, such as in Monsey, New York, which went from voting about 50% for each major party in 2000 to voting around 90% Republican in the following three elections. Modern Orthodox precincts also increased their Republican vote after 2000, but most did not increase to a level as high as the precinct in Teaneck, New Jersey, which jumped from 15% Republican in 2000 to around 60% thereafter.

While the 2013 Pew survey did not ask about voting, 62% of the Orthodox disapproved of Obama's performance as president, which likely means that most voted against him five months earlier.[9] The responses of Orthodox Jews on political issues were less conservative than might be expected. One-third of them wanted a larger government with more services, one-third favored society accepting homosexuality, and one-third felt that Israel could coexist peacefully with an independent Palestinian state (see the left half of table 13.3). Those with liberal views on these issues were mostly Democrats. Those who had conservative positions on the same issues were mostly Republicans but were not overwhelmingly so, which creates a possibility for the GOP to convert more Orthodox voters to their party.[10]

TABLE 13.3. Partisanship of Orthodox and Conservative Jews by Their Issue Positions

	Orthodox Jews			Conservative Jews		
	% with this position	Party identification		% with this position	Party identification	
		% Dem.	% Rep.		% Dem.	% Rep.
Favor more federal government services	35%	63%	29%	50%	82%	14%
Favor smaller federal government	61%	21%	74%	42%	38%	47%
Favor accepting homosexuality	34%	62%	32%	81%	73%	20%
Favor discouraging homosexuality	62%	23%	71%	15%	37%	62%
Israel and Palestine could coexist	32%	56%	38%	66%	70%	21%
Israel and Palestine could not coexist	64%	27%	67%	32%	52%	37%
Settlements hurt peace prospects	16%	50%	49%	36%	82%	11%
Settlements neither help nor hurt	50%	36%	54%	41%	60%	28%
Settlements help peace prospects	34%	29%	66%	23%	44%	49%

Source: Analysis of the 2013 Pew Jewish survey.

An important aspect of ultra-Orthodox voting is that the rabbis of some Hasidic sects negotiate with political leaders on behalf of their followers. That has resulted in virtually unanimous bloc voting by those sects in some elections, especially local elections in a few New York communities. That pattern creates opportunities for Republicans to gain votes among the ultra-Orthodox, though Hillary Clinton's 2000 Senate campaign and 2016 presidential campaign showed that Democratic candidates could attract some sects (Nathan-Kazis 2016).

Studies have not examined the extent to which ultra-Orthodox women vote. In other religious communities that have limited contact with the secular world, women generally participate in politics less than men. If ultra-Orthodox women vote at lower rates, they might be among the "missing Republicans" who could be mobilized into Republican voting.

Non-Orthodox Jews. While the Orthodox are trending Republican already, the much more numerous non-Orthodox have kept Jews in the Democratic camp. In the Pew survey, 54% of Jews who identify with the Conservative movement said they were Democrats when first asked, 65% when asked to which party they were closer. Only 15% first said they were Republican, 27% when pushed to choose between the parties. Their partisanship has been relatively stable (see my compilation of poll results in Fulcrum table A).

The right half of table 13.3 shows the issue stands of Conservative Jews. They are only somewhat more liberal than the Orthodox on size of the federal government. Those who feel that the settlements help the peace process are evenly split between the two parties, but those who believe that Israel and a Palestinian state could not coexist peacefully are still more Democratic than Republican. Both their focus on Israel and the substantial minority who favor a smaller government provide opportunities for the Republican Party to make inroads among Jews who belong to the Conservative movement. Yet many Conservative Jews are older and therefore less likely to change long-standing partisan ties.[11]

Other non-Orthodox Jews are less likely to convert politically. Pew found that Democrats outnumbered Republicans 63% to 10% when Reform Jews were asked if they are Republican, Democratic, or Independent, 78% to 17% when leaners are included. Surveys since 2000 have been consistent in finding that less than one-sixth of Reform Jews initially answer that they are Republican. Surveys (see the post-1990 results compiled in Fulcrum table A) consistently show that Reform Jews are more Democratic and less Republican than Conservative Jews, though that difference is generally within 10 percentage points. The nondenominational "just Jewish" are also heavily Democratic, 75% Democratic to 15% Republican in the Pew data.

The issue stands of Reform Jews and the "just Jewish" are generally within a few percentage points of one another (table 13.4). Both are more liberal than Conservative Jews, though one-third of both groups favor a smaller federal government that provides fewer services. There are large partisan differences between those who take liberal and conservative positions on domestic issues. The issue positions of most Reform Jews and the "just Jewish" make them unlikely to convert to the Republican Party, though those favoring small government are already not strongly Democratic.

Libertarian Jews. Jews who oppose "big government" have received little attention in previous studies of Jews' politics. These Jews include doctors

TABLE 13.4. Partisanship of Reform Jews and the "Just Jewish" by Their Issue Positions

	Reform Jews			Just Jewish		
		Party identification			Party identification	
	% with this position	% Dem.	% Rep.	% with this position	% Dem.	% Rep.
Favor more government services	58%	96%	2%	62%	87%	6%
Favor smaller federal government	37%	49%	41%	35%	54%	32%
Favor accepting homosexuality	93%	81%	13%	88%	79%	12%
Favor discouraging homosexuality	4%	17%	74%	9%	47%	34%
Israel and Palestine could coexist	61%	85%	10%	74%	80%	10%
Israel and Palestine could not coexist	36%	64%	29%	25%	64%	23%
Settlements hurt peace prospects	51%	89%	7%	48%	86%	6%
Settlements neither help nor hurt	36%	66%	26%	39%	67%	19%
Settlements help peace prospects	13%	64%	29%	13%	55%	34%

Source: Analysis of the 2013 Pew Jewish survey.

and lawyers who complain about high taxes or about progressive taxation, as well as businesspeople who object to government overregulation. Those complaints sometimes extend to arguing that labor unions have too much power or to objections to government welfare programs. These complaints are usually associated with political conservatives, but most small-government Jews are not traditional on moral issues and do not challenge the Supreme Court's liberal decisions on abortion and gay marriage. As described in chapter 11, these small-government social liberals can be termed "Libertarians," because they favor minimal government regulation of both the economic and morality realms. Estimates based on the Pew and PRRI surveys put one-quarter of Jews into this category, which is a plausible estimate because many Jews are professionals or businesspeople.

As shown earlier, Libertarian Jews are in the middle on partisanship, and their party identification varies more with their positions on Middle East policy than is the case for the other categories of Jews. They are ripe for political change, though it could be in either direction. If they become Republicans, it would probably be because of their desire for small government with low taxes; if they instead become more Democratic, it would likely be due to their liberal views on moral issues. Also, some might be pulled over to one side or the other on the basis of their views on Middle East issues.

Forces of Partisan Stability

While millennials, the Orthodox, members of the Conservative movement, and Libertarians might be likely targets for partisan change, there are still strong forces keeping Jews' partisanship stable. Social issues, like abortion and gay rights, give the Democrats considerable advantages among the non-Orthodox. Science issues also continue to work in their favor. The more Democrats focus on morality and science issues, the more likely it is that they can maintain their sizable majority among Jews and keep non-Orthodox millennials from going over to the Republican side. Fortunately for the Democrats, it is difficult for the GOP to change the ingrained Democratic partisanship of older Jews, and potential Republican near-term gains among the Orthodox are limited by their relatively small size.

Yet the Democratic Party has to wend its way carefully around two potential danger spots. One has to do with economic justice. The Democratic left emphasizes reducing the income gap that has grown between the rich and the poor. Many Jews strongly support economic justice, but that emphasis could push Libertarians out of the Democratic Party. The second potential danger spot for the Democratic Party is the Palestinian issue. Sympathy for the Palestinians has increased among the Democratic left, along with support for a more evenhanded American policy in the Middle East. Many American Jews are dissatisfied with Israeli policies, though most would be upset if American support for Israel's security were decreased. Additionally, Jews who support Israel unconditionally will watch how congressional Democrats respond to the Boycott, Divestment, Sanctions (BDS) movement.

Himmelfarb (1978, 305) argued that for Jews to remain liberal, it would be necessary for the "left of center to be at least not anti-Jewish." Similarly, continued support by Jews for the Democratic Party requires it to avoid taking stands that can be depicted as anti-Israel. In 2012 and 2016, platform disputes about U.S. policy toward Israel had the potential of alienating many of the Democratic Party's Jewish supporters. These incidents were forgotten once the party retained its usual platform planks, but they demonstrate that the Democratic Party is not as cohesively pro-Israel as the Republican Party. How the Palestinian issue is framed will determine whether it pushes many Jews to leave the Democratic Party.

Conclusions

Jews are the one part of Franklin Delano Roosevelt's New Deal coalition that has not yet left the Democratic Party. Political analysts have long waited for Jews to realign toward the Republican Party, but that has not yet occurred. Jews' level of Democratic presidential voting has gone up and down over the years. In the 2010s, it was back to its 1932 level. Mobilization of nonvoters into the electorate was crucial to the New Deal realignment of the 1930s, but there are too few Jewish nonvoters for such a dynamic to realign them into the Republican Party today. Instead, dramatic realignment of Jews would occur only if they felt pushed out of the Democratic Party, with prominent Jewish Democratic politicians leading the party switch.

As previous chapters have shown, the main reason that more Jews are not Republicans is the nature of the Republican Party, with its stances on cultural issues and its closeness to evangelicals. Still, the Republican Party's stands on economic issues and on Israel could attract more Jews. On the one hand, if the Democratic Party becomes focused on eliminating economic inequality, that might make well-off Libertarian Jews feel deserted by their party. A major impediment to Jews voting more Republican would be removed if cultural issues recede in importance. On the other hand, if the Republican Party nominates a presidential candidate who speaks of moving the government in a more theocratic direction, Jewish Republicans might move over to the Democratic side. In any case, most Jews consider it safe, at least for the moment, to remain with their current politicized social identity, without feeling that their self-interest is threatened enough to make them switch parties.

In the end, waiting for Jews to realign politically may be as endless as waiting for Godot. Indeed, distinguished Yale political scientist David Mayhew (2002) has argued that the very concept of political realignment is not useful, because political change is more of a gradual process. Furthermore, it is rare for a political party to radically change its policies on a matter that is essential to the self-interest of one of its constituent groups.

Theoretically, the fissures among Jews create an opening for voting change, but what always matters is how the choice of presidential nominees and their campaigns take advantage of such opportunities. Whereas party positions on most issues of special interest to Jews have been relatively stable over the past several presidential elections, that stability was upset in 2016, both because a strong candidate for the Democratic nomination departed from the usual Democratic playbook and because the Republican nominee embodied a dramatic departure from Republican Party orthodoxy. The next chapter of this study turns directly to the 2016 presidential election, to examine, first, how Jews responded to the challenges that campaign generated and, second, how Donald Trump's election may impact their future voting.

CHAPTER 14

The 2016 Election and Beyond

The 2016 presidential election confirmed the political mainstreaming of American Jews. There were previous contests in which a candidate had a Jewish grandparent, spouse, or brother or in which a Jewish person was nominated for vice president, but the 2016 election was the first in which both major-party candidates had Jewish sons-in-law and in which a Jew strongly contested the party's presidential nomination. That election also had a potential that transcended even those remarkable firsts.

The 2016 election could have upended the period of "normal politics" for Jewish Americans that had lasted from 1928 through 2012. As seen in the previous chapters, there were already fissures in Jewish support for the Democrats. With the rocky relations between the United States and Israel during the Obama presidency, particularly concerning the Iran nuclear accord, there was a greater chance than usual of change in Jews' politics. Regardless of this potential for change, the Jewish vote stayed remarkably stable.

This chapter begins by reviewing the role of Jewish candidates prior to 2016, as a prelude to considering the Jewish connections of the 2016 candidates. It then examines the 2016 primaries and general election campaign, summarizes Jewish voting in that year, and discusses the post-election period, including the election's implications for both Middle East policy and anti-Semitism. The chapter ends with a discussion of the future of Jews' voting in the aftermath of Donald Trump's presidential victory.

Jews in Pre-2016 Presidential Politics

Jews played an increasingly prominent role in presidential politics in the 13 elections from 1964 through 2012. The first candidate with a known Jewish heritage was Barry Goldwater, the 1964 Republican nominee; his paternal grandfather, Michael, was Jewish, though this heritage did not play a role in the election. The run of Pennsylvania governor Milton Shapp for the 1976 Democratic nomination was the first attempted presidential candidacy by a Jewish person, but he did not excite any interest in the primaries that year. The first candidate with a Jew in his immediate family was Michael Dukakis, the 1988 Democratic nominee whose wife, Katherine (Kitty), was Jewish; there is no reason to believe that connection affected how Jews voted. The 1996 run of Pennsylvania senator Arlen Specter for the Republican nomination was as unsuccessful as Shapp's two decades earlier.

A breakthrough occurred in 2000, when Al Gore chose Connecticut senator Joe Lieberman as his vice presidential running mate, making Lieberman the first Jewish major-party nominee for national office. Any initial concern that non-Jews would react negatively to his nomination proved unwarranted. Instead, his being an observant Orthodox Jew led to acceptance of his nomination in religious circles that respected piety. Jeffrey Cohen (2005) analyzed surveys of the general public to assess the Lieberman effect. Cohen found that voters who identified as born-again Christians and who were moral traditionalists did not have negative attitudes toward Lieberman. There was no evidence that raw anti-Semitism, such as feeling that Jews had too much influence, hurt the Democratic ticket. Still, Cohen showed that voters with less warm feelings toward Jews were significantly less likely to vote Democratic if they knew that Lieberman was Jewish, but that effect was still much smaller than the effects of traditional vote predictors, such as party identification. The name recognition that Lieberman gained in 2000 made him a leading 2004 presidential contender in early 2003 polls. However, his support for the 2002 Iraq War resolution put him out of step with the liberal antiwar mood of Democratic primary voters. As a result, he withdrew from the race in early February 2004.

When John Kerry won the Democratic nomination in 2004, he became the party's first presidential nominee with a Jewish heritage. Kerry's family was always considered to be Irish Catholic, though John's brother

Cameron had converted to Judaism in 1983 when he married Kathy Weinman. In 2003, it was discovered that the Kerry line was actually Jewish. John descended from a Kohn family from a town then in the Austrian Empire, now in the Czech Republic. John's grandfather from that family had changed the family name to *Kerry* when he converted to Catholicism in 1901, before immigrating to America a few years later. Following Kerry's unsuccessful run in 2004, billionaire New York mayor Michael Bloomberg considered running for the presidency as an Independent in 2008. However, the results of national polls that he commissioned convinced him to stay out of the race.

The 2016 Primary Campaign

Jews had a more central role in the 2016 presidential campaign. Bernie Sanders became the first Jewish presidential candidate to win a presidential primary. His run for the Democratic nomination received considerable support among liberal Democrats. Sanders contested the nomination through all the primaries, finally endorsing Hillary Clinton on July 12, two weeks before the party's national convention. Nearly 40% of the delegates voted for him at the convention.

Sanders's position on the Israeli-Palestinian dispute departed from usual Democratic stands. While he described himself as "100% pro-Israel" during a debate with Clinton on April 14, he labeled Israel's 2015 assault on Gaza as "disproportionate" and argued that the United States needed to play "an evenhanded role," including "recognizing the serious problems that exist among the Palestinian people." Those positions appealed to the increasing number of liberal Democrats (including Jews) who were upset with Israel because of the Netanyahu government's right-of-center policies. Two of Sanders's supporters on the party's platform committee were vocal proponents of a more-neutral American stance on the Middle East. Regardless of that position, Middle East policy did not become a major issue in the primary season or at the convention.

The candidates for the Republican nomination ran on opposition to the Iran nuclear agreement. Even though it was a multinational agreement, some candidates promised to tear it up on their first day in office. Opposition to the agreement pleased many Jewish voters, especially the Orthodox. However, the Christian-based conservatism and God Talk of several of the 2016 Republican candidates, especially Ben Carson, Ted Cruz, Mike Huckabee, Bobby Jindal, and Rick Santorum, would have seriously concerned more Jews. Cruz, Jeb Bush, Chris Christie, Carly Fiorina, and Marco Rubio were strongly pro-Israel, but their positions on social issues were problematic for many Jews. Cruz campaigned directly for Orthodox votes in the New York primary, including visiting a matzo factory before Passover. Rand Paul's early calls to end foreign aid would have diminished any potential Jewish support for his candidacy, although he later campaigned among Jewish groups after exempting Israel from his original blanket proposal. A spring poll conducted by the Republican Jewish Coalition indicated that Ohio governor John Kasich was the overwhelming favorite Republican among Jews, with Cruz in the middle and Donald Trump least popular (Peoples and Bykowicz 2016). Kasich's moderation might have appealed to many liberal Jews, though most would likely have preferred Clinton or Sanders to Kasich.

Other Jews in the 2016 race included the Green Party presidential candidate, Dr. Jill Stein, who was raised in Reform Judaism. She described herself as culturally Jewish but not actively practicing Judaism. She supported the Boycott, Divestment, Sanctions movement and accused Israel of war crimes in its 2015 Gaza War. As in 2008, Michael Bloomberg actively considered running an Independent candidacy for the presidency. However, he decided against it after polls that he conducted led him to conclude that his candidacy would ensure Trump's election.

The Fall Campaign

When she ran for the Democratic nomination in 2008, Hillary Clinton benefited from considerable Jewish support, partly based on the enthusiasm among most Jews for Bill Clinton's presidency. Her subsequent service as secretary of state linked her with Obama's Middle East policies, including the Iran nuclear accord, though the final agreement was negotiated by her successor, John Kerry. Hillary was seen as more supportive of Israel than Sanders, and it was expected that she would be able to get along better with the Israeli government than Obama had. There was speculation that she would resume efforts to bring about an Israeli-Palestinian settlement based on a two-state solution, perhaps enlisting her husband to broker a settlement. She also had a personal Jewish connection: in an interfaith ceremony, her daughter, Chelsea, married Marc Mezvinsky, who is Jewish.

In the early Republican debates, Donald Trump claimed that he would be neutral in peace negotiations between Israel and the Palestinians and that he could settle their dispute. Relatively quickly, he changed his tactic to emphasizing how pro-Israel he would be, though he still asserted that he could settle that dispute. His daughter Ivanka had converted to Judaism when she married newspaper owner and real estate developer Jared Kushner, an Orthodox Jew. Trump referred to her being Jewish and to his Jewish grandson in arguing that a Trump presidency would be good for Jews. During the fall campaign, Ivanka Trump visited the grave of the Lubavitcher Rebbe.

Still, Trump displayed a surprising lack of sensitivity to Jewish sensibilities. His association with white-identity politics disturbed many Jews. His midsummer tweet of an image including a six-pointed star in an attack of Hillary Clinton as corrupt was attacked as anti-Semitic because it used a Star of David. Trump's August 2016 choice of alt-right Breitbart News chairman Steve Bannon as his campaign director further concerned many Jews, since Breitbart News was accused of being anti-Semitic as well as white nationalist and anti-Muslim.

Prominent Jewish Republicans were conflicted on whether to endorse Trump. William Kristol, the editor of the *Weekly Standard*, was a vigorous Trump opponent. Former White House press secretary Ari Fleischer endorsed Trump in May while criticizing him as "personally offensive," whereas he termed Clinton "professionally offensive." Shortly before the election, Fleischer rescinded his endorsement and announced he would leave his presidential ballot blank. Trump eventually gained the financial support of billionaire Sheldon Adelson, but the lukewarm support of many other leading Jewish Republicans sent a message to Jewish voters.

Notably, the Israeli government stayed out of America's 2016 election. Benjamin Netanyahu's tacit support for Mitt Romney in the 2012 election had only sharpened the conflicts the prime minister was having with the Obama administration. This time, Israel recognized that it needed to be on good terms with anyone who might win the presidency.

The Jewish Vote in 2016

As the 2016 campaign progressed, the question became whether Trump's candidacy would lead to decreased Republican support among the Jewish electorate. Polls suggest that a minor Republican vote loss may have occurred, while Clinton's vote percentage was about the same as Obama's four years earlier. Whereas Clinton won the popular vote over Trump by a margin of 48% to 46%, the national exit poll showed Clinton winning the Jewish vote over Trump by 71% to 24%, with 5% voting for other candidates. The large Cooperative Congressional Election Study (CCES) found a 68% Clinton vote, versus 28% for Trump.[1]

The 2012 and 2016 CCES results for Jews are compared in table 14.1. As to be expected, nearly all Democratic identifiers (95%) voted for Clinton. Whereas the national exit poll found that 90% of Republicans in the general electorate voted for Trump, only 83% of Republican Jews voted for him, well below the 95% who voted for Romney in 2012. Independent Jews went narrowly for Clinton over Trump, with their vote for Trump being substantially lower than that for Romney four years earlier. Liber-

TABLE 14.1. 2012 and 2016 Jewish Presidential Vote by Demographics

	2016			2012	
	Clinton	Trump	Other	Obama	Romney
All Jews	68%	28%	4%	66%	33%
Democratic	95%	4%	2%	95%	5%
Independent	44%	37%	19%	33%	62%
Republican	12%	83%	4%	4%	95%
Orthodox	40%	51%	9%	16%	83%
Conservative	65%	30%	5%	65%	34%
Reform	75%	22%	3%	74%	24%
Just Jewish	68%	28%	4%	72%	27%
Liberal	95%	3%	2%	97%	2%
Moderate	69%	25%	6%	59%	40%
Politically conservative	23%	72%	5%	16%	82%
Men	64%	30%	6%	57%	41%
Women	72%	25%	3%	73%	26%
18–29 years	82%	12%	6%	70%	28%
30–45 years	68%	25%	6%	60%	38%
46–64 years	61%	34%	4%	69%	31%
65 and over	68%	30%	2%	66%	33%
No college	65%	32%	3%	52%	47%
Some college	71%	25%	5%	63%	34%
College graduate	64%	32%	4%	74%	25%
Postgraduate	72%	23%	5%	68%	32%

Source: Analysis of Cooperative Congressional Election Study surveys.

als solidly backed Clinton, while Trump lost some support among Jewish political conservatives.

The non-Orthodox denominational groups voted strongly for Clinton, from a low of 65% among Conservative Jews to a high of 75% among Reform Jews. By contrast, Orthodox Jews voted narrowly for Trump, by a margin of 51% to 40%, with a greater Democratic vote than in 2012.[2] The Republican vote in Modern Orthodox areas that Rocklin (2017) examined fell, but not drastically, and the vote in those areas remained much less Democratic than that of Jews as a whole. Clinton won the endorsement and vote of the Skver Hasidim,[3] but Satmar Hasidim precincts tended to vote for Trump, even though Satmar leaders had endorsed Hillary Clinton as a "longtime friend" of Jews. The Republican vote in ultra-Orthodox areas stayed fairly steady from 2012, declining about five percentage points in some areas while increasing a couple points in others. The Hasidic area of Borough Park in Brooklyn voted 69% for Trump versus 27% for Clinton, while the Satmar town of Kiryas Yoel, New York, went for Trump by 49% to 40% (Deutsch 2017).

The demographics of the Jewish vote changed in 2016 in two notable ways. First, the gender gap decreased among Jews, with a higher percentage of Jewish men voting for Clinton than had voted for Obama. By contrast, the gender gap increased nationally, moving up to 12%, due to the nature of Trump's candidacy. Second, there were age differences: Clinton's vote was highest (82%) among Jewish voters under 30, which was 12 percentage points higher than among that age-group four years earlier. Trump did best (34%) with Jewish voters in the 45–64 age-group; national exit polls similarly found that he won the votes of 63% of whites in that age-group, his best showing.

Most striking is the constancy in the Jewish vote across the 2012 and 2016 elections. Clinton's vote parallels Obama's 2012 vote in most categories. Her vote held steady among Democratic and liberal voters, gaining slightly among other political groups. She did a little better with Orthodox Jews, men, and young people. The Trump candidacy apparently cost the Republicans some votes among Jews. The slightly greater third-party vote among younger people is in accord with the usual finding that young people are more independent politically. Djupe's (2017) analysis of the CCES data found that the considerable difference in the Trump vote between Orthodox and Reform Jews could be entirely attributed to their differences on social issues (abortion and same-sex marriage), although he was not able to test if it could instead be due to attitudes toward the Christian Right.

The August 2016 AJC survey, further discussed later in this chapter, asked about Israel but not about domestic issues. The results for vote intention three months before the election are fairly routine. As expected, party identification and ideology had the strongest effects on intention, though ideology mattered somewhat more than partisanship. Income had the third-largest effect, with higher-income Jews being significantly less likely to vote for Clinton than those with lower incomes, though that tendency was partly counterbalanced by the fact that people with more education were more likely to vote for her. The question on the Middle East was the only other significant variable in the analysis. That Jews who felt that Israel and Palestine could coexist planned to vote more Democratic[4] reinforces the conclusion in chapter 12 that Jews' voting is related to attitudes on Israeli policies.

Political Implications of the Election

Politics is always a matter of what-ifs. Had Bernie Sanders won the Democratic nomination, his leftist campaign might have pushed the missing Jewish Republicans and Libertarian Jews to become full-fledged Republicans. Trump's Populism held less appeal to Jews than a Libertarian emphasis might have had. Instead, the Trump campaign turned off many college-educated women, a category that includes many Jews. Trump's claims that he understood Jews because of his daughter's conversion and because his grandson is Jewish did not win over Jewish Democrats. The spectacles of the 2016 GOP presidential nomination campaign and of Donald Trump's fall election campaign put at least a temporary damper on the possibility of large-scale party switches by Jews. The Iran agreement gave the Republicans an opening to increase their vote among Jews, but Trump's unusual candidacy kept most Jews voting Democratic for at least one more election.

The larger question became whether the Trump phenomenon would lead to a permanent change in the Republican Party that would affect Jews' partisan alignment. There was early speculation that Trump would disrupt the association between the Christian right and the Republican Party. He did not have a close relationship with the Christian right before his candidacy, but most evangelical leaders backed him, even after the release of videotape in which he made vulgar comments. Exit polls found that Trump won 81% of the white evangelical vote, partly because of his promise to appoint conservative Supreme Court justices who would overturn previous rulings on abortion. Several of his cabinet appointments and his nomination of Neil Gorsuch for the Supreme Court were particularly popular with evangelicals. As a result, the close association of the Republican Party with the Christian right, a relationship that makes many Jews uncomfortable, is likely to continue. Additionally, the future of Jews' voting could be affected by the resolution of differences in the Democratic Party between its centrist Obama-Clinton wing and its more leftist Sanders-Warren wing.

The Early Trump Administration. Trump became the first Republican president to appoint Jews to his initial cabinet. Dr. David Shulkin was continued for a year as secretary of veterans affairs, and Steven Mnuchin was appointed Treasury secretary. Trump's other Jewish advisors included his son-in-law Jared Kushner, who served as a senior adviser to the president, with a focus on the Middle East and Israel.

While Trump's campaign had often sounded Populist notes, the beginning of his administration came off as more Libertarian. Its initiatives to cut regulations, to decrease taxes, and to diminish the size of the government were the type of economic policies that would appeal to Libertarian Jews. Still, the general tone of the administration was not likely to attract Progressive Jews.

Jews remained primarily Democratic in their party identification after the election. Pew's 2017 polling found that 68% of registered Jewish voters identified as Democrats and 22% as Republicans, a fall from 27% Republicans during the Obama years and back to the 2013 value in fig. 7.1 (Pew Research Center 2018a).[5] An early October 2018 online poll of Jews conducted by the pro-Democratic Mellman Group for the Jewish Electorate Institute similarly showed that 68% identified with the Democratic Party and 25% with the Republican Party. An online 2018 election-day poll sponsored by J Street found a Democratic lead in identification among Jewish voters of 71% versus 20% Republican.

Middle East Policy. Trump made several large shifts in American policy on the Middle East in his first two years in office. In February 2017, he professed indifference between a two-state or one-state solution to the Israeli-Palestinian dispute, though he did not specify what type of one-state solution he would accept. Additionally, he gave his son-in-law Jared Kushner the responsibility for working to achieve a settlement of the dispute. Kushner worked with Israel and the Persian Gulf states to prepare the administration's own peace proposals for the Middle East. By the end of 2017, Trump ordered the U.S. embassy to be moved to Jerusalem, which resulted in the Palestinians refusing to participate in peace negotiations. The embassy in Jerusalem was opened in May 2018, and Trump pulled out of the Iran nuclear accord that same month.

Early polling showed that American Jews' views on Israel-related issues were less positive toward Trump's policy shifts than Israeli Jews were. The April-May 2018 AJC survey found that 59% of U.S. Jews favored and 30% opposed a two-state solution through establishment of a demilitarized Palestinian state on the West Bank, while a parallel AJC survey of Israeli Jews showed they were marginally opposed, with 44% favorable and 48% against. U.S. Jews were split fairly evenly (45% in favor and 47% opposed) on the decision to recognize Jerusalem as Israel's capital and relocate the U.S. embassy there, while Israeli Jews were overwhelmingly favorable (85% to 7%). Approval of Trump's handling of U.S. relations with Israel was at 34% in the AJC survey and 51% in an October 2018 Mellman Group poll, which contrast with the 77% approval in the survey of Israeli Jews.

Anti-Semitism and the Trump Administration. As described in chapter 5, a dramatic increase in anti-Semitic acts followed the 2016 election, with bomb threats phoned in to Jewish community centers across the nation in early 2017, along with cemetery desecration in Saint Louis and Philadelphia. Unusually, on at least two occasions when he was asked about the bomb threats in early 2017, President Trump's reply was to claim how strong the vote for him was in the election. That nonresponse was interpreted as condoning the action, though Trump later gave a strong denunciation of such acts at the beginning of his speech to Congress on February 28, 2017: "Recent threats targeting Jewish community centers and vandalism of Jewish cemeteries . . . remind us that while we may be a nation divided on policies, we are a country that stands united in condemning hate and evil in all its forms." The threats abated in March, after Israeli authorities arrested a disturbed American Jewish teenager who they considered to be the prime source of the threats and after the FBI arrested a Missouri man who allegedly made copycat threats.[6]

Trump's response to the "Unite the Right" march of white supremacists in Charlottesville, Virginia, on August 12, 2017, raised further concerns in the Jewish community. Neo-Nazis shouted such slogans as "Seig Heil" and "Jews will not replace us" as they marched past Congregation Beth Israel synagogue, whose congregants had to leave through the back door for their safety. Trump's initial statement condemned "the egregious display of hatred, bigotry, and violence on many sides," which seemed to equate the counterprotestors with the neo-Nazis. Even the Republican Jewish Coalition asked Trump to "provide greater moral clarity in rejecting racism, bigotry, and anti-Semitism," while the American Israel Public Affairs Committee urged "all elected officials to reject moral equivalence between those who promote hate and those who oppose it." Within a couple of days, Trump read a prepared statement condemning the "hatred, bigotry, and violence," including manifestations by "the KKK, neo-Nazis, white supremacists, and other hate groups." However, speaking extemporaneously a few days later, he emphasized that "there are two sides to a story," and he repeated that "there is blame on both sides."

There have been occasional attacks against Jews and Jewish institutions in single communities over the years, but the threats to Jewish community centers across the nation in early 2017 were unprecedented. They created anxiety among Jews across the nation, about whether their community would be targeted next, even though the threats were eventually traced to two isolated individuals who were not anti-Semitic. Trump's delay in denouncing such threats was noticed by Jewish Americans. His creating a moral equivalence between neo-Nazi marchers and those protesting the Charlottesville march further distressed Jews, who expected their political leaders to condemn neo-Nazis unequivocally. Accordingly, Gallup's 2017 polling (Newport and Davis 2017) showed Trump approval rate among Jews was 28%, which was 11 percentage points lower than among the general public.

While some Democratic Jews may be appreciative of Trump's move of the American embassy to Jerusalem, anecdotally there has been more rethinking among Jewish Republicans as to whether they want to remain Republicans. Trump's response on Charlottesville and his position on immigration were among the points mentioned when a Jewish Republican mega-donor in Ohio and another in New England separately announced in September 2018 that they were no longer contributing to the Republican Party. At the same time, Republican Jewish Coalition leaders emphasized the importance of their maintaining a channel to represent Jewish concerns with the Republican White House.

The increased salience of anti-Semitism had direct effects on Jewish public opinion. As shown in the right-hand column of table 14.2, perceptions of anti-Semitism directly affected evaluations of Trump's performance as president in the August 2017 poll, with its impact below only those of partisanship and ideology. Education level and the issue of moving the American embassy were the other significant predictors. Those who wanted the embassy moved immediately to Jerusalem were more likely to approve of Trump, while those with the most education were less approving. Views on the establishment of a Palestinian state were not significantly related to Trump approval.

Table 14.2 additionally compares the August 2016 and the 2017 AJC surveys to show the effects of several variables on major-party vote and on presidential approval. In the 2017 AJC poll, assessments of the seriousness of anti-Semitism in the United States had the third-greatest impact on recalled 2016 vote as well as on Trump approval. Many surveys over the years have asked Jews how serious they regarded anti-Semitism, but rarely, in any of the previous analysis done for this book, was there any indication of it having statistically significant ef-

TABLE 14.2. Logit Analysis of Presidential Vote and Approval

	Aug. 2016	Aug. 2017	
Variable	Vote intention	Recalled vote	Presidential approval
Party identification (Democratic = 1)	.21***	.19***	−.16***
Ideology (liberal = 1)	.24***	.12***	−.15***
Antisemitism is very serious	.03	.12***	−.11**
Israel and Palestinian state could coexist	.08**		
Support independent Palestinian state		.05*	−.02
Move U.S. embassy immediately to Jerusalem		−.10**	.07*
Education	.09*	.08*	−.07*
Income	−.10*	−.01	−.02
Orthodox	−.09	−.08*	.04
Conservative	−.00	.00	.01
Reform	.04	.04	−.03

Source: Analysis of surveys by the American Jewish Committee.

Note: Entries are effect coefficients showing the impact of changes from the mean values on voting for Clinton and on approval of President Trump according to logit analysis. Positive values represent voting for Clinton and approving of Trump's performance. The analysis also controlled on whether being Jewish is important, whether caring for Israel is important, gender, marital status, age, and living in the South, but they were not significant in any of the equations.

***$p < .001$; **$p < .01$; *$p < .05$.

fects on Jews' politics. By 2017, however, perceived seriousness of anti-Semitism had a greater effect than any variables other than party identification and ideology.

It is curious that views on the seriousness of anti-Semitism were significantly related to recalled vote, even though they were not significant in the August 2016 survey. This emphasizes how much the salience of anti-Semitism increased over the 12 months between the two surveys, possibly even during the last few months of the election campaign. It suggests that the Jews most concerned by the postelection anti-Semitic incidents may have turned most strongly against Trump and/or that Trump's Jewish supporters were more willing than his opponents to discount the seriousness of anti-Semitism.[7] That a comparable analysis (not shown) did not find anti-Semitism assessments to be a significant predictor of party identification in the August 2017 AJC survey suggests that this concern did not affect Jews' partisan loyalties at least through that date.

The October 27, 2018, killing of 11 people at the Tree of Life Synagogue in the heavily Jewish Squirrel Hill area of Pittsburgh during Shabbat morning services created further concern among Jews about their safety. President Trump condemned the act as a "wicked act of mass murder" and "pure evil," and said that anti-Semitism "must be confronted anywhere and everywhere it appears." Yet his claim that the outcome might have been different if the synagogue had an armed guard was regarded by some Jews as an instance of blaming the community and the victims themselves.

The November 2018 midterm election occurred 10 days after the Pittsburgh shootings. The election was expected to be a referendum on the Trump administration, particularly given the president's extensive campaigning. The early October 2018 Mellman Group poll showed that 76% of Jews had an unfavorable view of Trump (Mellman Group 2018). J Street's 2018 election-day online poll similarly found a 75% rate of disapproval of Trump's handling his job as president, with 72% of Jewish voters considering Trump's comments and politics as at least somewhat responsible for the Pittsburgh shootings.

The Jewish vote remained strongly Democratic according to three election-day polls. A weighted average of the poll results shows about 78% of Jews voted for Democratic rather than Republican candidates.[8] These midterm surveys may have under-sampled Republican-voting ultra-Orthodox Jews, but these results suggest an increase in Jews' support for the Democratic Party.

Conclusions

Jews and Israel were unusually important in the 2016 election. For the first time ever, a Jewish politician mounted a strong campaign for a major party's presidential nomination, and both parties' nominees had Jewish members in their immediate families. Due to the controversy over the Iran nuclear agreement, Bernie Sanders's acknowledgment of Palestinians' rights, and the unconditional support for Israel offered by nearly all Republican presidential candidates, Middle East policy became a topic in the election. Yet, in the end, there was little sign of real change in the Jewish vote: the Democratic vote among Jews was fairly steady, the number of Jews supporting Trump was a few percentage points below the number who had voted for Romney four years earlier, and a small percentage of Jews cast ballots for minor-party candidates.

An important question is how Jews will respond if liberal politicians continue to focus on reducing the income gap between the rich and the poor. That was the main focus of the Sanders campaign that energized many young Jews, but emphasizing that issue could move Libertarian Jews into the Republican camp. Trump's Populist appeal in the election also had the potential of upending traditional party alignments. Both the Trump administration's Middle East policies and the rise of anti-Semitism have the potential of further changing Jews' political views. The longer-term implications of any election depend considerably on whether the following election continues the trends or reverses them. The party alignments may permanently change if Trump or a Republican committed to his policies wins the presidency in 2020, but a Democratic win would likely shift politics back in the pre-2016 direction.

Large-scale movement of Jews toward the Republican Party has been possible at several times since the 1940s, but each time, changing circumstances have led to strengthening of Democratic ties. Political fissures exist in the American Jewish community. Realignment in the Republican direction seemed like a possibility in 2015. However, Trump's 2016 unexpected victory gave new energy to supporters of the Democratic Party. Reactions to Trump's actions and rhetoric, along with the increased threat of anti-Semitism, make it possible that Jews' voting will turn even more Democratic for at least the near future. The following chapter presents a summary of the results of this book's investigation of Jewish voting and offers further reflections about the future.

CHAPTER 15

The Politics of Tradition

While no single survey has measured Jews' attitudes on a full range of relevant topics, the preceding chapters have analyzed several recent surveys together to gain new insights about their politics. Rather than care about the frequent shallow claim that Jews voting Democratic are ignoring their self-interest, these chapters have given attention to several novel points: Jews being more Democratic than liberal; the replacement of economic issues by sociocultural issues as the defining element of Jews' liberalism; the missing Jewish Republicans; the unexpectedly large number of Jewish Libertarians; and an attitude triad that includes attitudes about Israel as one voting issue (but not the main voting issue) for Jews. Even after this lengthy examination of Jews' politics, it is paradoxical that their politics has stayed fairly steady over more than eight decades even though American Jewry has changed considerably over that time period. This brief conclusion chapter revisits some of the themes of earlier chapters to consider ways in which American Jewry may keep changing, why Jews remain predominantly Democratic, and the possibilities for partisan change.

Changing American Jewry

Like all ancient religions, Judaism is steeped in rituals and traditions. However, the traditional Judaism of early 20th-century Jewish immigrants was displaced as the immigrants and their children adapted to the American culture. As the Reform movement became less radical theologically, it has become the largest branch of Judaism, while the nondenominational "just

Jewish" are also a large component. At the same time, Orthodox Judaism has been reinvigorated. With the notable exception of the Orthodox, more Jews focus on being Jewish than on being religious. Being Jewish has become a matter of ancestry, culture, and ethnicity, at least as much as religion, for a large number of American Jews. Similarly, more Jews describe their being Jewish as important to them than view their religion as important to them. As a result of these considerations, the politics of most Jews is not a direct reflection of their Judaism as much as part of their shared ethnocultural Jewishness.

Five dynamics may affect the shape of American Judaism into the future. The first involves a continuation of trends in denominational attachment. The Reform movement is likely to continue to grow, due to both its greater acceptance of intermarriage and its openness to gender equality and LGBT inclusion. The number of nondenominational "just Jewish" is also likely to continue to increase, due to intermarriage and to millennials' seeming aversion to organization memberships. While those trends work to reinforce the liberal and Democratic leanings of American Jews, political conservatism and Republican identification are likely to increase as Orthodox Judaism continues to gain adherents, because of its higher fertility and retention rates as well as its outreach efforts to Jews who are less committed to Judaism.

Second, the polarization of politics may lead to some shifts in attachments to the different streams of Judaism. There are anecdotal accounts of politically conservative members of Reform synagogues avoiding going to services after fellow congregants made negative remarks about the Republican Party and/or about President Trump. Studies of the general public have found such partisan sorting in 2006–12 as liberal and moderate evangelicals left their churches when they disagreed with the Christian right and also when they disagreed with their clergy about Donald Trump during the fall 2016 campaign (Djupe, Neiheisel, and Sokhey 2017; 2018). Comparable patterns may occur for Jews, with politically conservative members shifting away from Reform congregations while liberal members of politically conservative congregations switch to Reform ones. Additionally, Michele Margolis (2018a; 2018b) has shown that young adults have been following their partisanship in choosing their religion, which suggests that young Jews who have not yet settled down may eventually choose a Jewish denomination that accords with their views of contemporary politics.

Third, according to the theory advanced in part II of this book, the increase in anti-Semitic threats and violence is likely to heighten the focus of Jews on their minority status, which could affect their self-interest and their values priorities. In turn, that might lead to modification of their politicized social identity. Their self-interest in physical safety for themselves and their children is certainly a primary concern. A small number of Jews may see this as a reason to move to Israel or to a different country, while the overwhelming majority will remain in the United States. The responses of the major political parties to the continued rise of white nationalism and to intensification of the Boycott, Divestment, Sanctions movement could reshape Jews' political loyalties, though there likely will continue to be debates as to whether anti-Semitism from the right or the left poses a more serious threat.

Fourth, the debates with regard to Iran and to the Palestinians could become so severe as to create a rupture in the Jewish community. Some strong advocates for Israel questioned whether Jews could legitimately vote for Obama's reelection in 2012, and they later challenged whether Jews could legitimately support the Iran nuclear accord in 2015. Major parts of the organized Jewish establishment pushed positions that were more hard-line than most American Jews would accept. If unconditional acceptance of Israel's policies becomes a defining condition for belonging to the American Jewish community, a large number of Jews would essentially be excommunicated. Such a schism is unlikely, but if it happened, the remaining diminished Jewish vote would be more politically conservative and Republican.

Fifth, the increased religionization of Israel has implications for the American Jewish community. Whereas Israel began as a secular society, the Orthodox—both the ultra-Orthodox, who expect accommodation from secular society, and the Modern Orthodox, who are militant Zionists—have become increasingly influential. This trend is not comfortable for American Jewish liberals, who expect separation between religion and state and are upset by how the Orthodox have influenced the Israeli government on matters from the role of women to the treatment of the Conservative and Reform movements. American Jews originally assumed that these trends would be reversed whenever the Likud government next loses power. However, as it increasingly becomes clear that these are manifestations of a trend that is likely to continue into the long term, many American Jews may readjust their feeling of attachment to Israel. Advocating for Israel might not continue to be a central project for American Jewry, though Jews would likely still expect the U.S. government to ensure Israel's security.

Why Are Jews Still Predominantly Democratic?

Most Jews have kept voting Democratic for president in the years since the New Deal. Lipset and Raab (1995, 148) described the variation in the Jewish vote as follows: "The Jewish vote for Democratic and other liberal-party nominees has, since early in the 20th century, gone up and down in the same directions as the vote of the general electorate, but it has always been much higher for Democratic and leftist third-party candidates than the general electorate." It is not quite true that Jews' votes have always followed the same trends as the public as a whole, though it has indeed been more Democratic than the general electorate.

The preceding chapters have confirmed that Jews' politics are still distinctively Democratic and liberal. Additionally, more Jews are Democratic than are liberal, with many politically conservative Jews not being Republican. The main explanation of the "missing Jewish Republicans" involves social/morality issues, with Jewish conservatives being more moderate on "cultural" matters than are non-Jewish conservatives. Only about one-tenth of Jews are "traditionalist" conservatives who oppose government action in the economic sphere while favoring government limitations on personal morality. By contrast, about one-quarter of Jews are small-government social liberals ("Libertarians") who favor minimal government regulation in both the economic and morality arenas, and many of them are not Republicans.

Most of the original components of the New Deal coalition peeled off from the Democratic Party over the second half of the 20th century, with Jews being a notable exception. Why have Jews stayed in the Democratic fold? The most basic answer to this question is that being Democratic has become tradition. Jews have voted Democratic for so long that Democratic voting has become ingrained in their political DNA. The sociopsychological version of this answer was described in chapter 3: Jews' social identity as Jews has become politicized, with being Democratic having become the dominant version, although some Jews have the Republican "gene" instead.

Understanding Jews' voting patterns requires considering their self-interest, values, and identity. The overall pattern is essentially self-interested voting based on Jews' values, combined with the entrenchment of habitual Democratic voting in most Jews' politicized social identity. Their universalistic and postmaterialist values and their self-interest in maintaining the political and economic system in which they have prospered have kept most Jews on the liberal and Democratic side of American politics. There are exceptions, of course, such as Jews whose social identity includes being conservative and Republican, whose self-interest focuses more on the pocketbook, or whose values are less universalistic and/or more materialist. As American society, the modern economy, and the threat of anti-Semitism continue to change, Jews' self-interest and values may also change and affect their politics.

While it is commonly claimed that Jews' Democratic voting is contrary to their economic self-interest, their voting has been in accord with their subjective self-interest. A key aspect is Jews' self-interest in protecting their rights as a minority, against both individual-level discrimination and government-level restrictions. In the first half of the 20th century, Jewish voters came to see the Democratic Party as more favorable to keeping religion separate from the public sphere, in addition to being more favorable to their economic concerns. Both the subsequent movement of more Jews into the managerial class and increasing tensions with blacks created a potential for shifting away from the Democratic Party. However, when the economic issues of the New Deal days became less pressing, Jews became liberal on new social issues on which they oppose the Christian right. The alignment of the Christian right with the Republican Party has helped the Democratic Party retain the support of Jews who fear that government legislation on morality would lead to weakening the separation of church and state, under which American Jews have prospered. The Democratic Party remains the party of urban minorities, and Jews are a primarily urban group that still feels that the Democratic Party best protects their minority rights. As a result, Republican identification remains low even among Jewish political conservatives.

Possible Party Change

As people in a social group vote for the same party over time, their partisanship becomes particularly resistant to change. They interpret news events through a partisan lens that is favorable to their party, and their discussion of politics with other members of their group reinforces their partisanship. When a president of their party takes actions that they do not like, they usually can discount those acts as an aberration, and they expect that the next president of their party will act in a manner they find more acceptable. As a result of that psychology, political realignments are usually slow.

Yet fractures have developed in the Jewish vote. Ultra-Orthodox Jews are predominantly Republican in their partisan loyalties. Jews from the former Soviet Union have been more supportive of the GOP. Businesspeople who have had negative experiences with government regulations and/or labor unions are also more Republican. There is even some indication that higher-income Jews vote somewhat more Republican.[1] These fractures, taken together, still involve only a minority of the Jewish community, but they are notable changes in the once-solid phalanx of Democratic support by Jews, and they have the potential of leading to meaningful change in Jews' voting patterns.

Groups are most likely to change those ties when their party pushes them away as the other party pulls them over. That situation has not occurred for Jews, though the Republican Party has been attempting to use its support for Israel as a wedge issue to pull Jews over. Views on Israeli policy and attachment to Israel are significantly related to Jews' party identification, and many of the Jews who primarily care about Israel are already voting Republican. Additionally, many liberal Jews have come to regard the Netanyahu government as being a barrier to a solution to the Israeli-Palestinian disputes, which makes it harder for the Republican Party to attract them. As a result, GOP emphasis on the Israel issue may serve more to bolster the Republican vote among evangelical Christians than to increase Republican support among Jews, at least as long as the Democratic Party continues to emphasize Israel's security and does not adopt positions of Palestinian support that make Jews feel pushed away.

Rather than wait for an across-the-board realignment, it makes more sense for political parties to target particular groups of Jews. Most ultra-Orthodox Jews are already Republican, but mobilizing them further could have political effects, particularly if their large number of young people can be mobilized. The Israel issue could be crucial to moving Modern Orthodox and Conservative Jews more toward the Republicans, though the Trump administration's domestic and foreign policies and the increase in anti-Semitic acts may instead lead to movement of Jews toward the Democratic Party.

The battle for the Jewish vote will likely be fought over Libertarian Jews who oppose both government regulation of the economy and government interference on social issues. Small-government non-Orthodox Jews could theoretically be drawn more to the Republican side, at least to the extent to which the Republican Party emphasizes its small-government focus rather than traditional morality, particularly if the party's tone moderates in the post-Trump era.

Like other Americans, Jewish Americans have several identities. In addition to religious identities, they have gender identities, racial identities, class identities, occupational identities, and so on. For many or perhaps most Jews, their identity as Jewish is probably less salient than those other identities when they vote. They may notice Israel-related issues more than other Americans (at least, more than other nonevangelical Americans), but that does not mean that most Jews normally bring those issues directly into their voting calculus. Thus, attitudes related to Israel are relevant for Jews' voting but are not among the two most important factors.

This book has proposed an "attitude triad" theory in which economic issues are most important to the Jewish vote, with attitudes on Israel policy and on cultural issues also being significant. Jews' political positions depend on which threats they consider most serious: some Jews are more concerned about potential security threats to Israel, while most Jews are more apprehensive about possible domestic limitations on their personal liberties.

Breaking Tradition

The mainstreaming of Jews in American politics makes it possible that Jews' political distinctiveness will cease. But that claim has been made for decades, across which the politics of tradition has always won out. The developing fissures could lead to dramatic changes in Jews' political leanings, but similar opportunities for the Republican Party proved illusionary in the 1950s and 1980s. The Iran dispute in 2015 made the possibility of Jews breaking away from the Democratic Party more real, especially when Jews heard Jewish organizations and leaders arguing from both sides of the matter.

It looked like these possibilities for Jewish political realignment could come to a head in the 2016 U.S. election. Instead, the 2016 campaign went in unexpected directions when Donald Trump emerged as a leading contender for the Republican nomination. His campaign raised enough concern among Jews that even many prominent Jewish Republican leaders did not support him. Rather than showing a shift of Jewish voters in the Republican direction, the best evidence indicates that the Jewish vote for the Republican presidential candidate fell a few percentage points from 2012. Early readings of party identification find that the Trump administration has not drawn more Jews over to the Republican camp. Trump's electoral victory seems to have made this into another missed realignment opportunity. Indeed, the postelection anti-Semitic incidents and Trump's refusal to repudiate his supporters from the alt-right movement could sour most Jews on the GOP for another generation, though Trump's policy shifts regarding Iran and Jerusalem are wild cards that could shuffle the partisan deck. Additionally, assuming right-wing anti-Semitic violence subsides, some Jews might move away from the Democratic Party if it is seen as entangled with anti-Semitism from the political left.

As a minority that feels vulnerable, Jews recognize that their position in society is always fragile. Their values and their subjective self-interest have become embedded in their politicized social identity, making their party ties resistant to change. Their politics of tradition is based on their recognition that they have prospered under the policies and economics of a liberal, pluralistic society and that it is much safer to maintain their political allegiances than to take the risks inherent in moving to a less-regulated economy and to more culturally conservative politics.

Thus, the puzzle of Jews' partisan stability from 1932 through 2016 that was mentioned at the beginning of the introduction to this book can largely be explained by this "politics of tradition." Traditions can, of course, be changed, just as most American Jews have shed many of the traditions of Judaism that their ancestors followed. Still, tradition is a powerful force, and the Jewish politics of tradition is likely to win out for at least a while longer.

Data Appendix

The surveys discussed in this book are listed alphabetically below and, where applicable, by the abbreviations that are used in the text. The Pew and PRRI surveys are the main Jewish surveys analyzed in this book; the ANES and GSS surveys are the main surveys used for comparisons of Jews with the general public. Some of the other surveys used in this book are sponsored by advocacy organizations, which can introduce bias in question wording. Survey weights are used in analysis when they are available.

ADL: Anti-Defamation League Survey of Attitudes towards Jews in America, 2016. This national telephone survey taken in October included 1,532 adults. Reports are available at ADL.org

AJC: American Jewish Committee Annual Survey of American Jewish Opinion; most years between 1981 and 2018. Also, 2018 Comparative Survey of Israeli Jews. Telephone surveys taken by SSRS since 2016 included people of Jewish religion or background who were prescreened in the SSRS Omnibus Survey. The 2012–15 AJC surveys (including their 2015 poll on the Iran nuclear accord) were conducted by GfK using its web-based KnowledgePanel® and included Jews by religion as well as people who considered themselves Jewish for other reasons. AJC surveys up through 2010 used Synovate's Consumer Opinion Panel for samples, amplified in some years by adding a list of distinctive Jewish names; the early AJC surveys included only Jews by religion (see Perlmann 2007a; 2007b). Generally, the samples include just over 1,000 Jews. Data for several years is available at JewishDataBank.org

ANES: American National Election Studies, Cumulative, 1992–2012. The ANES surveys of the general public started in 1948. The face-to-face surveys (plus a telephone component in 2000 and an Internet component in 2012) included 202 Jews in presidential election years.

The data is available at ElectionStudies.org

Brandeis University American Jewish Attitudes about Israel Survey, 2010. This Internet survey is based on an online panel of 1,243 Jews, which includes some who identified as Jewish by criteria other than religion. See Sasson et al. 2010.

CCES: Cooperative Congressional Election Study, Common Content. This Internet survey of the general public, including 944 Jewish voters in 2012 and 1,177 in 2016, used matched random sampling.

The data is available at CCES.gov.Harvard.edu

Faith Matters Survey, 2006 and 2011. This telephone survey included 56 Jews in 2006 and 41 in 2011. See Putnam and Campbell 2010, 2012.

The data is available at AmericanGrace.org

GSS: General Social Survey, Cumulative, 1972–2016. The face-to-face surveys of the general public for 1992–2016 include 639 Jews. See Smith et al. 2018.

The data is available at GSS.NORC.org and at ICPSR.UMich.edu

Israel Project U.S. National Survey of Jewish Community on the Iran Nuclear Deal, late July 2015. This survey of 1,034 Jews was conducted by Olive Tree Strategies for an advocacy group.

The data is available at TheIsraelProject.org

Jewish Public Opinion Study, 2000. This Internet survey was based on an online panel of 531 Jews. See Greenberg and Wald 2001.

JJLA: *Jewish Journal of Greater Los Angeles* Survey on the Iran Nuclear Agreement, mid-July 2016. SSRS conducted this phone survey of 501 Jews, prescreened through the SSRS Omnibus Survey.

The data is available at JewishDataBank.org

J Street National Election Survey, 2012, 2016, and 2018; National Survey of Jewish Voters on Iran Nuclear Accord, late July 2015. J Street is an advocacy group for a two-state solution in the Middle East. Its election-day Internet surveys of Jewish voters were conducted by GBA Strategies and included 800 Jews in 2012, 731 in 2016, and 903 in 2018. The Internet survey on the Iran accord included 1,000 Jews.

Reports are available at JewishDataBank.org

Los Angeles Times 50th Anniversary of the State of Israel poll, 1998. The poll surveyed a stratified telephone sample with 848 Jews.

The data is available at RoperCenter.org

NAES: National Annenberg Election Survey, 2008. This telephone survey of the general electorate included 1,383 Jews.

The data is available at AnnenbergPublicPolicyCenter.org

National Survey of American Jews, 2007. This mail and Internet survey polled 1,828 self-identified Jews.

The data is available at JewishDataBank.org

NJDC: National Jewish Democratic Council survey of Jews, Summer 2004. This survey polled an Internet sample of 817 likely Jewish voters.

NJPS: National Jewish Population Survey, 1971; 1990; 2000–01. Unless otherwise stated, results from the 2000–01 stratified telephone survey using random-digit dialing include 4,484 Jews and 664 people of Jewish background. Noncitizens have been excluded. See Goldberg 2003; Kotler-Berkowitz 2006; Kadushin, Phillips, and Saxe 2005; Perlmann 2007b. The 1990 NJPS conducted RDD telephone interviews with 2,441 respondents; the 1971 NJPS conducted face-to-face interviews with 5,790 respondents, sampling from Jewish federation lists, supplemented by probability samples and distinctive Jewish names for areas without available lists. The data is available at JewishDataBank.org

Pew Research Center Survey of U.S. Jews, 2013. Unless otherwise stated, results from this stratified telephone survey using random-digit dialing, conducted by Abt SRBI, include 3,475 Jews by religion and Jews of no religion, but no people of Jewish background or people with Jewish affinity.[1] Results were recomputed to exclude noncitizens.

The data is available at PewForum.org. See also Fischer 2013; Klausner 2013; Eliezrie 2013; Cooperman and Smith 2013.

PRRI: Public Religion Research Institute Jewish Values Survey, 2012. The early 2012 Internet survey of 1,004 Jews in the Knowledge Networks' KnowledgePanel® (recruited by randomly selecting households using address-based sampling and providing Internet access and a computer to households without them) included people who considered themselves Jewish for reasons other than religion. See Jones and Cox 2012.

The data is available at JewishDataBank.org

Republican Jewish Coalition Post-Election Poll, 2012. This one-day telephone survey polled 1,000 Jews.

Reports are available at JewishDataBank.org

RLS: U.S. Religious Landscape Study, 2007 and 2014. This Pew telephone survey using random-digit dialing included 682 Jews in 2007 and 650 Jews by religion in 2014. See Lugo 2008. See Pew Research Center 2015.

The data is available at PewForum.org

WC: 2012 Workmen's Circle Survey of American Jews; postelection survey of 2,067 Jews; American Jews' Political Values Survey; spring Internet survey of 1,000 Jews. Workmen's Circle is an advocacy group for social and economic justice. See Cohen and Abrams 2012; 2013.

Reports are available at BJPA.org

WVS: World Values Survey, 1992–2014. This face-to-face survey of several nations includes 130 U.S. Jews.

The data is available at WorldValuesSurvey.org

Notes

Introduction

1. To give some rough values, the margin of error for a survey employing simple random sampling (using the *t* distribution) would be 9.9% for 100 respondents, 4.4% for 500, 3.1% for 1,000, 2.2% for 2,000, and 1.8% for 3,000. Few samples are simple random samples, so the margin of error for most samples would likely be at least 25% higher than those values. These values do not take non-sampling errors into account.

2. Some survey analysts argue that low response rate in phone surveys is not a serious problem, because studies (e.g., Keeter et al. 2000; Weisberg 2005) have shown that survey results do not change materially when extraordinary effort is made to increase the response rate. Consumer panels and Internet surveys that recruit ongoing panels of respondents avoid the problem of low response rate, but people who join them may not be representative of the population. Even RDD telephone samples pose difficulties for surveying ultra-Orthodox Jews, since those who are willing to participate in surveys likely differ from those who are too separated from secular society to participate.

Chapter 1

1. The biblical basis for that phrase is Numbers 23:9, "I see a people who live apart."

2. Some terms used in religious surveys of the general public may be interpreted differently by Jews than by Christians. For example, the lower proportion of Jews feeling that the Bible is the word of God may be partly due to some associating the term *Bible* with the New Testament instead of the Torah.

3. This scenario is adapted freely from an Irish joke repeated by Achen and Bartels (2016, 228).

4. Horowitz 1999 provides an overview of different understandings of Jewish identity, and Shapiro 2005 describes the history of the development of Jewish identity in the United States.

5. I am choosing to refer to this as "cultural," rather than "ethnic," Judaism. The limit of viewing being Jewish as an ethnicity was shown when the 2014 Religious Landscape Study (Pew Research Center 2015, 43) found that one-sixth of American Jews were raised in a different religious group.

6. Unless otherwise stated, references to the "Pew survey" and "Pew report" are to the 2013 Pew Research Center Survey of U.S. Jews (Pew Research Center 2013). Because of the political focus of this book, the Pew statistics have been recalculated to include only U.S. citizens. That calculation drops 1.8% of their original sample and explains the slight differences between percentages shown in this book and those given in the original Pew report.

7. That "being part of a Jewish community" was chosen primarily by the Orthodox and at a much lower proportion than the 2004 AJC poll found for Jews who emphasize being part of the Jewish people suggests that people may have interpreted that response's wording as referring not to being part of the Jewish people but as living in a predominantly Jewish neighborhood, as the Orthodox do so they can walk to their synagogue.

8. Goldwater's paternal grandfather Michael was Jewish.

9. Phillips (2010) found that 68% of the JNRs in the 2000–01 National Jewish Population Survey had intermarried parents and that most had little Jewish experience while growing up (see also the analysis of "partly Jewish" Jews in Cohen, Ukeles, and Miller 2013).

10. Pew Research Center (2013, 23) extrapolated from its 2013 survey that there were 4.2 million "Jews by religion" and 5.3 million Jews including the JNR. The Steinhardt Social Research Institute estimated a Jewish population of just over 7 million, including 1 million partly Jewish. A 2010 study estimated that about 14% of American Jews identified as Jewish by nonreligious criteria (Tighe, Saxe, and Kadushin 2011, 33).

11. Early surveys, including the main exit polls for 1970s elections, asked people which religion they were brought up in, a question that did not measure their current religion (see Best and Krueger 2012).

12. The Pew survey collected limited data on two additional sets of people, not included in their main statistics: (1) "non-Jewish people of Jewish background," who had a Jewish parent and/or were raised Jewish but do not consider themselves Jewish; and (2) "non-Jewish people with a Jewish affinity," who consider themselves at least partly Jewish but (a) have a different religion than Judaism or no religion and (b) neither had a Jewish parent nor were raised Jewish. Those groups manifest some Jewish practices—for example, 31% of the people of Jewish background reported fasting on Yom Kippur, as did 26% of the affinity group (Pew Research Center 2013, 114).

Chapter 2

1. Garland 2014 describes illegal Jewish immigration during this period.

2. There are claims, however, that the ultra-Orthodox were overrepresented in the 2012 Jewish Community Study of New York because their rabbis instructed them to participate if they were contacted.

3. Unless otherwise stated, subsequent citations to Cohen are to Steven M. Cohen.

4. Young adults are less likely to join a synagogue than older adults, but that tendency does not account for lower religious service attendance among Jews than among non-Jews, since non-Jewish young adults are also less likely to attend church services. By contrast to other studies, a nonrandom survey of 599 Jewish millennials (Barna Group 2017) found that 80% consider themselves "religious Jews," with one-fifth thinking that Jesus was God in human form. But that survey controversially included Messianic Jews in its sample and was sponsored by the Jews for Jesus movement (Sales 2017).

5. Likewise, Pew's 2014–2015 survey of Israeli Jews (Pew Research Center 2016b) found that 70% of the ultra-Orthodox (Haredi) chose "religion" by itself in answering a similar question, while 83% of secularists (Hitoni) chose "ancestry/culture" without "religion." The responses of the remaining two groups fell in between: the religious Zionists (Dati) tended to choose "religion" only (52%), while the plurality (41%) of the traditional Conservatives (Masorti) answered "ancestry/culture."

6. See also Hartman, Sheskin, and Cohen 2017.

7. See also Liebman's (1990) description of Jewish identity on a continuum from particularism with ritualism at one end to universalism and moralism at the other end (see also Cohen and Eisen 2000, 68).

8. However, Klaff's (2006) analysis of the 2000–01 National Jewish Population Survey found that those with stronger religious connections to Judaism also have a stronger ethnic Jewish identity.

Chapter 3

1. Social identity theory views group membership as creating biased intergroup comparisons that bolster self-esteem. A variant of social identity theory, known as "self-categorization theory" (Tajfel and Turner 1986), instead emphasizes the importance of salience of group identity to generating group cohesion, but I here use the term *social identity theory* generically to encompass such variants.

2. Other theoretical explanations of ethnocentrism (Kinder and Kam 2009) include (1) realistic group conflict theory, which is based on intergroup competition over scarce resources; (2) genetics, as in studies that consider identical twins and attribute much of the variation between individuals in political conservatism to heredity (e.g., Alford, Funk, and Hibbing 2005); and (3) personality, as in the finding that attitudes on cultural issues are structured by a person's degree of authoritarianism (e.g., Hetherington and Weiler 2009). Each of these explanations could be relevant to Jewish political behavior: a Jewish sense of liberal identity can be created (1) by competition with conservative non-Jews, (2) through a liberal gene (if one exists), or (3) because of personality tendencies toward individualism (e.g., Mondak 2010 found that liberals and Democrats are more open to experience, and Dunkel et al. 2015 found that Jews are high on openness to experience).

3. As discussed in chapter 9, Wald and Williams (2006) have used the related concept of "politicized ethnic identity" to describe American Jews' incorporation of sup-

port for Israel into their Jewish ethnicity. See also Huddy's (2013) discussion of the process by which a group identity becomes politicized.

4. It may be common for ethnoreligious groups to be predominantly of one party; see the discussion by Campbell, Green, and Monson (2014, 97). However, those authors suggest that it would be befitting for religion to shape the politics of an ethnoreligious group (101), which is not necessarily the case for Jews. Further, whereas those authors claim, "The sharper those boundaries [that distinguish Mormons from secular society], the stronger the partisan attachment" (101), the political distinctiveness of Jews is greatest for Reform Jews, who have the least-sharp boundaries.

5. The NJPS sample appears less Democratic because Independents were not asked to which party they were closer.

6. Few respondents whose parents were intermarried were themselves inmarried, which is why there is no column in table 3.3 for that combination. The Orthodox are excluded from the table, since so few are intermarried.

Chapter 4

1. The Orthodox were mainly older traditional Jews when Fuchs wrote, so they may have been as liberal as other Jews.

2. An early study by Milton Rokeach (1969) had people rank the importance to them of several values. While his study included relatively few Jews, it is still the only empirical study that explicitly identified a "Jewish value system" of American Jews. The "terminal values" that Jews chose more than did adherents of other religions included a sense of accomplishment, equality, pleasure, family security, inner harmony, and wisdom. The "instrumental values" Jews emphasized included being capable, independent, intellectual, and logical.

3. Religiosity was correlated with tradition at 0.61, with conformity at 0.20, with hedonism at –0.32, and with self-direction at –0.31.

4. The difference remains significant and unchanged with statistical controls on gender, age, and education in a regression analysis.

5. Significant differences of 0.10 on egalitarianism and 0.17 on traditionalism remain when comparing Jews with non-Jews who are similar on education, income, age, gender, and living in the South.

6. Wald (2015) argues that because Jews in many countries support conservative parties, Jewish values do not intrinsically lead to liberalism. However, the conservative parties in most of those countries favor social welfare programs that are more liberal than those advanced by the Democratic Party, so Jews voting for those parties are still supporting liberal values, even if they are not voting for the most liberal parties in their country.

7. By contrast, Lipset and Raab (1995, 161) could still write in the 1990s that "American Jews, unlike their European brethren, have not been pressed to choose between their commitment to Israel and their traditional ties to the left."

8. While this famous line does not appear in Himmelfarb's published work, it is likely a paraphrase from Himmelfarb 1973, 81.

9. Feingold (2014, 51; 1992, 204–5) attributes Jews' becoming liberal to their being urban, urbane, and cosmopolitan.

10. Though it would not be an explanation of Jews being liberal, one could argue that the self-interest of minorities is to be respected. That explanation is sometimes given for many Jews being Republican in the late 1800s, due to the unprecedented recognition that Republican presidents were giving Jews. However, one sometimes hears the opposite explanation: that Jews became Democrats because the Democrats helped the Jewish immigrants settle during the Great Migration (1881–1924).

Chapter 5

1. The high average for Jews is particularly notable because people always give a high score to their own religion. The scores of 58 for members of the Catholic and mainline Protestant religions reflect that their large memberships gave their own religions high ratings, whereas only 2% of the sample was Jewish.

2. The average ratings of Jews were 71 by white evangelicals, 68 by white mainline Protestants and Catholics, 67 by agnostics, 66 by black Protestants, and 62 by atheists.

3. The high level of acceptance of Jews was also shown in a survey experiment that found participants were more likely to reprimand a speaker attacking Jews than to reprove similar negative comments made about Catholics, Mormons, or Muslims (Karpowitz, Monson, and Patterson 2016).

4. A comparison of 2003 and 2014 surveys found increases in anti-Jewish answers: those agreeing that Jews "do not at all agree with my vision of American society" rose from 7% to 18%, and those who would disapprove if their child wanted to marry a Jew went up from 12% to 18% (Edgell et al. 2016, 619).

5. While not all of these incidents may have been motivated by anti-Semitism, the publicity given them considerably increased Jews' sense of vulnerability.

6. Millennials and Gen Xers had higher rates of reporting having experienced anti-Semitism, partly because more of those generations are Orthodox.

7. Staetsky (2017) has provided an insightful explanation of why perceptions of anti-Semitism remain high even when Jews achieve greater acceptance. He argued that people with extreme anti-Semitic views are unlikely to have much contact with Jews, but Jews are likely to come into contact with people in the middle category regarding anti-Semitism (the 28% in the ADL survey), who might make occasional anti-Semitic comments. Such comments would make Jews cringe and believe that there is considerable anti-Semitism even when extreme anti-Semitism is relatively low.

8. Surveys in 1988 showed that the Democratic vote by Jews would have fallen considerably had Jackson been on the ticket, just as the Republican vote by Jews would have fallen if Rev. Pat Robertson had been on the Republican ticket (S. Cohen 1989, 9–12; Wald and Sigelman 1997, 153).

9. About a quarter of the PRRI sample could not rate the Christian right.

Chapter 6

1. Or the 614th commandment, since there are 613 commandments according to Jewish tradition.

2. Voting is rational only if the costs (C) of voting are exceeded by the benefits of your candidate winning (B) discounted by the tiny probability that your vote causes that candidate to win (p), that is, if $pB > C$.

3. The epitome of the Jewish vote swinging the outcome of an election occurred unintentionally when Florida's Palm Beach County used a confusing "butterfly ballot" design in 2000. Statistical analysis (Brady et al. 2001) shows that many voters trying to vote for Al Gore accidentally cast a ballot for Pat Buchanan. There is a sizable elderly Jewish population in that county, and it seems that many in that population accidentally cast a ballot for Buchanan, who many Jews consider to be anti-Semitic. The Florida outcome was in recount territory, and those miscast votes likely gave George W. Bush the presidency (Hasen 2012), though the same could be said about miscast votes by other groups in that county.

4. A related argument is that one cannot complain about an election's outcome if one has not voted, so Jews vote in order to protect their right to complain if the election does not come out as they want. Another version of that argument would be that Jews vote so that fellow Jews cannot shame them for not voting. A more recent explanation of voting turnout, offered from a political science perspective, is that the partisanship-directed anger that has resulted from the increased polarization of American politics motivates more political participation, though Jews were voting at high rates well before American politics became so polarized.

5. To expand the equation from note 2, if satisfying one's civic duty (D) provides a psychological benefit, then voting is rational if $pB + D > C$.

6. The values for the general public are from Pew Research Center 2013, 42.

7. While the ANES and GSS surveys started in 1948 and 1972 respectively, only the surveys since 1992 are used in this book, to focus on the contemporary period. The results for both surveys apply only to the 1992–2012 presidential elections, because the religion coding for the 2016 ANES survey was not available in the cumulative data when this book was completed in early 2018 and because the 2016 GSS survey was conducted before that year's presidential election.

8. The distinctiveness values are regression coefficients from predicting turnout by whether the respondent is Jewish, controlling for other variables, with blacks excluded as means of controlling for race, since very few Jews are black. Fixed-effects regressions are used, to control for effects associated with different election years. The turnout analysis includes 179 Jews in the ANES and 571 in the GSS.

9. A similar analysis of the 2000 Social Capital Benchmark Survey by Wuthnow and Hackett (2003, 657–659) showed that Jews still have a significantly higher level of turnout when just urban/rural residence, age, gender, and citizenship are statistically controlled. However, that the turnout difference is insignificant when education is also controlled emphasizes the importance of education to voter turnout.

10. There are 256 Jews in the ANES data on campaigns, political donations, and contributions.

Chapter 7

1. Specifically, Pew asked, "In politics today, do you consider yourself a Republican, a Democrat, or Independent?" Those who said they were Independent, had no preference, supported another party, answered "Don't know," or refused to answer the question were then asked, "As of today do you lean more to the Republican Party or the Democratic Party?" The focus on "today" in the questions, which is also how Gallup words its polling question on party identification, emphasizes respondents' current views. The ANES and GSS surveys instead ask, "Generally speaking, do you usually think of yourself as a Republican . . . ," which emphasizes long-term identifications.

2. A small proportion of Pew respondents have been dropped from all of the analysis because they are not U.S. citizens and thus cannot vote.

3. On the ideology question, 3% of Jews answered "Don't know" or did not answer. Similarly, 1% did not answer the party question. Since they did not take a position, they have been merged into the middle categories throughout the rest of this book.

4. Part of the reason that there are more Democrats than liberals in figure 7.1 is that Pew did not ask moderates which side they lean toward, as they asked Independents. Still, there were more Democrats than liberals even before Independents were asked how they leaned.

5. To minimize confusion within this discussion, the term *conservative* is given an uppercase *C* when referring to Jews adhering to the Conservative movement in Judaism and a lowercase *c* when referring to politically conservative Jews.

6. The party split for JBR in the Pew survey was 68% Democratic, 7% Independent, and 25% Republican, versus 78%, 10%, and 12% for JNR. The difference was even larger on ideology: JBR split 43% liberal, 35% moderate, and 22% conservative, versus 67%, 22%, and 11% for JNR.

7. The distinctiveness values are regression coefficients from Democratic identification and liberal ideology by whether the respondent is Jewish, controlling for other variables (first gender, age, education, and living in the South; then income), with blacks excluded as a means of controlling for race, since very few Jews are black. Partisanship and ideology are treated as dichotomous: Democrats (including Independents who lean toward the Democratic Party) are coded 1, others 0; liberals are coded 1, others 0. These are fixed-effects regressions, to control for effects associated with different election years. There are 280 Jews in the ANES analysis of party identification and 608 in the GSS analysis; in the analysis for ideology, the numbers are 247 in ANES and 552 in GSS.

8. Mazur's (2016) comparison of Jews and non-Jews with similar demographics (white, college-educated, and residing regionally) in the 1972–2014 GSS data also finds Jews more distinctive on partisanship (21% more Democratic than the control group) than on ideology (8% more liberal than the control).

9. The income results omit the 12% of respondents who refuse to answer the income question.

10. Djupe's (2007, 201) analysis of the 1972–2004 GSS data likewise found Jews' GOP identification peaking in the mid-1980s.

11. Djupe's (2007, 188–88) analysis of the 1972–2004 GSS data found that the

liberal advantage among Jews nearly disappeared in the mid-1980s, rebounded sharply thereafter, and then moderated somewhat.

Chapter 8

1. As a means of controlling for race, comparisons are of Jews with nonblacks.

2. Distinctiveness is computed by fixed-effects regression analysis, examining only whites and controlling for socioeconomics. To obtain enough Jewish respondents for analysis, the examination of 1992–2012 ANES data and of 1992–2016 GSS data was restricted to questions asked over several years. For comparability across issues, attitude questions have been converted to dichotomies, coded 1 for liberal positions and 0 for conservative opinions. The distinctiveness scores have been multiplied by 100 to be comparable to percentage differences.

3. This ideology control is intended as a substitute for Cohen and Liebman's (1997) comparison of Jews with other liberal religious groups.

4. Goren et al. (2016) found that racial issues, including affirmative action and immigration, invoked both conservation and self-transcendence values, with conservation dominating. People who favor tradition and security were most conservative on racial issues, while those who favor universalism were, to a lesser extent, more liberal.

5. Glaser's (1997) analysis of 1980–92 ANES surveys found that Jews' distinctiveness on these questions was due to their attribution of the black condition to societal issues rather than to personal characteristics of blacks, presumably because of Jews' own experience with discrimination.

6. Jews were more likely than non-Jews to support increasing immigration, but the real dispute was whether to curtail immigration, so table 8.3 compares responses to decrease versus not decrease immigration. Jews were more liberal than the population as a whole on an ANES question asking whether immigrants strengthen this country or are a burden (Abrams and Cohen 2016, 107–11).

Chapter 9

1. "Just Jewish" is the baseline denomination category for this analysis.

2. Only non-Orthodox Jews are included in the table, since few Orthodox are intermarried.

3. Two late-July Jewish 2015 polls sponsored by policy advocate organizations obtained opposite results. J Street found 60% support and 40% opposition, while the Israel Project found that only 40% wanted Congress to approve the deal and that 45% favored rejection, which became 30% approval and 58% disapproval after respondents were shown arguments on both sides.

4. Neither Hertzberg (1979, 223) nor Fein (1988, 86–87) contains the "heresy" statement attributed to them by several later authors (e.g., Silberstein 2012, 619).

5. Not only liberals have challenged Israeli policies over the years. For example, the hard-line Zionist Organization of America (ZOA) tried lobbying Congress to derail

the Oslo process by stopping U.S. aid to the Palestinian Authority and opposed Israel prime minister Ariel Sharon's unilateral Israeli withdrawal from Gaza (Waxman 2016, 159–63, 173).

Chapter 10

1. Independents who lean toward a party are included as partisans. The results are equally striking even when not including Independents who lean toward a party: 79% of liberal Jews were Democratic, whereas just 45% of conservative Jews were Republican.

2. Weisberg (2011) reported comparable differences in the 1974–2010 data from the General Social Survey, the 2000–01 National Jewish Population Survey, the 2007 National Survey of American Jews, and the phone survey of the 2008 National Annenberg Election Study.

3. Using Pew data, if 93%, rather than 61%, of the 19% of Jews who are politically conservative were Republican, there would be an increase of 32% × 19% = 6%.

4. The 2012 PRRI Jewish Values Survey similarly finds a lower rate of Republicans among Conservative Jews who are politically conservative: 61% are Republican, versus 84% of politically conservative Orthodox Jews and 78% of conservative Reform Jews.

5. By contrast, 91% of political conservatives who gave the conservative answers to both of those questions about domestic issues were Republicans. Of the 40% of political conservatives who did not give consistently conservative or liberal answers on the two questions, 60% were Republicans.

Chapter 11

1. This classification is based on Janda, Berry, and Goldman 2002; see Swedlow and Wyckoff 2009 for national survey results. See also Abrams and Cohen 2016, 112.

2. "Right conservatives" could also be referenced as "Tories" or "Conservativists."

3. Comparable questions appear in the ANES surveys but were asked of only half the samples in 2000 and 2008, so the number of Jews asked such questions across the 1992–2012 ANES surveys is too few for detailed statistical analysis.

4. Pew's telephone survey permitted respondents to not answer a question, so 13% of its respondents did not answer at least one of these questions. The PRRI online survey apparently required respondents to choose an answer, so only 2% of the PRRI sample could not be classified.

5. The reliance on just two questions in creating this typology might seem insufficient. The overwhelmingly liberal answers to the questions about social issues are typical for Jews, as was seen in table 8.5 earlier in the present study. PRRI also asked about abortion, but the answers on that issue were even more one-sided, with 93% being pro-choice. There was a greater spread in Jews' answers to economic questions (see table 8.1), but responses for the economic items used for the typology are in the range of those for other PRRI economic questions. The use of different questions for

the typology would produce only slightly different percentages of Jews in each category.

6. Most liberals and moderates who could not be categorized did not answer the question on government size. They may have wanted a smaller government that provided more services, rather than accepting that getting more services requires a larger government. An alternative possibility is that some simply found this trade-off question too complicated to understand in a telephone interview. Most political conservatives who could not be categorized did not answer the homosexuality question.

7. In the Pew survey, the party variable is coded 1 for Democrats, 0.5 for Independents, and 0 for Republicans, with Independents who lean toward a party being included with that party; the same coding is used for PRRI except that only a handful of Independents did not indicate the party to which they were closer. Similarly, the ideology variable is coded 1 for liberals, 0.5 for moderates and respondents answering "Don't know," and 0 for conservatives.

Chapter 12

1. The ANES data is based on interviews within two months after the election, so they are probably more accurate, since GSS interviews often require recall of one's vote two to four years afterward.

2. Studies of earlier elections find similarly large gaps even with statistical controls. Using ANES data, Jews were 45 percentage points more Democratic than a control group in 1956 (A. Campbell et al. 1960, 306) and 31 points more Democratic in 2004 (Lewis-Beck et al. 2008, 310). Erikson, Lancaster, and Romero (1989) estimated that Jewish presidential voting was 27 to 79 percentage points more Democratic during 1952–84 than it would have been if they were not Jewish, with an average of 45 points over those nine elections.

3. More detailed vote analysis using questions on domestic issues is not possible because there were too few major-party Jewish voters (under 90) in the ANES 1992–2012 data.

4. Since timing is relevant in election surveys, the tables in this chapter show the season or month in which the polls were taken. Survey questions that ask about approval of specific presidential policies are generally avoided in this chapter, since respondents often base their responses on their voting plans.

5. The partial correlations are based on three-category party identification, with leaners included as partisans.

6. Uslaner's (2015) analysis of the 2012 J Street election-day survey also found Israel questions significant, along with party identification, thermometer ratings of the Tea Party, the direction of the country, and income.

7. None of these studies employed random-digit dialing.

8. People answering "Don't know" or "Other" in the PRRI survey were scored 0.5 for calculating these averages. The basic patterns in table 12.3 hold in a separate analysis (not shown) of only the non-Orthodox, showing that denomination does not determine these results.

9. Cohen and Abrams (2012, 4) also found social issues, economic matters, and Israel attachment significant in their analysis of the presidential vote intentions expressed in a spring 2012 survey sponsored by Workmen's Circle, a Jewish advocacy group for social and economic justice.

10. Looking just at small-government hard-liners in the two surveys, more than 60% were liberal on the social issue; 30% of them were Democrats, showing that the social issue compensated in their politics for Middle East attitudes even for many economic conservatives.

11. Feelings about evangelicals were not significant in a comparable analysis of the data for the general public from the 2004 ANES survey, so the authors concluded that attitudes toward evangelicals were uniquely relevant for Jews' voting.

Chapter 13

1. Additionally, at least 4% of Jews voted for third-party candidates in 1928, 1932, 1948, 1980, 1992, and 1996 (Weisberg 2012), as well as in 2016.

2. An analysis of foreign-born adult males in the 1910 census for one heavily Jewish New York district found that less than one-fifth were naturalized and could therefore vote at the time (Goren 1961). Rischin (1962, 231) admits that "the Lower East Side districts recorded the smallest proportion of registered voters in the city in 1912." A random sample of 1,500 New York City Jewish families in 1925 found only 20% on the voting rolls (Kessner 1981, 232). See also Howe 1976, 312. Additionally, the Republican and Democratic parties were different in those days than today. In some of these elections, neither major party nominated a progressive presidential candidate who would have appealed to new immigrants. The Socialist Party energized many Jewish immigrants, but its main influence was through such means as political rallies, protest (as after the Triangle Shirtwaist Factory fire), and labor litigation.

3. The neoconservatives who moved to the Republican Party in the 1970s included several Jews, such as the editor of the Jewish political magazine *Commentary*, but those neocons were intellectuals rather than well-known Jewish politicians. The neocons' subsequent involvement in the 2003 Iraq War did not increase their credibility among American Jews, whose feelings about the war were lukewarm at best.

4. After losing the Democratic Senate primary in 2006, Lieberman was reelected to the Senate as an Independent. Though he endorsed Republican John McCain in the 2008 presidential election, Lieberman continued to caucus with Senate Democrats until he retired in 2012.

5. A limitation of this analysis is that these surveys, particularly the PRRI survey, had to give unusually heavy weight to the data for younger generations, probably because it is harder to obtain interviews with young respondents.

6. This large difference could be partially due to sampling issues. It also reflects how several ultra-Orthodox sects have exploded in size because of their high fertility rate after being brought to America by small numbers of Holocaust survivors.

7. The splits between Republicans and Democrats were virtually identical for the ultra-Orthodox (58% to 35%) and the Modern Orthodox (56% to 38%).

8. Except for election-day polls, most recent surveys concur that the Orthodox are predominantly identifying with the Republican Party. Fulcrum table A gives the proportion of the Orthodox who said they were Republican in a variety of surveys taken since 1990.

9. Those who disapproved of Obama's performance included 66% of the ultra-Orthodox and 57% of the Modern Orthodox. The 2012 election-day polls by J Street and the Republican National Committee found Obama leading over Romney among the Orthodox, but that result may reflect difficulty getting ultra-Orthodox respondents in a one-day poll. The 2012 CCES poll found that Romney carried the Orthodox vote over Obama by 83% to 16%.

10. A major nonprobability survey of Modern Orthodox Jews (Nishma Research 2017) found considerable variety in their beliefs, practices, and demographics. The splits it found between Republicans and Democrats varied correspondingly: 79% to 21% for the most observant group (the "right centrists"), 62% to 38% for the large middle, and 21% to 79% for the least observant (the "Open Orthodox").

11. As is the case among the Modern Orthodox, there is a spectrum of beliefs among adherents to the Conservative movement: those close to the Orthodox side are likely more Republican, and those close to the Reform side are likely most Democratic, with the large middle group being Democratic.

Chapter 14

1. An August 2016 telephone survey by the American Jewish Committee found 61% of Jews saying that they most likely would vote for Clinton, versus 19% for Trump, 9% for minor-party candidates, and 11% saying "Don't know" or that they would not vote. Corresponding percentages for Jews planning on voting would be 69% for Clinton, 21% for Trump, and 10% for other candidates. J Street's election-day poll, based on emails to Jews in a web-based panel, showed a split of 70% Democratic to 25% Republican. The August 2017 AJC poll had 71% remembering voting for Clinton and only 20% for Trump.

2. Polls varied considerably on the Orthodox vote. The J Street one-day poll had Clinton winning the Orthodox vote by a margin of 56% to 39%, while an August 2017 poll by the American Jewish Committee showed a Trump lead of 67% to 15%. This disparity emphasizes the difficulty in obtaining reliable estimates of the Orthodox vote.

3. Before leaving office, Bill Clinton controversially shortened the federal prison sentences of four Skver men, shortly after the predominantly Skver town of New Square, New York, voted for Hillary Clinton by a margin of 1,400 to 12 in her 2000 Senate race (Russakoff 2002).

4. This analysis is based on a logit analysis, controlling on estimates of anti-Semitism, denomination, importance of being Jewish, caring about Israel, views as to whether Israel is overly religious, and demographic controls on gender, age, region, and marital status, all of which were insignificant.

5. The autumn 2017 and spring 2018 AJC polls found only about 15% of Jews to

be Republicans, though both findings would likely be in the low-20% range if Independents had been asked which party they lean toward.

6. While Trump's security briefings might have given him early indications of law-enforcement authorities' belief that the threats were from abroad, that information was not known by American Jews, who expected their president to condemn those threats.

7. The low percentage of respondents in the 2017 AJC poll who said they had voted for Trump (20% versus at least 24% in polls closer to the election) suggests that Trump voters may have been less willing to participate in the 2017 poll.

8. The early exit polls from Edison Research showed 79% of Jews voting Democratic for Congress versus 15% Republican. The larger J Street poll (which included Jews of No Religion) gave a 76%-19% split, but the AP VoteCast survey conducted by the University of Chicago's NORC found a 71%-28% division.

Chapter 15

1. See figure 12.2 and tables 12.2 and 14.2.

Data Appendix

1. Pew screened 70,000 people. Disproportionate stratified sampling was used, omitting 1,431 counties where there were no Jews by religion and no Jewish educational institutions or synagogues. The remaining counties were sampled by strata based on their Jewish populations as estimated from previous samples, plus an Orthodox stratum of three counties in which the Orthodox account for at least 35% of the Jewish population, as well as a Russian stratum of census tracts where at least 10% of the population was born in the former Soviet Union.

References

Abrams, Samuel J., and Steven M. Cohen. 2016. "The Persisting Liberalism of (Most) American Jews: The Pew Survey of 2013 in Historical Context." In Kyle L. Kreider and Thomas J. Baldino, eds., *Minority Voting in the United States*, 2:95–123. Santa Barbara, CA: Praeger.

Achen, Christopher H., and Larry M. Bartels. 2016. *Democracy for Realists*. Princeton: Princeton University Press.

ADL (Anti-Defamation League). 2017. "A Survey about Attitudes towards Jews in America." https://www.adl.org/sites/default/files/documents/ADL_MS_Survey_Pres_1_25_17.pdf. Accessed 12 Apr. 2017.

ADL. 2018. "2017 Audit of Anti-Semitic Incidents." https://www.adl.org/resources/reports/2017-audit-of-anti-semitic-incidents. Accessed 15 Mar. 2018.

Alba, Richard. 2006. "On the Sociological Significance of the American Jewish Experience." *Sociology of Religion* 67 (4): 347–58.

Alford, John R., Carolyn L. Funk, and John R. Hibbing. 2005. "Are Political Orientations Genetically Transmitted?" *American Political Science Review* 99 (2): 153–67.

Allinsmith, Wesley, and Beverly Allinsmith. 1948. "Religious Affiliation and Politico-Economic Attitude: A Study of Eight Major U.S. Religious Groups." *Public Opinion Quarterly* 12 (3): 377–89.

American National Election Studies. 2014. Time Series Cumulative Data File, 1948–2012. Data set. Produced and distributed by Stanford University and the University of Michigan.

Andersen, Kristi. 1979. *The Creation of a Democratic Majority, 1928–1936*. Chicago: University of Chicago Press.

Aronson, Janet, Matthew Boxer, Matthew A. Brookner, Charles Kadushin, and Leonard Saxe. 2016. *2015 Greater Boston Jewish Community Study*. Waltham, MA: Steinhardt Social Research Institute, Brandeis University.

Balinska, Maria. 1988. "The Jewish Vote in the 1988 United States Presidential Election." Research report 9, Institute of Jewish Affairs, Dec.

Barna Group. 2017."The Evolving Spiritual Identity of Jewish Millennials." https://www.barna.com/research/beliefs-behaviors-shaping-jewish-millennials/. Accessed 2 Mar. 2018.

Barnett, Michael N. 2016. *The Star and the Stripes: A History of the Foreign Policies of American Jews*. Princeton: Princeton University Press.

Barreto, Matt A., and Francisco I. Pedraza. 2009. "The Renewal and Persistence of Group Identification." *Electoral Studies* 28:595–605.

Bartels, Larry. M. 2018. "Partisanship in the Trump Era." *Journal of Politics* 80 (4): 1483–94.

Baumgartner, Jody C., Peter L. Francia, and Jonathan S. Morris. 2008. "A Clash of Civilization? The Influence of Religion on Public Opinion of U.S. Foreign Policy in the Middle East." *Political Research Quarterly* 61 (2): 171–79.

Beck, Paul Allen. 1979. "The Electoral Cycle and Patterns of American Politics." *British Journal of Political Science* 9 (2): 129–56.

Beinart, Peter. 2012a. "American Jews and the Religion-Intensity Gap." *Newsweek*, 23 Jan.

Beinart, Peter. 2012b. *The Crisis of Zionism*. New York: Times Books.

Bellah, Robert N. 1967. "Civil Religion in America." *Daedalus* 96 (1): 1–21.

Ben-Nun Bloom, Pazit, Gizem Arikan, and Marie Courtemanche. 2015. "Religious Social Identity, Religious Belief, and Anti-Immigration Sentiment." *American Political Science Review* 109 (2): 203–21.

Berger, Peter L., and Thomas Luckmann. 1966. *The Social Construction of Reality*. Garden City NY: Doubleday.

Best, Samuel J., and Brian S. Krueger. 2012. *Exit Polls: Surveying the American Electorate, 1972–2010*. Los Angeles: Sage / CQ Press.

Brady, Henry E., Michael C. Herron, Walter R. Mebane Jr., Jasjeet Singh Sekhon, Kenneth W. Shotts, and Jonathan Wand. 2001. "Law and Data: The Butterfly Ballot Episode." *PS: Political Science and Politics* 34 (1): 59–69.

Brodkin, Karen. 1998. *How Jews Became White Folks and What That Says about Race in America*. New Brunswick, NJ: Rutgers University Press.

Brown, Clifford W., Jr., Lynda W. Powell, and Clyde Wilcox. 1995. *Serious Money: Fundraising and Contributing in Presidential Nomination Campaigns*. Cambridge: Cambridge University Press.

Burris, Val. 2001. "The Two Faces of Capital: Corporations and Individual Capitalists as Political Actors." *American Sociological Review* 66 (3): 361–81.

Campbell, Angus, Philip E. Converse, Warren E. Miller, and Donald E. Stokes. 1960. *The American Voter*. New York: Wiley.

Campbell, David E. 2006. *Why We Vote*. Princeton: Princeton University Press.

Campbell, David E., John C. Green, and J. Quin Monson. 2014. *Seeking the Promised Land: Mormons and American Politics*. Cambridge: Cambridge University Press.

Carroll, Andrew Silow. 1988. "1988's Election and the Jews: Voters Buck the Trend by Favoring Dukakis." *Jewish Exponent*, 11 Nov.

Cavari, Amnon. 2013. "Religious Beliefs, Elite Polarization, and Public Opinion on Foreign Policy: The Partisan Gap in American Public Opinion toward Israel." *International Journal of Public Opinion Research* 25 (1): 1–22.

Center for Public Integrity. 2012. "Top 25 Super PAC Donors for 2012 Election Cycle." http://www.publicintegrity.org/2012/12/20/11970/top-25-super-pac-donors-2012-election-cycle. Accessed 19 Nov. 2015.

Chanes, Jerome A. 2001. "Who Does What? Jewish Advocacy and Jewish 'Interest.'" In L. Sandy Maisel and Ira N. Forman, eds., *Jews in American Politics*, 99–119. Lanham, MD: Rowman and Littlefield.

Chyet, Stanley F. 1958. "The Political Rights of Jews in the United States, 1776–1840." *American Jewish Archives* 10 (1): 14–75.

Cohen, Jeffrey E. 2005. "The Polls: Religion and the 2000 Presidential Election; Public Attitudes toward Joseph Lieberman." *Presidential Studies Quarterly* 35 (2): 389–402.

Cohen, Steven M. 1983. *American Modernity and Jewish Identity*. New York: Tavistock.

Cohen, Steven M. 1989. *The Dimensions of American Liberalism*. New York: American Jewish Committee.

Cohen, Steven M. 2015. "New Poll: U.S. Jews Support Iran Deal, Despite Misgivings." *Jewish Journal*, 23 July. http://www.jewishjournal.com/nation/article/new_poll_u.s._jews_support_iran_deal_despite_misgivings. Accessed 17 Aug. 2015.

Cohen, Steven M. 2018. "The Shrinking Jewish Middle—and What to Do about It." Ann Arbor, MI: Frankel Center for Judaic Studies.

Cohen, Steven M., and Samuel Abrams. 2012. *Workmen's Circle / Arbeter Ring 2012 American Jews' Political Values Survey*. http://www.bjpa.org/Publications/details.cfm?PublicationID=14166. Accessed 20 Aug. 2015.

Cohen, Steven M., and Samuel Abrams. 2013. *The Workmen's Circle Survey of American Jews: Jews, Economic Justice, and the Vote in 2012*. New York: Workmen's Circle.

Cohen, Steven M., and Lauren Blitzer. 2008. "Belonging without Believing: Jews and Their Distinctive Patterns of Religiosity—and Secularity." New York: Florence G. Heller–JCC Association Research Center.

Cohen, Steven M., and Arnold M. Eisen. 2000. *The Jew Within: Self, Family, and Community in America*. Bloomington: Indiana University Press.

Cohen, Steven M., and Ari Y. Kelman. 2007. *Beyond Distancing: Young Adult American Jews and Their Alienation from Israel*. New York: Andrea and Charles Bronfman Philanthropies.

Cohen, Steven M., and Ezra Kopelowitz. 2015. *The Jewish Impact of the Jerusalem Journey: Increasing Jewish Engagement among Conservative, Reform, and Non-Denominational Youth*. NCSY, April. https://www.ou.org/assets/Anne-Samson-TJJ-Report.pdf. Accessed 15 Nov. 2018.

Cohen, Steven M., and Charles S. Liebman. 1997. "American Jewish Liberalism: Unraveling the Strands." *Public Opinion Quarterly* 61 (3): 405–30.

Cohen, Steven M., Jacob B. Ukeles, and Ron Miller. 2012. *Jewish Community Study of New York: 2011*. New York: UJA-Federation of New York.

Cohen, Steven M., Jacob B. Ukeles, and Ron Miller. 2013. "Special Study on 'Partly Jewish' Jews." New York: UJA-Federation of New York. https://www.jewishdatabank.org/content/upload/bjdb/597/JCSNY-2011-Special-Study-on-Partly-Jewish-Jews.pdf. Accessed 12 Oct. 2015.

Cohn, Werner. 1958. "The Politics of American Jews." In Marshall Sklare, ed., *The Jews: Social Patterns of an American Group*, 614–26. Glencoe, IL: Free Press.

Cooperman, Alan, and Greg Smith. 2013. "Explaining Pew's Findings on Orthodox

Jews." *Jewish Week,* 21 Oct. http://www.thejewishweek.com/editorial-opinion/opinion/explaining-pews-findings-orthodox-jews. Accessed 5 Oct. 2015.

Cramer, Katherine J. 2016. *The Politics of Resentment: Rural Consciousness in Wisconsin and the Rise of Scott Walker.* Chicago: University of Chicago Press.

Dalin, David G. 2017. *Jewish Justices of the Supreme Court.* Waltham, MA: Brandeis University Press.

Dawidowicz, Lucy S., and Leon J. Goldstein. 1974. "The American Jewish Liberal Tradition." In Marshall Sklare, ed., *The Jewish Community in America,* 285–300. New York: Behrman House.

Dawson, Michael. 1994. *Behind the Mule: Race and Class in African-American Politics.* Princeton: Princeton University Press.

Deutsch, Nathaniel. 2017. "'Borough Park Was a Red State': Trump and the Haredi Vote." *Jewish Social Studies,* n.s., 22 (3): 158–73.

Djupe, Paul A. 2007. "The Evolution of Jewish Pluralism: The Public Opinion and Political Preferences of American Jews." In J. Matthew Wilson, ed., *From Pews to Polling Places,* 185–212. Washington, DC: Georgetown University Press.

Djupe, Paul A. 2017. "The Jewish Vote and the Culture Wars." *Religion in Public* (blog), 31 Oct. https://religioninpublic.blog/2017/10/31/the-2016-jewish-vote-fragmenting-or-consolidating/. Accessed 5 Nov. 2017.

Djupe, Paul A., Jacob R. Neiheisel, and Anand E. Sokhey. 2017. "How Fights over Trump Had Led Evangelicals to Leave Their Churches." *Washington Post,* 11 Apr. https://www.washingtonpost.com/news/monkey-cage/wp/2017/04/11/yes-many-voters-left-their-congregations-over-trump-so-what-else-is-new/?utm_term=.1e93779fa09b. Accessed 15 Nov. 2018.

Djupe, Paul A., Jacob R. Neiheisel, and Anand E. Sokhey. 2018. "Reconsidering the Role of Politics in Leaving Religion." *American Journal of Political Science* 62 (1): 161–75.

Dunkel, Curtis S., Charlie L. Reeve, Michael A. Woodley of Menie, Dimitri van der Linden. 2015. "A Comparative Study of the General Factor of Personality in Jewish and Non-Jewish Populations." *Personality and Individual Differences* 78:63–67.

Edgell, Penny, Douglas Hartmann, Evan Stewart, and Joseph Gerteis. 2016. "Atheists and Other Cultural Outsiders." *Social Forces* 95 (2): 607–38.

El Azhary, M. S. 1980. *Political Cohesion of American Jews in American Politics: A Reappraisal of Their Role in Presidential Elections.* Washington, DC: University Press of America.

Eliezrie, David. 2013. "Pew Missed the Newest Trend in Jewish Life." *Jewish Week,* 18 Oct. http://www.thejewishweek.com/editorial-opinion/opinion/pew-missed-newest-trend-jewish-life. Accessed 5 Oct. 2015.

Ellis, Christopher, and James A. Stimson. 2012. *Ideology in America.* Cambridge: Cambridge University Press.

Erikson, Robert S., Thomas D. Lancaster, and David W. Romero. 1989. "Group Components of the Presidential Vote, 1952–1984." *Journal of Politics* 51 (2): 337–46.

Fein, Leonard. 1988. *Where Are We? The Inner Life of America's Jews.* New York: Harper and Row.

Feingold, Henry L. 1992. *A Time for Searching: Entering the Mainstream, 1920–1945*. Baltimore: Johns Hopkins University Press.

Feingold, Henry L. 2014. *American Jewish Political Culture and the Liberal Persuasion*. Syracuse, NY: Syracuse University Press.

Feldman, Stanley. 2003. "Values, Ideology, and the Structure of Political Attitudes." In David O. Sears, Leonie Huddy, and Robert Jervis, eds., *Oxford Handbook of Political Psychology*, 477–508. 2nd ed, New York: Oxford University Press.

Ferejohn, John A., and Morris P. Fiorina. 1974. "The Paradox of Not Voting." *American Political Science Review* 68 (2): 525–36.

Ferziger, Adam S. 2015. *Beyond Sectarianism: The Realignment of American Orthodox Judaism*. Detroit: Wayne State University Press.

Fingerhut, Eric. 2008. "Some Stats on the Orthodox Jewish Vote." JTA, 25 Nov. http://www.jta.org/2008/11/26/news-opinion/the-telegraph/some-stats-on-the-orthodox-jewish-vote. Accessed 25 Apr. 2016.

Firestone, David. 2002. "Billy Graham Responds to Lingering Anger over 1972 Remarks on Jews." *New York Times*, 17 Mar.

Fischer, Dov. 2013. "Making an Orthodox Sense of an Unorthodox Census." *Jewish Journal*, 4 Oct. http://www.jewishjournal.com/opinion/article/making_an_orthodox_sense_of_an_unorthodox_census. Accessed 26 May 2015.

Fisher, Alan M. 1979. "Realignment of the Jewish Vote?" *Political Science Quarterly* 94 (1): 97–116.

Fitzgerald, Frances. 2017. *The Evangelicals: The Struggle to Shape America*. New York: Simon and Schuster.

Forman, Ira N. 2004. "The Politics of Minority Consciousness: The Historical Voting Behavior of American Jews." In L. Sandy Maisel and Ira N. Forman, eds., *Jews in American Politics*, 141–60. Langham, MD: Rowman and Littlefield.

Francia, Peter L., John C. Green, Paul S. Herrnson, Lynda W. Powell, and Clyde Wilcox. 2003. *The Financiers of Congressional Elections*. New York: Columbia University Press.

Francia, Peter L., John C. Green, Paul S. Herrnson, Lynda W. Powell, and Clyde Wilcox. 2005. "Limousine Liberals and Corporate Conservatives: The Financial Constituencies of the Democratic and Republican Parties." *Social Science Quarterly* 86 (4): 761–78.

Friedman, Murray. 2003. "The Changing Jewish Political Profile." *American Jewish History* 91 (3): 423–38.

Fuchs, Lawrence H. 1955. "American Jews and the Presidential Vote." *American Political Science Review* 49 (2): 385–401.

Fuchs, Lawrence H. 1956. *The Political Behavior of American Jews*. Glencoe, IL: Free Press.

Gamm, Gerald H. 1989. *The Making of the New Deal Democrats: Voting Behavior and Realignment in Boston, 1920–1940*. Chicago: University of Chicago Press.

Gans, Herbert J. 1994. "Symbolic Ethnicity and Symbolic Religiosity: Toward a Comparison of Ethnic and Religious Acculturation." *Ethnic and Racial Studies* 17 (4): 577–92.

Garland, Libby. 2014. *After They Closed the Gates: Jewish Illegal Immigration to the United States, 1921–1965*. Chicago: University of Chicago Press.

Gerstein, Jim, Steven M. Cohen, and J. Shawn Landres. 2013. *Connected to Give: Key Findings from the National Study of American Jewish Giving*. Los Angeles: Jumpstart.

Ginsberg, Benjamin. 1993. *The Fatal Embrace: Jews and the State*. Chicago: University of Chicago Press.

Ginsberg, Benjamin. 2001. "Identity and Politics: Dilemmas of Jewish Leadership in America." In L. Sandy Maisel and Ira N. Forman, eds., *Jews in American Politics*, 3–27. Lanham, MD: Rowman and Littlefield.

Glaser, James M. 1997. "Toward an Explanation of the Racial Liberalism of American Jews." *Political Research Quarterly* 50 (2): 437–58.

Gold, Matea, and Anu Narayanswamy. 2016. "How Mega-Donors Helped Raise $1 Billion for Hillary Clinton." *Washington Post*, 24 Oct. https://www.washingtonpost.com/politics/how-mega-donors-helped-raise-1-billion-for-hillary-clinton/2016/10/22/a92a0ee2-9603-11e6-bb29-bf2701dbe0a3_story.html?postshare=6641477230109581&tid=ss_tw. Accessed 21 Nov. 2016.

Goldberg, J. J. 2003. "A Jewish Recount." *New York Times*, 17 Sept.

Goldstein, Eric L. 2008. *The Price of Whiteness: Jews, Race, and American Identity*. Princeton: Princeton University Press.

Goren, Arthur. 1961. "A Portrait of Ethnic Politics: The Socialists and the 1908 and 1910 Congressional Elections on the East Side." *Publication of the American Jewish Historical Society* 50 (3): 202–38.

Goren, Paul, and Christopher Chapp. 2017. "Moral Power: How Public Opinion on Culture War Issues Shapes Partisan Predispositions and Religious Orientations." *American Political Science Review* 111 (1): 110–28.

Goren, Paul, Harald Schoen, Jason Reifler, Thomas Scotto, and William Chittick. 2016. "A Unified Theory of Value-Based Reasoning and U.S. Public Opinion." *Political Behavior* 38 (1): 977–97.

Greeley, Andrew M. 1974. "Political Participation among Ethnic Groups in the United States." *American Journal of Sociology* 80 (1): 170–204.

Greenberg, Anna, and Kenneth D. Wald. 2001. "Still Liberal after All These Years?" In L. Sandy Maisel and Ira N. Forman, eds., *Jews in American Politics*, 161–93. Lanham, MD: Rowman and Littlefield.

Greenberger, Robert S. 2009. "Can Eric Cantor Save the GOP?" *Moment* Mar.–Apr.

Guttman, Nathan. 2014. "Does Intermarriage Drive Young Jews Away from Israel?" *Forward*, 15 May. https://forward.com/news/israel/198206/does-intermarriage-drive-young-jews-away-from-isra/. Accessed 14 Nov. 2018.

Guttman, Nathan. 2015. "Where Do Jews Stand on Iran Deal? Don't Ask the Polls." *Forward* 7 Aug. http://forward.com/news/318762/nathan-polls/. Accessed 10 Sept. 2015.

Handlin, Oscar, and Mary F. Handlin. 1955. "The Acquisition of Political Rights by the Jews in the United States." In Morris Fine, ed., *American Jewish Year Book 1955*, 43–98. New York: American Jewish Committee.

Hartman, Harriet J., and Moshe Hartman. 2000. "Denominational Differences in the Attachment to Israel of American Jews." *Review of Religious Research* 41 (3): 394–417.

Hartman, Harriet J., Ira M. Sheskin, and Erik H. Cohen. 2017. "Multi-dimensional Analysis of Jewish Identity in 22 American Communities." *International Journal of Religions and Tradition* 3 (1): 19–31.

Hasen, Richard L. 2012. *The Voting Wars: From Florida 2000 to the Next Election Meltdown*. New Haven: Yale University Press.

Heilman, Samuel C., and Steven M. Cohen. 1989. *Cosmopolitans and Parochials: Modern Orthodox Jews in America*. Chicago: University of Chicago Press.

Herda, Daniel. 2013. "Innocuous Ignorance? Perceptions of the American Jewish Population Size." *Contemporary Jewry* 33 (3): 241–55.

Hertzberg, Arthur. 1979. *Being Jewish in America*. New York: Schocken Books.

Hertzberg, Arthur. 1985. "Reagan and the Jews." *New York Review of Books*, 31 Jan.

Hertzberg, Arthur. 1989. "What Future for American Jews?" *New York Review of Books*, 23 Nov.

Hetherington, Marc J., and Jonathan D. Weiler. 2009. *Authoritarianism and Polarization in American Politics*. Cambridge: Cambridge University Press.

Himmelfarb, Milton. 1973. "The Jewish Vote (Again)." *Commentary* 55 (6): 81–85.

Himmelfarb, Milton. 1978. "The Case of Jewish Liberalism." In Seymour Martin Lipset, ed., *Emerging Coalitions in American Politics*, 297–305. San Francisco: Institute for Contemporary Studies.

Himmelfarb, Milton. 1981. "Are Jews Becoming Republican." *Commentary* 72 (2): 27–31.

Himmelfarb, Milton. 1989. "American Jews: Diehard Conservatives." *Commentary* 87 (4): 44–49.

Hogg, Michael A. 2006. "Social Identity Theory." In Peter J. Burke, ed., *Contemporary Social Psychological Theories*, 111–36. Stanford: Stanford University Press.

Horowitz, Bethamie. 1998. "Connections and Journeys: Shifting Identities among American Jews." *Contemporary Jewry* 19 (1): 63–94.

Horowitz, Bethamie. 1999. "Indicators of Jewish Identity: Developing a Conceptual Framework for Understanding American Jewry." Discussion paper prepared for the Mandel Foundation. http://bjpa.org/Publications/details.cfm?PublicationID=2285. Accessed 12 Oct. 2015.

Howe, Irving. 1976. *The World of Our Father*. New York: Harcourt Brace Jovanovich.

Huddy, Leonie. 2013. "From Group Identity to Political Cohesion and Commitment." In Leonie Huddy, David O. Sears, and Jack S. Levy, eds., *Oxford Handbook of Political Psychology*, 511–58. 2nd ed. New York: Oxford University Press.

Inglehart, Ronald. 1977. *The Silent Revolution: Changing Values and Political Styles among Western Publics*. Princeton: Princeton University Press.

Isaacs, Steven D. 1974. *Jews and American Politics*. Garden City, NY: Doubleday.

Janda, Kenneth, Jeffrey M. Berry, and Jerry Goldman. 2002. *The Challenge of Democracy*. 7th ed. Boston: Houghton Mifflin.

Johnson, George E. 2017. "What Will the Jewish World Look Like in 2050?" *Moment* 42 (1): 44–55.

Jones, Jeffrey M. 2016. "U.S. Religious Groups Disagree on Five Key Moral Issues."

Gallup, 26 May. http://www.gallup.com/poll/191903/religious-groups-disagree-five-key-moral-issues.aspx. Accessed 16 Sept. 2016.

Jones, Robert P., and Daniel Cox. 2012. *Chosen for What? Jewish Values in 2012: Findings from the 2012 Jewish Values Survey.* Washington, DC: Public Religion Research Institute.

JTA (Jewish Telegraphic Agency). 1972. "Jewish Vote Triples for Nixon." 9 Nov.

Kadushin, Charles, and Laurence Kotler-Berkowitz. 2006. "Informal Social Networks and Formal Organizational Membership among American Jews." *Sociology of Religion* 67 (4): 465–85.

Kadushin, Charles, Benjamin T. Phillips, and Leonard Saxe. 2005. "National Jewish Population Survey 2000–01: A Guide for the Perplexed." *Contemporary Jewry* 25 (1): 1–32.

Karpowitz, Christopher F., J. Quin Monson, and Kelly D. Patterson. 2016. "Who's In and Who's Out: The Politics of Religious Norms." *Politics and Religion* 9 (3): 508–36.

Keeter, Scott, Carolyn Miller, Andrew Kohut, Robert M. Groves, and Stanley Presser. 2000. "Consequences of Reducing Nonresponse in a National Telephone Survey." *Public Opinion Quarterly* 64 (2): 125–48.

Keith, B. E., D. B. Magleby, C. J. Nelson, E. Orr, M. C. Westlye, and R. E. Wolfinger. 1992. *The Myth of the Independent Voter.* Berkeley: University of California Press.

Kelman, Ari Y., Tobin Belzer, Ziva Hassenfeld, Ilana Horwitz, and Matthew C. Williams. 2017. "The Social Self: Toward the Study of Jewish Lives in the Twenty-First Century." *Contemporary Jewry* 37 (1): 53–79.

Keren-Kratz, Menachem. 2017. "Rabbi Yoel Teitelbaum—the Satmar Rebbe—and the Rise of Anti-Zionism in American Orthodoxy." *Contemporary Jewry* 37 (3): 457–79.

Kessner, Thomas. 1981. "Jobs, Ghettoes, and the Urban Economy, 1880–1935." *American Jewish History* 71 (2): 228–38.

Kinder, Donald R., and Nathan P. Kalmoe. 2017. *Neither Liberal nor Conservative: Ideological Innocence in the American Public.* Chicago: University of Chicago Press.

Kinder, Donald R., and Cindy D. Kam. 2009. *Us against Them: Ethnocentric Foundations of American Opinion.* Chicago: University of Chicago Press.

Klaff, Vivian. 2006. "Defining American Jewry from Religious and Ethnic Perspectives: The Transitions to Greater Heterogeneity." *Sociology of Religion* 67 (4): 415–38.

Klausner, Samuel Z. 2013. "Pew Study of American Jewry: A Few Grains of Salt." Jewish Free-Culture Society. http://jewishfreeculture.org/news/pew-study-of-american-jewry-a-few-grains-of-salt-by-dr-samuel-klausner-2/. Accessed 5 Oct. 2015.

Kliger, Sam. 2011. "Russian-Jewish Immigrants in the U.S." Paper presented at the Conference on the Contemporary Russian-Speaking Jewish Diaspora, Harvard University, 13–15 Nov.

Kotler-Berkowitz, Laurence A. 2005. "Ethnicity and Political Behavior among American Jews: Findings from the National Jewish Population Survey 2000–01." *Contemporary Jewry* 25 (1): 132–57.

Kotler-Berkowitz, Laurence A. 2006. "An Introduction to the National Jewish Population Survey 2000–01." *Sociology of Religion* 67 (4): 387–90.

Kotler-Berkowitz, Laurence A. 2014. "The Great Recession and American Jews." Berman Jewish DataBank. https://www.jewishdatabank.org/databank/search-results/study/742. Accessed 15 Nov. 2018.

Kotler-Berkowitz, Laurence A. 2017. "The Structure of Political Divisions among American Jews." *Contemporary Jewry* 37 (1): 5–27.

Kotler-Berkowitz, Laurence A., and Jonathon Ament. 2010. "The Israel Attachments of American Jews." *Contemporary Jewry* 30 (2/3): 165–73.

Kreider, Kyle L., and Thomas J. Baldino, eds. 2016. *Minority Voting in the United States*. Santa Barbara, CA: Praeger.

Kuo, Alexander, Neil Malhotra, and Cecilia Hyunjung Mo. 2017. "Social Exclusion and Political Identity: The Case of Asian American Partisanship." *Journal of Politics* 79 (1): 17–32.

Lazarowitz, Arlene. 2010. "Ethnic Influence and American Foreign Policy: American Jewish Leaders and President Jimmy Carter." *Shofar* 29 (1): 112–36.

Lazerwitz, Bernard, and Michael Harrison. 1979. "American Jewish Denominations: A Social and Religious Profile." *American Sociological Review* 44 (4): 656–66.

Lazerwitz, Bernard, J. Alan Winter, Arnold Dashefsky, and Ephraim Tabory. 1998. *Jewish Choices: American Jewish Denominationalism*. Albany: State University of New York Press.

Lederhendler, Eli. 2017. *American Jewry: A New History*. Cambridge: Cambridge University Press.

Lefkowitz, Jay P. 1993. "Jewish Voters and the Democrats." *Commentary* 95 (4): 38–41.

Lenski, Gerhard E. 1967. "Status Inconsistency and the Vote: A Four Nation Test." *American Sociological Review* 32 (2): 298–301.

Levey, Geoffrey Brahm. 1995. "Toward a Theory of Disproportionate American Jewish Liberalism." In Peter Y. Medding, ed., *Values, Interests, and Identity: Jews and Politics in a Changing World*, 64–85. Studies in Contemporary Jewry 11. New York: Oxford University Press.

Levey, Geoffrey Brahm. 1996. "The Liberalism of American Jews: Has It Been Explained?" *British Journal of Political Science* 26 (3): 369–401.

Lewin, Kurt. 1941. "Self-Hatred among Jews." *Contemporary Jewish Record*, June.

Lewis-Beck, Michael S., William G. Jacoby, Helmut Norpoth, and Herbert F. Weisberg. 2008. *The American Voter Revisited*. Ann Arbor: University of Michigan Press.

Liebman, Charles S. 1971. "Reconstructionism in American Jewish Life." In Morris Fine and Milton Himmelfarb, eds., *American Jewish Year Book 1970*, 3–99. Philadelphia: Jewish Publication Society of America.

Liebman, Charles S. 1973. *The Ambivalent American Jew*. Philadelphia: Jewish Publication Society of America.

Liebman, Charles S. 1990. "Ritual, Ceremony, and the Reconstruction of Judaism in the United States." In Ezra Mendelsohn, ed., *Art and Its Uses: The Visual Image and Modern Jewish Society*, 272–83. Studies in Contemporary Jewry 6. New York: Oxford University Press.

Liebman, Charles S., and Steven M. Cohen. 1990. *Two Worlds of Judaism: The Israeli and American Experiences*. New Haven: Yale University Press.

Liebman, Charles S., and Steven M. Cohen. 1996. "Jewish Liberalism Revisited." *Commentary* 102 (5): 51–53.

Lipka, Michael. 2016. "Few Americans Identify with More than One Religion." Pew Research Center. http://www.pewresearch.org/fact-tank/2016/10/26/few-americans-identify-with-more-than-one-religion. Accessed 16 Feb. 2018.

Lipset, Seymour Martin. 1963. *Political Man*. Garden City, NY: Anchor Books.

Lipset, Seymour Martin. 1985. "The Elections, the Economy and Public Opinion: 1984." *PS: Political Science and Politics* 18 (1): 28–38.

Lipset, Seymour Martin, and Earl Raab. 1995. *Jews and the New American Scene*. Cambridge, MA: Harvard University Press.

Lipstadt, Deborah, Charles Pruitt, and Jonathan Woocher. 1984. "Election '84: Where Are the Jews?" *Moment* 9 (9): 35–38.

Litt, Edgar. 1960. "Status, Ethnicity, and Patterns of Jewish Voting Behavior in Baltimore." *Jewish Social Studies* 22 (3): 159–64.

Lubell, Samuel. 1951. *The Future of American Politics*. New York: Harper and Brothers.

Lugo, Luis. 2008. *U.S. Religious Landscape Survey—Religious Affiliation: Diverse and Politically Relevant*. Washington, DC: Pew Forum on Religion and Public Life.

Maisel, Sandy L., and Ira N. Forman. (2001) 2004. *Jews in American Politics*. Reprint, Lanham, MD: Rowman and Littlefield.

Maller, Allen S. 1977. "Class Factors in the Jewish Vote." *Jewish Social Science* 39 (1/2): 159–62.

Manza, Jeff, and Clem Brooks. 1997. "The Religious Factor in U.S. Presidential Elections." *American Journal of Sociology* 103 (1): 38–81.

Marcus, Jacob Rader. 1989. *United States Jewry, 1776–1985*. Vol. 1. Detroit: Wayne State University Press.

Margolis, Michele F. 2018a. *From Politics to the Pews: How Partisanship and the Political Environment Shape Religious Identity*. Chicago: University of Chicago Press.

Margolis, Michele F. 2018b. "How Politics Affects Religion: Partisanship, Socialization, and Religiosity in America." *Journal of Politics* 80 (1): 30–43.

Mayer, Jeremy D. 2004. "Christian Fundamentalists and Public Opinion toward the Middle East: Israel's New Best Friends?" *Social Science Quarterly* 85 (3): 695–712.

Mayhew, David R. 2002. *Electoral Realignments: A Critique of an American Genre*. New Haven: Yale University Press.

Mazur, Allan. 2016. "How Distinct Are American Jews?" *Contemporary Jewry* 36 (2): 225–41.

McGinity, Keren R. 2009. *Still Jewish: A History of Women and Intermarriage in America*. New York: New York University Press.

Mearsheimer, John J., and Stephen M. Walt. 2007. *The Israel Lobby and U.S. Foreign Policy*. New York: Farrar, Straus and Giroux.

Medding, Peter Y. 1977. "Towards a General Theory of Jewish Political Interests and Behaviour." *Jewish Journal of Sociology* 19 (2): 115–44.

Medoff, Rafael. 2002. *Jewish Americans and Political Participation: A Reference Handbook*. Santa Barbara, CA: ABC-CLIO.

Mellman, Mark S., Aaron Strauss, and Kenneth D. Wald. 2012. *Jewish American Voting Behavior 1972–2008*. Washington, DC: Solomon Project.

Mellman Group. 2018. "American Jews Remain Strongly Supportive of the Democratic Party." Memo to the Jewish Electoral Institute. 16 Oct. mellmangroup.com/wp-content/uploads/2018/10/18mem1016-f2-JEI.pdf. Accessed 1 Nov. 2018.

Miller, Arthur H., Patricia Gurin, Gerald Gurin, and Oksana Malanchuk. 1981. "Group Consciousness and Political Participation." *American Journal of Political Science* 25 (3): 494–511.

Mondak, Jeffery J. 2010. *Personality and the Foundations of Political Behavior*. Cambridge: Cambridge University Press.

Morris, Benny. 2004. *The Birth of the Palestinian Refugee Problem Revisited.* 2nd ed. Cambridge: Cambridge University Press.

Nadeau, Richard, Richard G. Niemi, and Jeffrey Levine. 1993. "Innumeracy about Minority Populations." *Public Opinion Quarterly* 57 (3): 332–47.

Nathan-Kazis, Josh. 2016. "Why So Many Ultra-Orthodox Jews Will Vote for Hillary Clinton." *Forward,* 8 Nov. https://forward.com/news/353644/why-so-many-ultra-othodox-jews-will-vote-for-hillary-clinton-not-donald-tr. Accessed 1 Mar. 2018.

Newport, Frank. 2015. "About Three in 10 American Jews Identify as Republicans." Gallup, 6 Jan. http://www.gallup.com/poll/180422/three-american-jews-identify-republicans.aspx. Accessed 10 Jan. 2015.

Newport, Frank. 2016. "Jerusalem, Jews and the Presidential Candidates." Gallup, 24 Mar. http://news.gallup.com/opinion/polling-matters/190283/jerusalem-jews-presidential-candidates.aspx. Accessed 30 Mar. 2018.

Newport, Frank, and Alyssa Davis. 2017. "Trump's Job Approval among U.S. Jews." Gallup, 17 Mar. http://www.gallup.com/opinion/polling-matters/206666/trump-approval-among-jews.aspx. Accessed 12 Mar. 2018.

Nisbett, Richard E., and Timothy D. Wilson. 1977. "Telling More than We Can Know: Verbal Reports on Mental Processes." *Psychological Review* 84 (3): 231–59.

Nishma Research. 2017. *The Nishma Research Profile of American Modern Orthodox Jews.* http://nishmaresearch.com/assets/pdf/Report%20-%20Nishma%20Research%20Profile%20of%20American%20Modern%20Orthodox%20Jews%2009-27-17.pdf. Accessed 15 Nov. 2018.

Paul, David M., and Rachel Anderson Paul. 2009. *Ethnic Lobbies and US Foreign Policy*. Boulder, CO: Lynne Rienner.

Peoples, Steve, and Julie Bykowicz. 2016. "Cruz Rails against Trump as Republican Jews Ponder Options." *Washington Post,* 9 Apr. https://apnews.com/376cad29c7b948b8826c7a3d7fd2a4cf/cruz-rails-against-trump-republican-jews-ponder-options. Accessed 23 Aug. 2017.

Perlmann, Joel. 2007a. "The American Jewish Committee's Annual Opinion Surveys: An Assessment of Sample Quality." Working paper 508, Levy Economics Institute of Bard College, Annandale-on-Hudson, NY.

Perlmann, Joel. 2007b. "Two National Surveys of American Jews, 2000–01: A Comparison of the NJPS and AJIS." Working paper 501, Levy Economics Institute of Bard College, Annandale-on-Hudson, NY.

Perlmann, Joel. 2010. "Secularists and Those of No Religion: 'It's the Sociology, Stupid (not the Theology).'" *Contemporary Jewry* 30 (1): 45–62.

Petrocik, John R. 1981. *Party Coalitions: Realignments and the Decline of the New Deal Party System*. Chicago: University of Chicago Press.

Pew Research Center. 2011. "The Tea Party and Religion." 23 Feb. http://www.pewforum.org/2011/02/23/tea-party-and-religion/. Accessed 3 Dec. 2015.

Pew Research Center. 2013. *A Portrait of Jewish Americans: Findings from the Pew Research Center Survey of U.S. Jews*. 1 Oct. http://www.pewresearch.org/wp-content/uploads/sites/7/2013/10/jewish-american-full-report-for-web.pdf. Accessed 15 Nov. 2018.

Pew Research Center. 2014. "How Americans Feel about Religious Groups." 16 July. http://www.pewresearch.org/wp-content/uploads/sites/7/2014/07/Views-of-Religious-Groups-07-27-full-PDF-for-web.pdf. Accessed 15 Nov. 2018.

Pew Research Center. 2015. *America's Changing Religious Landscape*. 12 May. http://www.pewforum.org/wp-content/uploads/sites/7/2015/05/RLS-08-26-full-report.pdf. Accessed 15 Nov. 2018.

Pew Research Center. 2016a. "American and Israeli Jews: Twin Portraits from Pew Research Center Surveys." 27 Sept. http://www.pewforum.org/essay/american-and-israeli-jews-twin-portraits-from-pew-research-center-surveys/. Accessed 27 Aug. 2017.

Pew Research Center. 2016b. *Israel's Religiously Divided Society*. 8 Mar. http://www.pewforum.org/2016/03/08/israels-religiously-divided-society/. Accessed 11 May 2017.

Pew Research Center. 2017. *Americans Express Increasingly Warm Feelings toward Religious Groups*, 15 Feb. http://www.pewforum.org/wp-content/uploads/sites/7/2017/02/Feeling-thermometer-report-FOR-WEB.pdf. Accessed 15 Nov. 2018.

Pew Research Center. 2018a. "Party Identification Trends, 1992–2017." 20 Mar. http://www.people-press.org/2018/03/20/party-identification-trends-1992-2017/. Accessed 17 July 2018.

Pew Research Center. 2018b. "Republicans and Democrats Grow Even Further Apart in Views of Israel, Palestinians." 23 Jan. http://assets.pewresearch.org/wp-content/uploads/sites/5/2018/01/23085852/1-23-18-Middle-East-release.pdf. Accessed 8 May 2018.

Phillips, Benjamin, Eszter Lengyel, and Leonard Saxe. 2002. American Attitudes toward Israel. Waltham, MA: Maurice and Marilyn Cohen Center for Modern Jewish Studies, Brandeis University.

Phillips, Bruce A. 2010. "Accounting for Jewish Secularism: Is a New Cultural Identity Emerging?" *Contemporary Jewry* 30 (1): 63–85.

Putnam, Robert D., and David E. Campbell. (2010) 2012. *American Grace: How Religion Divides Us and United Us*. Reprint, New York: Simon and Schuster.

Raab, Earl. 1996. "Are American Jews Still Liberal?" *Commentary* 101 (2): 43–45.

Riker, William H., and Peter C. Ordeshook. 1968. "A Theory of the Calculus of Voting." *American Political Science Review* 62 (1): 25–42.

Rischin, Moses. 1962. *The Promised City*. Cambridge, MA: Harvard University Press.

Rocklin, Mitchell. 2017. "Are American Jews Shifting Their Political Affiliation?" *Mosaic*, 18 Jan. https://mosaicmagazine.com/observation/2017/01/are-american-jews-shifting-their-political-affiliation/. Accessed 6 Mar. 2017.

Rokeach, Milton. 1969. "Part I: Value Systems in Religion." *Review of Religious Research* 11 (1): 3–23.

Rosenblatt, Gary. 2011. "How Many U.S. Jews, and Who Cares?" *Jewish Week*, 11 Oct. http://www.thejewishweek.com/editorial_opinion/gary_rosenblatt/how_many_us_jews_and_who_cares. Accessed 26 Dec. 2011.

Ross, Dennis. 2015. *Doomed to Succeed: The U.S.-Israel Relationship from Truman to Obama*. New York: Farrar, Straus and Giroux.

Rubin, Neal. 2012. *American Jewry and the Oslo Years*. New York: Palgrave Macmillan.

Russakoff, Dale. 2002. "Clinton Cleared in New Square Pardon Case." *Washington Post*, 21 June. https://www.washingtonpost.com/archive/politics/2002/06/21/clinton-cleared-in-new-square-pardon-case/5a4d8f1d-4f69-494f-904c-0e6c2b689baa/?utm_term=.ef4469fd367b. Accessed 7 May 2017.

Ryan, John B., and Caitlin Milazzo. 2015. "The South, the Suburbs, and the Vatican Too: Explaining Partisan Change among Catholics." *Political Behavior* 37 (2): 441–63.

Saad, Lydia. 2018. "Americans Remain Staunchly in Israel's Corner." Gallup, 13 Mar. http://news.gallup.com/poll/229199/americans-remain-staunchly-israel-corner.aspx. Accessed 2 Apr. 2018.

Sales, Ben. 2016. "Few Republican Jewish Coalition Leaders Open Wallets for Donald Trump." JTA, 1 Nov. http://www.jta.org/2016/11/01/news-opinion/politics/few-republican-jewish-coalition-leaders-open-wallets-for-donald-trump. Accessed 21 Nov. 2016.

Sales, Ben. 2017. "Jews for Jesus Commissioned a Study of Jewish Millennials." JTA, 31 Oct. https://www.jta.org/2017/10/31/news-opinion/united-states/jews-for-jesus-commissioned-a-study-on-jewish-millennials-heres-what-it-found. Accessed 2 Mar. 2018.

Sarna, Jonathan D. 2012. *When General Grant Expelled the Jews*. New York: Schocken Books.

Sarna, Jonathan D., and Zev Eleff. 2017. "The Immigration Clause That Transformed Orthodox Judaism in the United States." *American Jewish History* 101 (3): 357–76.

Saroglou, Vassilis, Vanessa Delpierre, and Rebecca Dernelle. 2004. "Values and Religiosity: A Meta-analysis of Studies using Schwartz's Model." *Personality and Individual Differences* 37:721–34.

Sasson, Theodore, Janet Krasner Aronson, Fern Chertok, Charles Kadushin, and Leonard Saxe. 2017. "Millennial Children of Intermarriage." *Contemporary Jewry* 37 (1): 99–123.

Sasson, Theodore, Charles Kadushin, and Leonard Saxe. 2010. "Trends in American Jewish Attachment to Israel: An Assessment of the 'Distancing' Hypothesis." *Contemporary Jewry* 30 (2/3): 297–319.

Sasson, Theodore, Benjamin Phillips, Charles Kadushin, and Leonard Saxe. 2010. *Still Connected: American Jewish Attitudes about Israel*. Waltham, MA: Maurice and Marilyn Cohen Center for Modern Jewish Studies, Brandeis University. http://www.bjpa.org/Publications/details.cfm?PublicationID=5822. Accessed 5 Aug. 2015.

Schwartz, Shalom H. 1994. "Are There Universal Aspects in the Structure and Contents of Human Values?" *Journal of Social Issues* 50 (4): 19–45.

Schwartz, Shalom H., and Sipke Huismans. 1995. "Value Priorities and Religiosity in Four Western Religions." *Social Psychology Quarterly* 58 (2): 88–107.

Schwartz, Shalom H., et al. 2014. "Basic Personal Values Underlie and Give Coherence to Political Values: A Cross National Study in 15 Countries." *Political Behavior* 36 (4): 899–930.

Sellers, Charles. 1965. "The Equilibrium Cycle in Two-Party Politics." *Public Opinion Quarterly* 29 (1): 16–38.

Shain, Michelle, Leonard Saxe, Shahar Hecht, Graham Wright, and Theodore Sasson. 2015. *Discovering Israel at War: The Impact of Taglit-Birthright Israel in Summer 2014.* Waltham, MA: Maurice and Marilyn Cohen Center for Modern Jewish Studies, Brandeis University.

Shapiro, Edward S. 1991. "Charles S. Liebman and American Jewish Liberalism." *American Jewish History* 80 (4): 451–64.

Shapiro, Edward S. 1992. *A Time for Healing: American Jewry since World War II.* Baltimore: Johns Hopkins University Press.

Shapiro, Edward S. 2000. "Waiting for Righty? An Interpretation of the Political Behavior of American Jews." *Michael: On the History of the Jews in the Diaspora,* 155–79.

Shapiro, Edward S. 2005. *We Are Many: Reflections on American Jewish History and Identity.* Syracuse, NY: Syracuse University Press.

Shavit, Ari. 2013. *My Promised Land: The Promise and Tragedy of Israel.* New York: Spiegel and Grau.

Sheskin, Ira M. 2013. "Geography, Demography, and the Jewish Vote." In Dan Schnur, ed., *American Politics and the Jewish Community,* 37–76. West Lafayette, IN: Purdue University Press.

Sheskin, Ira M. 2016. "An Introduction to the Jewish Voter." In Kyle L. Kreider and Thomas J. Baldino, eds., *Minority Voting in the United States,* 2:61–94. Santa Barbara, CA: Praeger.

Sheskin, Ira M. 2017. *The 2017 Jewish Federation of Greater Indianapolis Population Study.* Jewish Federation of Greater Indianapolis. https://www.jewishindianapolis.org/community. Accessed 10 July 2018.

Sheskin, Ira M., and Arnold Dashefsky. 2018. "United States Jewish Population, 2017." In Arnold Dashefsky and Ira M. Sheskin, eds., *American Jewish Year Book 2017,* 179–284. Dordrecht: Springer.

Sigelman, Lee. 1991a. "If You Prick Us, Do We Not Bleed? If You Tickle Us, Do We Not Laugh? Jews and Pocketbook Voting." *Journal of Politics* 53 (4): 977–92.

Sigelman, Lee. 1991b. "Jews and the 1988 Election: More of the Same?" In James L. Guth and John C. Green, eds., *The Bible and the Ballot Box: Religion and Politics in the 1988 Election,* 188–203. Boulder: Westview Press.

Silberstein, Laurence J. 2012. "American Jewry's Identification with Israel." In Alan T. Levine, ed., *The Wiley-Blackwell History of Jews and Judaism,* 619–42. Chichester: Blackwell.

Skocpol, Theda, and Vanessa Williamson. 2012. *The Tea Party and the Remaking of Republican Conservatism.* New York: Oxford University Press.

Smith, Tom W. 2005. *Jewish Distinctiveness in America: A Statistical Portrait.* New York: American Jewish Committee.

Smith, Tom W., Michael Davern, Jeremy Freese, and Michael Hout. 2018. General Social Surveys, 1972–2016. Machine-readable data file. Produced by NORC at the University of Chicago and distributed by the Roper Center for Public Opinion Research, University of Connecticut.

Solomon, Herbert L. 1988. "The Republican Party and the Jews." *Judaism* 37 (3): 276–87.

Sonenshein, Raphael J., and Nicholas A. Valentino. 2000. "The Distinctiveness of Jewish Voting: A Thing of the Past?" *Urban Affairs Review* 35 (3): 358–89.

Spiegel, Steven L. 1982–83. "Religious Components of U.S. Middle East Policy." *Journal of International Affairs* 36 (2): 235–46.

Spinrad, William. 1990. "Explaining American-Jewish Liberalism: Another Attempt." *Contemporary Jewry* 11 (1): 107–19.

Staetsky, L. Daniel. 2017. *Antisemitism in Contemporary Great Britain*. London: Institute for Jewish Policy Research.

Stammer, Larry B. 1996. "Baptists Seek to Convert Jews in U.S." *Los Angeles Times*, 15 June. http://articles.latimes.com/1996-06-15/local/me-15213_1_southern-baptist. Accessed 14 Nov. 2018.

Stanley, Harold W., and Richard G. Niemi. 2006. "Partisanship, Party Coalition, and Group Support, 1952–2004." *Presidential Studies Quarterly* 36 (2): 172–88.

Swanson, Emily. 2013. "Christianity as State Religion Supported by One-Third of Americans, Poll Finds." *HuffPost*, 6 Apr. http://www.huffingtonpost.com/2013/04/06/christianity-state-religion_n_3022255.html. Accessed 11 Aug. 2015.

Swedlow, Brendon, and Mikel L. Wyckoff. 2009. "Value Preferences and Ideological Structuring of Attitudes in American Public Opinion." *American Politics Research* 37 (6): 1048–87.

Tajfel, Henri. 1978. "Social Categorization, Social Identity, and Social Comparisons." In Henri Tajfel, ed., *Differentiation between Social Groups*, 61–76. London: Academic Press.

Tajfel, Henri C., and John C. Turner. 1986. "The Social Identity Theory of Intergroup Behavior." In S. Worchel and W. G. Austin, eds., *Psychology of Intergroup Relations*, 7–24. Chicago: Nelson-Hall.

Thompson, Jennifer A. 2014. *Marrying Out: Jewish Men, Intermarriage, and Fatherhood*. Bloomington: Indiana University Press.

Tighe, Elizabeth, Leonard Saxe, and Charles Kadushin. 2011. *Estimating the Jewish Population of the United States: 2000–2010*. Waltham, MA: Maurice and Marilyn Cohen Center for Modern Jewish Studies, Brandeis University.

Turner, John C. 1991. *Social Influence*. Milton Keynes, UK: Open University Press.

Uhlaner, Carole J. 1989. "Rational Turnout: The Neglected Role of Groups." *American Journal of Political Science* 33 (2): 390–422.

Uslaner, Eric M. 2013. "American Jews and the Elephant Question." In Dan Schnur, ed., *American Politics and the Jewish Community*, 77–98. West Lafayette, IN: Purdue University Press.

Uslaner, Eric M. 2015. "What's the Matter with Palm Beach County?" *Politics and Religion* 8 (4): 699–717.

Uslaner, Eric M., and Mark Lichbach. 2009. "Identity versus Identity: Israel and Evangelicals and the Two-Front War for Jewish Votes." *Politics and Religion* 2 (3): 395–419.

VanderHei, Jim. 2006. "Future of Orthodox Jewish Vote Has Implications for GOP." *Washington Post*. 3 Aug. http://www.washingtonpost.com/wp-dyn/content/article/2006/08/02/AR2006080201692.html. Accessed 26 Dec. 2015.

Verba, Sidney, Kay Lehman Schlozman, and Henry E. Brady. 1995. *Voice and Equal-*

ity: Civic Voluntarism in American Politics. Cambridge, MA: Harvard University Press.

Wald, Kenneth D. 2015. "The Choosing People: Interpreting the Puzzling Politics of American Jewry." *Politics and Religion* 8 (1): 4–35.

Wald, Kenneth D. 2016. "Politically Hyperactive? The Civic Participation of American Jews." *Politics, Groups, and Identities* 4 (4): 545–60.

Wald, Kenneth D., and Michael D. Martinez. 2001. "Jewish Religiosity and Political Attitudes in the United States and Israel." *Political Behavior* 23 (4): 377–97.

Wald, Kenneth D., and Lee Sigelman. 1997. "Romancing the Jews: The Christian Right in Search of Strange Bedfellows." In Corwin E. Smidt and James M. Penning, eds., *Sojourners in the Wilderness*, 139–68. Lanham, MD: Rowman and Littlefield.

Wald, Kenneth D., and Bryan D. Williams. 2006. "American Jews and Israel: The Sources of Politicized Ethnic Identity." *Nationalism and Ethnic Politics* 12:205–37.

Walzer, Michael. 1995. "Liberalism and the Jews: Historical Affinities, Contemporary Necessities." In Peter Y. Medding, ed., *Values, Interests, and Identity: Jews and Politics in a Changing World*, 3–10. Studies in Contemporary Jewry 11. New York: Oxford University Press.

Waxman, Dov. 2016. *Trouble in the Tribe: The American Jewish Conflict over Israel*. Princeton: Princeton University Press.

Weisberg, Herbert F. 2005. *The Total Survey Error Approach: A Guide to the New Science of Survey Research*. Chicago: University of Chicago Press.

Weisberg, Herbert F. 2011. "The Distinctiveness of the Jewish-American Voter." Paper presented at the Symposium on Jewish Political Behavior, Frankel Institute for Advanced Judaic Studies, University of Michigan, Ann Arbor, 10–11 Nov.

Weisberg, Herbert F. 2012. "Reconsidering Jewish Presidential Voting Statistics." *Contemporary Jewry* 32 (3): 215–36.

Weisberg, Herbert F. 2014. "Tradition! Tradition? Jewish Voting in the 2012 Election." *PS: Political Science and Politics* 47 (3): 629–35.

Wentling, Sonja Schoepf, and Rafael Medoff. 2012. *Herbert Hoover and the Jews*. Washington, DC: Wyman Institute.

Wertheimer, Jack. 2002. "The Jewish Debate over State Aid to Religious Schools." In Alan Mittleman, Robert Licht, and Jonathan D. Sarna, eds., *Jews and the American Public Square: Debating Religion and Republic*, 217–37. Lanham, MD: Rowman and Littlefield.

Wolfson, Ron. 2013. *Relational Judaism: Using the Power of Relationships to Transform the Jewish Community*. Woodstock, VT: Jewish Lights.

Woocher, Jonathan S. 1986. *Sacred Survival: The Civil Religion of American Jews*. Bloomington: Indiana University Press.

Wuthnow, Robert, and Conrad Hackett. 2003. "The Social Integration of Practitioners of Non-Western Religions in the United States." *Journal for the Scientific Study of Religion* 42 (4): 651–67.

Yaffe, James. 1968. *The American Jews*. New York: Random House.

Zaller, John. 1992. *The Nature and Origins of Mass Belief Systems*. Cambridge: Cambridge University Press.

Author Index

Subject Index